Whither the Child?

Whither the Child?

Causes and Consequences of Low Fertility

Edited by

Eric Kaufmann

and

W. Bradford Wilcox

Paradigm Publishers

Boulder • London

All Web Figures and Tables can be seen at the book website:
http://www.paradigmpublishers.com/Books/BookDetail.aspx?productID=287423

Published in the United States by Paradigm Publishers, 5589 Arapahoe Avenue, Boulder, CO 80303 USA.

Paradigm Publishers is the trade name of Birkenkamp & Company, LLC,
Dean Birkenkamp, President and Publisher.

Library of Congress Cataloging-in-Publication Data

Whither the child? : causes and consequences of low fertility / edited by Eric Kaufmann and W. Bradford Wilcox.
     p. cm.
 Includes bibliographical references and index.
 ISBN 978-1-61205-094-2 (pbk. : alk. paper)
 1. Fertility, Human. 2. Family policy. 3. Birth control—Government policy. I. Kaufmann, Eric P. II. Wilcox, William Bradford, 1970–
 HB901.W49 2012
 304.6'32—dc23

                                                                    2012017754

Printed and bound in the United States of America on acid-free paper that meets the standards of the American National Standard for Permanence of Paper for Printed Library Materials.

Designed and Typeset by Straight Creek Bookmakers.

17 16 15 14 13   1 2 3 4 5

Contents

Introduction

Eric Kaufmann and W. Bradford Wilcox

Increasingly, demography is front-page news. During just one year, the *Economist* (October 2009), *Foreign Affairs* (January/February 2010), *Time* (July 2010), and *Foreign Policy* (October 2010) all featured cover stories on the effects of demography. Meanwhile, the economic crisis has forced governments to scale back public spending, reduce child allowances and raise the retirement age, causing immense social conflict in countries such as France. "In 2050," writes Ted Fishman in the *New York Times,* "developed countries are on track to have half as many people under 15 as they do over 60. In short, the age mix of the world is turning upside down and at unprecedented rates. This means profound change in nearly every important relationship we have—as family members, neighbors, citizens of nations and the world" (Fishman 2010). As an only child and a mother of one, Lauren Sandler remarks in a *Time* cover story: "It's a marvel to me these days that anyone can manage a second kid … since I celebrated my 35th birthday, I have to ask myself not when but if. My parents asked themselves that question when I was my daughter's age and decided the answer was no" (L. Sandler, "The Only Child: Debunking the Myths," *Time,* July 8, 2010).

In the last four decades, birth rates have fallen dramatically throughout the world. Europe and East Asia lead the way, with fertility rates well below the replacement level of 2.1. The economic, technological, and social sources of the Demographic Transition toward smaller families, which began in the late eighteenth century, are well understood (Coale and Watkins 1986). However, more recently, the so-called Second Demographic Transition (SDT) has come to the fore. Characterized by below-replacement fertility and based more on cultural than material shifts, it demands further exploration (Surkyn and Lesthaeghe 2004). This book arises out of an Experts Meeting in 2010, "Whither the Child? Causes, Consequences, and Responses to Low Fertility," sponsored by the Social Trends Institute in Barcelona, Spain, which was designed to do precisely that. The book brings together leading demographers and social scientists and asks how changing gender roles, religious values, belief systems, and family norms affect fertility.

But beyond traditional demographic approaches that probe the causes of fertility change, this work turns the question on its head to ask how demography affects individuals and society. What does it feel like to live in a low-fertility world? What exactly are the consequences of falling fertility rates and aging populations—for children, adults, communities, nation-states, and religions? What have individuals, policymakers, and politicians done to address the problem? *Is* there even a problem—economically, culturally, and morally? No other book encapsulates so many dimensions of the low-fertility issue and none engage with the thorny issues of child psychology, parenting, family, and social policy that we tackle head-on here. Throughout, this book turns on several key debates. Are cultural or economic forces driving low fertility? Are liberal or communitarian values the answer? Should we aim for a fertility increase or learn to live with decline?

Some of the pressing questions that our contributors—leaders in their fields—address include the following:

- Is fertility decline caused by a loss of religious faith and a diminishing hope for the future in modern societies?
- Are patriarchal family norms and traditional gender roles contributing to low fertility?
- What are the social and emotional consequences of being an "only child"?
- How do children influence the emotional and spiritual lives of adults?
- Does parenthood affect the extent to which adults engage with society?
- Is low fertility linked to a rising secularism, permitting orthodox religions to eclipse moderate faiths and nonreligion through their comparative fertility advantage?
- If low fertility—or at least the "lowest low fertility" found in much of Europe and East Asia—can be viewed as a social problem, how should governments respond?

- What is the optimum level of fertility in society? Might we be better off with a declining population?

The book begins by taking stock of demographic trends of the past few decades and tries to make sense of them. In the first chapter, Alícia Adserà asks why fertility rates vary from little more than one child per woman in southern and eastern Europe to near-replacement levels in France, Scandinavia, and many Anglo-Saxon societies. Two important developments coincide with fertility declines across Europe since the 1960s: a steep drop in religious piety and growing female labor force participation. At the same time, intra-European variation maps onto both religious and economic differences. Using the latest economic and social survey data for Europe and the OECD, Adserà weighs competing cultural and economic explanations for the variation in fertility rates across Europe and the OECD. She finds that while cultural differences delineate differences in ideal family size, economic constraints best explain individual women's abilities to meet their fertility goals.

Moving from the causes to the consequences of low fertility, David Eggebeen asks a novel question: Do rising levels of childlessness in a society result in reduced levels of civic voluntarism and engagement? Parenthood engenders its own set of norms and expectations, which some claim tend to increase levels of volunteering in society. This would imply more atomistic, disengaged societies in the Europe of tomorrow. But does the evidence support such a dramatic interpretation? Eggebeen examines the way gender, marital status, and education refract the influence of parenthood on civic engagement, and he provides an interesting answer.

Happiness with one's children is both a cause and consequence of fertility. Just how happy do children make parents? Hans-Peter Kohler takes a closer look at the association between children and the happiness of mothers and fathers. Critically, he doesn't find that parents are unswervingly positive about the parenthood experience. This is partly due to individual differences in neurological happiness "set points." However, much of the variation is mediated by other factors, such as the gender and marital status of the parent and the gender and birth order of the child in question. Specifically, Kohler raises the provocative suggestion that men may have children to enter into happiness-enhancing partnerships, while women may enter such partnerships to secure happiness-inducing children!

The emotional consequences of fertility decisions are also central to Elizabeth Marquardt's work. Peering at the problem from both normative and empirical angles, she asks how we might balance the rights of children against those of adults. Such concerns are thrown into relief by the question of assisted reproductive technologies (ART). These are increasingly prevalent fertility techniques, typically considered from the perspective of those who have experienced difficulty conceiving a child. Yet the "successes," the offspring of these treatments, have only rarely been studied. Marquardt cleverly deploys a survey to research this question. It highlights the troubling experiences of children born to anonymous sperm donors, thereby juxtaposing the rights of adults (to anonymity) and children (who wish to know their birth parents).

While Europe has captured much of the attention when it comes to low fertility, family sizes are actually considerably lower in East Asia. Susan Short, Hongwei Xu, and Ying Liu glimpse the ramifications of these changes as they affect this region of the world. In dissecting the impact of China's one-child policy on children's well-being, they discover that the policy's effects are manifold. In a society where child neglect has been a persistent problem, only children are better cared for, healthier, and more active in extra-curricular activities than those with siblings. Girls, especially those in sibling families, continue to show poorer health outcomes than boys, but in general, lower fertility seems to be accompanied by higher investment in children. On the other hand, the social and emotional consequences of being an only child—not just in terms of loneliness, but also in the form of increased parental expectations and pressure—are intangibles that may carry tumultuous consequences. This insecurity manifests itself in the finding that only children place a stronger emphasis than other children on the need to be liked by their friends.

Children are not the only actors affected by shifting fertility regimes. Parents and their marriages also register the effects. In the West, where the post–sexual revolution Second Demographic Transition is important, lower fertility has been associated with secularization and the eclipse of traditional gender roles. This is where W. Bradford Wilcox and Jeffrey Dew enter our story, asking whether wives' religiosity and gender role expectations affect their marital satisfaction. In a highly original departure, the authors gather information on the actual division of household labor among US couples and contrast it with wives' perceptions of marital fairness and happiness. Are marriages in which the housework is distributed unequally less happy? Not necessarily. Where children are present, wives who are religious and subscribe to traditional family norms are more content with the division of labor in the home—regardless of the actual division of housework. Moreover, Wilcox and Dew also find that wives with children at home do not prefer the strictly egalitarian option of sharing both paid work and housework but rather the "neo-traditional" arrangement featuring a male breadwinner who takes the lead in material providership but also shares in household duties.

Religion and traditionalism also loom large in Eric Kaufmann's chapter, which moves beyond the individual to ask how low fertility affects the culture and politics of society as a whole. Theorists of the Second Demographic Transition posit that a shift to secular values reduces fertility. The flipside of this equation, claims Kaufmann, is that the pious in secularizing societies resist the transition to lower fertility more than the nonreligious, regardless of income or education. Paradoxically, secularization appears to be self-limiting in that it sets the stage for a demographically induced return of religion. In the medium term, this largely takes place through religious immigration and ethnic religiosity. In the long run, native differences in fertility between the strongly religious and the secular rise to the fore. To be sure, this is not religion in its traditional guise: the religions that prosper best in secular Western environments are closed, pronatalist sects like Holland's Orthodox Calvinists or America's ultra-Orthodox Jews.

Religious pronatalism and secular feminism are often juxtaposed. Alícia Adserà's chapter, as noted, nicely navigates the contentious terrain between those who pin the blame for below-replacement fertility on secular cultures and those who cite inhospitable economies. Leonard Schoppa addresses the latter point by walking us through the policy debate over whether "feminism is the new natalism," that is, that governments seeking to raise fertility should concentrate on restructuring the national labor market to permit women to more easily combine work and family. His paper forms the first of three chapters that make up the second section of the book. Though policy issues inform the work of all the authors, in the articles that follow Schoppa's, the authors pay special attention to concrete policy options and their consequences.

Schoppa's paper largely reserves judgment on whether feminist economic policies work to trace the evolution of European policy discourse on the subject. Through a special focus on Germany, Japan, and Italy, three "lowest-low" fertility countries, his chapter examines the steps OECD countries have taken to render their labor markets more child friendly. Subsidized childcare, child benefits, flexible labor markets, and maternity leave have all been flagged as vital elements of economic reform by government officials in these countries. Nevertheless, policies have been implemented piecemeal and have yet to pay significant fertility dividends.

Catherine Hakim, in a fast-paced chapter that is certain to provoke debate, tries to explain why. In her review of recent research, she contends that women differ in their lifestyle preferences: some are career-oriented while others remain home-centered. The median woman in fact seeks a part-time mix of work and childcare. Realistic fertility gains are more likely to emerge from among the ranks of stay-at-home than careerist women. Ergo, home-centered women and those who seek to work part-time must figure centrally in government policy. Accordingly, this evidence calls for a retargeting of fertility policy toward these less "sexy" categories. Too often, she argues, governments are drawn into allocating scarce political and economic resources to enticing highly resistant career-oriented women to reproduce when they are not disposed to do so. On the other hand, homecare allowances for stay-at-home mothers are, for Hakim, a population policy intervention that is popular, simple, and effective.

Hakim, like Schoppa, Adserà, and a number of other contributors, takes it as axiomatic that below-replacement fertility is a negative development. But is this necessarily the case? In a highly innovative, blue-sky reconsideration of our taken-for-granted notions, leading macro-demographers Wolfgang Lutz, Stuart Basten, and Erich Striessnig question the received wisdom. The chapter begins by taking stock of the big picture of global fertility patterns, placing these in historical and theoretical context. Fertility rates will not fall to zero, but nor are they likely to rise to pre-Transition levels of 3 or above.

Those who claim that recent increases in European fertility portend an end to sub-replacement fertility may be seeing what they wish to see. These increases, say the authors, have more to do with an end to the decades-long rise in the age at which women have children. Indeed, family-size norms as low as one child per woman remain a distinct possibility, as the case of coastal China reveals. Lutz et al. use the Chinese case as a platform from which to interrogate the shibboleth that 2.1 is the optimal population level for society. Actually, if one factors in the costs and benefits of education (to say nothing of climate change), a society's optimal total fertility rate may well be as low as 1.5. Economic success is not the only factor to consider when setting population targets, but the notion that below-replacement fertility may be economically rational will strike many as counterintuitive.

The common thread running through all the papers is that our new low-fertility environment is a product of society and has consequences for all aspects of our individual and collective lives. Beyond that, however, our authors offer no unitary explanations. Few deny the importance of changing women's roles and the erosion of religious traditionalism in lowering fertility. Equally, few contest the idea that aspects of economic structure—some of which may be amenable to policy interventions—can enable or inhibit fertility gains. The same broad consensus holds for the consequences of low fertility: lower fertility does enable greater investment in children's health and education, but this may also carry certain costs in terms of children's emotional lives and parents' civic engagement. At the level of society, lower fertility enables greater development of human resources, but this must be balanced against the costs associated with a higher proportion of elderly dependents and the possibility that population decline will threaten the viability of nation-states and cultures.

These are, however, broad parameters within which our commentators are far from united. Differences of opinion often stem from contrasting normative concerns. Some approach their subject from a communitarian standpoint, urging an end to below-replacement fertility and a revaluation of traditional motherhood, religion, and family norms. Others are feminist egalitarians. For them, patriarchal gender roles, proscriptions on out-of-wedlock births, insufficient support for working mothers, and inflexible workplaces prevent women from realizing their desired fertility. Finally, a minority are individualists who remain agnostic about the need to raise fertility rates, arguing instead for whatever policies best maximize the self-interests of society's individuals. Some combine several of these political philosophies.

As the developing world follows the wealthy global North into a low-fertility future, the concerns elucidated in this book will only grow in relevance. Few will be able to sidestep these tectonic issues in their personal and public lives. This book therefore represents an important step forward. Here, for the first time, scholars, policymakers, journalists, and concerned members of the public will find a wealth of relevant work in one place. These experts' analyses, data, and policy recommendations provide an impressive set of tools to help all of us make sense of, and navigate, our new demographic environment.

References

Coale, A. J., and S. C. Watkins (1986). *The Decline of Fertility in Europe: The Revised Proceedings of a Conference on the Princeton European Fertility Project.* Princeton, NJ: Princeton University Press.

Economist, The (2009). "Falling Fertility: Astonishing Falls in the Fertility Rate Are Bringing with Them Big Benefits." October 29.

Fishman, T. (2010). "As Populations Age, a Chance for Younger Nations." *New York Times,* October 14.

Goldstone, J. (2010). "The New Population Bomb: The Four Megatrends That Will Change the World." *Foreign Affairs* 1(89).

Sandler, L. (2010). "The Only Child: Debunking the Myths." *Time,* July 8.

Surkyn, J., and R. Lesthaeghe (2004). "Value Orientations and the Second Demographic Transition (STD) in Northern, Western and Southern Europe: An Update." *Demographic Research* Special Collection 3: Article 3.

Chapter 1

Fertility, Feminism, and Faith

The Influence of Secularism and Economic Conditions

Alícia Adserà

Fertility rates in developed countries have fallen to previously unseen levels. Within that general downward trend, fertility has varied significantly across countries, plummeting to 1.3 or less in southern European countries, Germany, and Austria—to what some refer to as "lowest-low" fertility levels (Kohler et al. 2002). Conversely, fertility has remained comparatively high, though still below the replacement rate, in Anglo-Saxon and Nordic countries where norms of intra-household equality are more widespread. At the same time, Western societies have undergone differential processes of secularization—though its extent is subject to heated academic debate (Bumpass 1990; Lesthaeghe and Moors 1996; Voas 2009). Contemporaneous with the decrease in fertility and with "secularization," labor markets in developed countries have been transformed by rising female labor force participation and economic uncertainty. Periods of high and persistent unemployment since the late 1980s as well as an upward trend in the share of temporary employment characterize many countries within the Organisation of Economic Co-operation and Development (OECD, the focus of this chapter), notably those in Europe (Adsera 2004, 2005, 2011).

There is no unique answer to the question of what explains those sharp reductions in family size. Are changes in religious practice behind these shifts? Are beliefs about the ideal number of children related to particular religious views or affiliations? Are economic constraints limiting the number of children families can afford? Do labor market institutions constitute a barrier for women to combine active careers and motherhood? There is a big debate between those who suggest that cultural values are the key to explaining variation in fertility (with the religious emphasizing community and motherhood over individualism and career) and those who give the nod to material factors such as labor market flexibility, subsidized childcare, and egalitarian gender roles (which enable women to combine work and family). In this chapter I hope to present analyses that can help to arbitrate between these competing arguments.

Figure 1.1 presents data on total fertility rates across a subset of OECD countries from the mid-1960s into 2003. Beginning at levels close to 3 children per woman, all these countries underwent a dramatic transformation, particularly those in southern Europe. In Italy and Spain, for example, fertility dropped later than in northern Europe, but reached levels close to 1.1 children per woman by the late 1990s. Fertility rates in the US and Nordic countries stabilized at relatively higher levels close to (or slightly below) the replacement level of 2.1 children per woman. Changes in the preferences of couples toward smaller families, larger investments per child, and dual careers help explain the general decrease in fertility across developed countries (Becker 1981; Butz and Ward 1979, 1980; Galor and Weil 1996). The widespread access to family planning in OECD countries made those changes possible (Goldin and Katz 2002).

Furthermore, part of the decrease in fertility can be attributed to the delay in motherhood. When women postpone having their first child, they may be unable to bear even their (lower) desired number of children (Morgan 2003). That said, the differing extent to which women postpone their fertility only provides part of the explanation for the observed variation in fertility levels across countries (Sobotka 2004). Of greater importance is that differences in the number of children that women *say* they desire only account for a small

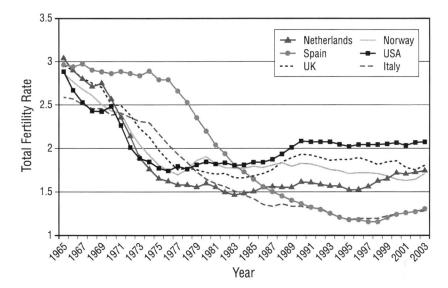

Figure 1.1 Total Fertility Rate, Selected OECD Countries, 1965–2003
Source: Council of Europe. Various years. *Recent Demographic Developments in Europe.* Strasbourg, France: Council of Europe Publishing.

portion of the *actual* variation in fertility levels between European countries (Bongaarts 2002; Goldstein et al. 2003).

Fahey and Speder (2004) show how in Europe the gap between the number of children women state they want and the total number of children they actually have has started to move from negative into positive, meaning that many women do not attain their desired fertility. Even if measuring the desired number of children involves a whole set of methodological problems (see Adsera 2006a and 2006b for a discussion), Morgan and Rackin (2010) have recently noted a gap between desired and achieved fertility across developed countries. They add that this is a result of many women failing to attain their preferred fertility rather than the traditional problem of women being unable to limit their fertility.[1]

The first part of the chapter reviews the existing literature that contends that greater individualism, as well as changes in religious attendance and beliefs, is linked to changes in family size across countries and denominations. It then explores these questions employing the five waves of the World Values Survey and the European Values Survey (WVS-EVS). It shows estimates of fertility patterns across denominations both for the whole world and developed countries.

Next, using data of the European Community Household Panel (ECHP), 1993–2001, the chapter explores the role of economic constraints in the decline of family size. This adds to the cultural explanation advanced in the first part. It highlights the barriers and opportunities that different labor market conditions and welfare state regimes constitute to those confronting the trade-offs of career and family. It presents some results on how the country's unemployment rate, form of labor contracts, and available family benefits, among other factors, affect women's paths to motherhood.

Finally the chapter attempts to understand whether the effect of religion depends on labor market institutions and the opportunity costs they impose on professional women. In particular, I look at a few questions from the International Social Survey Program (ISSP) module Religion II (1998) and WVS-EVS that tackle issues of work-family arrangements and the value couples put in having more offspring. I comment on whether the answers vary over different denominations and countries according to their welfare and labor market arrangements.

Religion and Fertility

Rapid secularization in many countries has been associated with the adoption of patterns of behavior often described as the "second demographic transition." These include increases in the age at marriage and at first birth together with increases in extramarital childbearing and cohabitation (Van de Kaa 1987, 2004). At the core of these changes are an accentuation of individual autonomy, rapid secularization (defined as a reduction in religious practice), the abandonment of traditional religious beliefs, and a decline in religious sentiment (Lesthaeghe and Surkyn 1988; Bumpass 1990; Lesthaeghe and Moors 1996). This transformation, which had already become widespread in northern and western Europe, has become increasingly apparent in southern Europe since the mid-1980s. It was probably boosted by the massive entrance of women into the labor market and by information flowing from neighboring countries (Becker and Murphy 2001; Surkyn and Lesthaeghe 2004). A similar trend was noted with religious practice: in those countries where it used to be higher, we observe a rapid decline in attendance. Still, the degree of secularization of Western countries has been the subject of a heated debate (Stark 1999; Bruce 2001; Voas and Crockett 2005; Voas 2009), and religiosity seems to continue to influence individuals' demographic choices (Voas 2007). The rise of the Muslim population in OECD countries also poses questions regarding the religiosity of future generations, though it hinges on the inter-generational transmission of the faith (Westoff and Frejka 2007; Kaufmann 2010).

The major religious traditions confer a central role on the family in society. Thus membership in a religious group is assumed to be associated with a desire for larger families. In modern societies, individuals without a religious affiliation display different demographic behavior. In data from the European Values Surveys, for instance, individuals with lower levels of adherence to institutional religion prefer fewer children and are less likely to live in traditional families (Lesthaeghe and Surkyn 1988; Bumpass 1990; Surkyn and Lesthaeghe 2004). Unaffiliated women have fewer children than any other group in the US (Mosher et al. 1992; Lehrer 1996). Conversely, affiliated individuals, particularly those belonging to a denomination with strong pro-natalist teachings, prefer larger families than those without religion. Conservative Protestants exhibit differentially lower contraceptive use and higher fertility than other affiliations (Goldscheider and Mosher 1991; Lehrer 1996). McQuillan (2004) notes that the guidelines of the Catholic Church on abortion, family planning, and sexuality within marriage also may affect other childbearing patterns such as spacing between births. Nonetheless, different norms in family planning do not seem to be driving observed fertility differences. For example, despite the extensive contraceptive use among practicing Catholics in Spain, they still have larger families than their non-practicing and unaffiliated fellow citizens (Adsera 2006c, 2007).

Religion is relevant for demographic preferences and behavior not only because of the specific teachings of each religious denomination but also through its influence on the norms and structures of society (Goldscheider and Mosher 1991; McQuillan 2004). With a fading of the influence of religious institutions on society (e.g., weakening of adherence to the Catholic Church norms on contraception among Catholics), we expect only individuals with active participation to remain committed to the teachings of their religious denomination.

As the influence of religious institutions in society has waned, religious practice has emerged as a more salient predictor of family norms. Many recent papers find a strengthening relationship between religiosity and fertility (Adsera 2005 for OECD; Adsera 2006b, 2006c, and 2007 for Spain; Philipov and Berghammer 2007 for Europe; Frejka and Westoff 2008 for the OECD). Might more fertile families gravitate toward religion? Recent work by Berghammer (2009) more closely addresses the direction of the causal relationship between fertility and religiosity by exploiting the longitudinal nature of a Dutch data set. In so doing, it refutes the reverse causality hypothesis that adults attend more religious services once they have little children in the house.

Previous research using data from the International Social Survey Program (ISSP), Family and Changing Gender Roles II 1994, finds the ideal number of children in many OECD countries to be higher for conservative Protestants and Catholics, affiliations with more pro-natalist teachings, than for more liberal Protestants or unaffiliated individuals (Adsera 2006b). In all countries, a higher share of men than women claims to be non-religious. Further, the intensity of religious practice is traditionally lower among men than women in most affiliations. Religious practice plays a lesser role for men than for women, once membership is accounted for, except for conservative Protestants. On the other hand, claiming membership in a religious group more greatly impacts the demographic behavior of men than women. Among women, the power of religious affiliation to predict family size preferences has dwindled across generations, while that of religious practice remains high and significant across denominations (Adsera 2006b).

To examine the role of both religion and religious practice as meaningful influences on family size, I use the five available waves of the WVS-EVS study (1981–2005). The survey provides ninety detailed codings for religious denomination, especially across Protestant denominations. I divide the sample into ten groups (Catholics, Jews, Muslims, Conservative Protestants, Liberal Protestants, Orthodox, Buddhist, Hindus, Other, and No Religion) as shown in Table 1.1. Following previous practice, I regroup all Protestant denominations in two main groups, conservative or liberal Protestants, defined by the strictness of their membership criteria.[2] I use the same guidelines to classify religious denominations absent in the US but present in other countries in the sample. The Other Religion group is a residual category that includes a great variety of non-Christian denominations. Finally, the No Religion group includes both individuals that explicitly report no religion as their affiliation as well as those who do not report any affiliation and declare that they never attend religious services.

Table 1.2 presents the shares of the religious groups and the number of individuals in both the pooled sample of countries in the WVS-EVS (with close to 300,000 observations) and in the sample limited to OECD countries (with close to 97,000 observations). Overall Catholics are the largest group, representing 30 percent of the world sample and 38 percent of the sample of selected OECD countries. Protestants comprise around 17 percent of world sample and 30 percent of the OECD sample. Unaffiliated individuals represent close to 20 percent in the world and almost one in four in the OECD sample. Muslims, even if rapidly rising in numbers across some OECD countries during recent years, still constitute a very small minority in the OECD sample, whereas they represent over 16 percent of the world sample. It is important to remember that the shares in Table 1.2 are obtained with data over the five waves from 1981 to 2005.

Table 1.1 Groups of Religious Denominations

Religion Variable	WVS-EVS Category
Catholic	Roman Catholic
Jewish	Inclusive
Muslim	Muslims, Druse, Shiite, Shia, Sunni, Al-hadis, Qadiani
Conservative Protestant	Baptist, Congregational, Evangelist, Mormons, Jehovah's Witness Charismatic, Christian Fellowship, Biblist, Pentecostal
Liberal Protestant	Methodist, Lutheran, Presbyterian, Church of England, Episcopal, Unitarian, Church of Sweden, Norwegian State Church, United Church of Canada, Other Christian
Orthodox	Greek, Gregorian, Armenian Apostolic, Russian
Buddhist	Buddhist
Hindu	Hindu, Jain
Other	Shinto, Sikh, Brethren, Ratana, Other Non-Christian, Ancestral, Bahai, Other Miscellaneous
No Religion	None

Source: Derived from the WVS-EVS data.

Table 1.2 Number and Share of Individuals by Religious Affiliation in the 1981–2005 WVS-EVS Sample

	All Countries		OECD	
Affiliation	N	%	N	%
Catholic	88,675	29.85	36,650	37.87
Jewish	707	0.24	426	0.44
Muslim	48,311	16.26	446	0.46
Conservative Protestant	17,883	6.02	4,152	4.29
Liberal Protestant	33,526	11.29	24,726	25.55
Orthodox	30,469	10.26	3,987	4.12
Buddhist	5,809	1.96	1,537	1.59
Hindu	7,076	2.38	164	0.17
Other	6,630	2.23	2,141	2.21
No Religion	57,958	19.51	22,562	23.31
Total	297,044	100.00	96,791	100.00

Source: Author's calculation from WVS-EVS, all waves.

Table 1.3 shows the percentage of individuals in each OECD country who attend religious services at least once a month or more and those who declare themselves to be religious. Consistent with other studies, the percentage of people who consider themselves religious is much higher than the share of those who practice (with the exception of Ireland). More than 80 percent of those surveyed in the US, Italy, Portugal, and Austria consider themselves to be religious. In terms of practice, Ireland has a distant lead (though participation has sharply decreased recently) followed by the US, Portugal, and Italy. Nordic

Table 1.3 Shares of Individuals Who Practice at Least Once a Month and Who Consider Themselves Religious for Selected Countries, 1981–2005 WVS-EVS

Country	% Practice at Least Once a Month	% Religious	N
Australia	25.8	56.5	4,172
Austria	43.8	81.1	2,932
Belgium	33.3	69.5	5,212
Canada	38.9	73.5	6,485
Denmark	12.0	75.4	2,801
Finland	12.4	60.4	3,461
France	14.2	49.4	4,356
Germany	22.8	48.1	9,393
Greece	33.3	80.0	1,096
Iceland	11.1	73.1	2,274
Ireland	83.3	73.1	2,545
Italy	52.7	86.2	5,540
Japan	12.0	25.3	4,020
Luxembourg	30.3	62.0	1,115
Netherlands	28.6	62.5	3,622
New Zealand	21.6	51.9	1,139
Norway	12.7	45.9	4,082
Portugal	50.2	80.7	2,179
Spain	39.9	64.3	9,801
Sweden	10.3	34.1	4,602
Ukraine	18.5	71.0	4,790
Great Britain	22.6	52.3	4,109
United States	59.9	83.9	5,902
Germany west	40.4	73.8	768
Northern Ireland	63.0	64.2	1,431
Total	30.4	62.7	97,827

Source: Author's calculation from WVS-EVS, all waves 1981–2005.

countries (Sweden, Denmark, Norway, and Finland) followed by Iceland, Japan, and France are at the other end—with barely 10 percent of individuals attending religious services at least once a month over the 1981–2005 period.

An increase in the share of individuals not identifying with a religious denomination and a widening of the fertility gap between affiliated and non-affiliated individuals appears to be a necessary condition to sustain the argument that secularization and value change explain the overall decrease in total fertility rates. Data from the International Social Survey Program (ISSP) module Religion II (1998) demonstrate the inter-generational change in the prevalence of non-affiliated adults across developed countries.[3] Within the ISSP, I analyze the sample of those ages 16 to 45 in thirteen European countries, the US, Australia, New Zealand, and Canada who live with a spouse (both in cohabiting unions and marriages).[4]

The share of unaffiliated among those surveyed compared to that among their mothers and fathers increases dramatically across all countries with the exception of Russia. It is highest in Japan, where 81 percent of men and 77 percent of women declare themselves to have no religion, and in Eastern Germany, where 76 percent of men and 78 percent of women are unaffiliated. It is important to note, however, that, in some countries where the share of unaffiliated individuals is large, the intensity of practice among the affiliated is also high.

In the Netherlands, for example, where 66 percent of men and 58 percent of women declare no affiliation, the share of the affiliated who actively participate in church activities is 42 percent for women and 32 percent for men (calculations available upon request). This is similar to levels of practice among affiliated Americans (58 percent of men and 48 percent of women), New Zealanders (31 percent), and Canadians (38 percent). Interestingly in Russia very few people attend religious services despite high religious affiliation. The identification with the Orthodox Church thus appears to indicate a national identity more than a religious one. Among the very few men who consider themselves religious in the former East Germany, the large majority attend church activities frequently.

Finally the lowest rates of religious participation are found in Nordic countries, with less than 6 percent attending services more than two to three times per month in Denmark. In Sweden the equivalent figure is 7–8 percent, and in Norway 12 percent. These numbers are consistent with those in Table 1.3 and with the finding by Stark and Iannaccone (1994) that countries with a state church, such as the Church of Sweden or the Norwegian State Church, have very low participation rates.

Nonetheless a complete understanding of the relationship between religiosity and fertility requires that we examine the link between religious beliefs and fertility. The ISSP 1998 Survey contains a question that asks respondents to self-identify as "a religious person" on a scale of 0 to 6.[5] The correlation of this measure of religiosity and religious attendance, 0.53 in the sample of all individuals, is high but far from one. This implies that religious practice may be only one of the dimensions through which religiosity is expressed and its relevance may depend on the expectations of service attendance within each denomination (e.g., not frequent among Muslim women).[6]

I ran a statistical analysis[7] of the total number of children individuals have by education, age, current activity, and marital status as well as by their religious affiliation and intensity of practice.[8] The reference group consists of those with no religion. For this table, religious practice was based on whether the individual of a certain affiliation attends services at least once a month. I have used a more restrictive measure of religious practice—whether individuals attend weekly or more—instead of at least once a month to see whether results were affected by the definition of religious practice. Neither the ranking of affiliations nor the implied differences in fertility across them vary from the results in the original analysis. Across faith traditions, Muslims are by far the most prolific—having a little over 0.4 more children than someone with no religion even when religious practice is taken into account.

I have calculated the predicted difference in the number of children for an individual of each affiliation compared to a person without religion.[9] The simulated gap is shown in Web Figure 1.1 both for those who attend services less than once a month and for those with more active participation. The distance between Muslim fertility and that of the No Religion group is larger in the OECD sample (0.39 and 0.62 for each degree of practice) than in the global sample (0.29 and 0.51, respectively). Again, it is important to keep in mind that the share of Muslims in OECD countries in the 1981–2005 WVS-EVS sample is fairly small and that, as Westoff and Frejka (2007) note, there is wide heterogeneity in the fertility of European Muslims. On the other end, the Jewish population is on average the one with fewest children. Nonetheless, predictions confirm, not surprisingly, a great divide within that affiliation between practicing and non-practicing Jews, the largest within any affiliation.[10]

Among major denominations, Catholics and conservative Protestants have the largest family sizes. Once the intensity of practice is accounted for, membership in these denominations still matters. Catholics in OECD countries are significantly more fertile than others. This is consistent with previous findings on the ideal number of children (particularly among men) in the ISSP 1994 sample (Adsera 2006b). Both practicing Catholics and conservative Protestants in the OECD have a similar advantage of around 0.32 children over those with no religion (a sizable difference given the low overall fertility rates in those countries), though the advantage in the world sample is slightly larger for practicing conservative Protestants over Catholics (0.22 versus 0.15 children).

It is, however, important to note that in the world sample the great majority of conservative Protestants are active church attendees (75 percent)—a much larger figure than among Catholics (57 percent). In the OECD sample the average rate of regular attendance stands at 51 percent for both denominations over the entire period 1981–2005. Nonetheless, the share of practicing Catholics has been dwindling (from 58 percent in the 1981 wave to 38 percent in the latest 2005 wave) and, as a result, the impact of their fertility advantage on the total fertility of the countries where they live is now smaller than twenty years ago. The trend in participation for conservative Protestants is precisely the opposite. They are increasingly energized, with the rate of regular attendance rising from 47 percent in 1981 to 67 percent in 2005. Even so, they remain a fairly small (though growing) element of the population.

The fertility differential between liberal Protestants, who constitute around 25 percent of the population in the OECD sample, and those without religion, is very modest (0.08 children in the OECD and negligible in the world sample). Even practicing liberal Protestants bear only 0.12 children more than those with no religion (and have only half that advantage in the global sample). Liberal Protestants' rate of attendance is also substantially lower than that of other groups: only 32 percent in the world sample and 22 percent in the OECD sample attend church at least monthly. Finally, in a model that contains an indicator for each survey wave to compare it with the first wave of 1981–1985, the negative and increasingly large numbers found for more recent surveys are consistent with the overall fall in fertility during the last decades.[11] In separate analyses, I do not observe any major shifts in the ranking of affiliations over the period 1981–2005, though the distance between groups changes somewhat over time. Practicing adults consistently display higher fertility than non-attendees across all five waves. Compared to those of no religious affiliation, Catholic fertility has significantly decreased over time worldwide. Conversely, Protestant fertility has increased in relative terms since 1981 closing the gap between liberal Protestants and Catholics in recent decades—as noted in other studies. The relative increase is particularly large among conservative Protestants since the early 1990s and is most noticeable within the OECD. Within each affiliation no appreciable shift in the distance between practicing and non-practicing individuals is found, except for a continuous decrease of the gap within Muslims—consistent with previous findings (Morgan et al. 2002; Westoff and Frejka 2007; Kaufmann 2010).

One's religion and religious intensity both clearly matter for fertility decisions, but how much of the variation in fertility do these factors explain? In this vein, Frejka and Westoff (2008) model the total fertility rates (TFRs) of European countries as if they had the same high level of religiosity as the US. They estimate that fertility for European women ages 18–44 would be around 14 (or 13) percent higher with a frequency of church attendance (or self-declared religiosity) at American levels. The increase would be closer to 30 percent for western Europe.

This is an important effect. Yet such changes are not sufficient to account for the fertility gap between the US and Europe or between different regions in Europe. Secularization is certainly part of the story, but far from all of it. Consider the gap between the *desired* and *actual* number of children people have. This is affected by unforeseen material circumstances (e.g., not finding a suitable spouse; inability to land a permanent job). In developed countries this gap has been widening recently (Fahey and Speder 2004), but in separate analyses with WVS-EVS data I do not find large differences in unrealized fertility between denominations (with the exception of Jews and Muslims in the OECD). Therefore the observed religious fertility differences shown in Web Table 1.2 and Web Figure 1.1 are related principally to differences in *desired* fertility (as in Adsera 2006b). The next section tackles economic conditions to explain recent observed shortfalls in *actual* fertility.

Economic Conditions, Labor Market Institutions, and Fertility

In the introduction I pointed to two main competing arguments purporting to explain the variation in fertility: a cultural theory that posits an increase in individualism and decrease in religiosity, and a materialist argument that focuses on economic conditions such as employment, family benefits, and the ability to combine career and motherhood. In this section I explore the second explanation. Secularization aside, the sharp decrease in fertility rates, particularly in Western countries, could be explained as the logical outcome of competing demands for women's time and the rise in the opportunity cost of having children (Butz and Ward 1979, 1980; Becker 1981). Improvement in access to family planning in these countries made the move to smaller families (and postponed motherhood) possible (Goldin and Katz 2002).

Indeed, across the OECD, fertility was initially much lower in countries where women had entered the job market in the 1960s. Yet the cross-country (though not the *within-country*) relationship between female workforce participation and fertility rates across the OECD turned positive by the late 1980s. Those countries with the lowest levels of participation, such as Spain, Italy, or Greece, also displayed the lowest fertility rates, around 1.2–1.3.[12]

The change in the correlation between fertility and female participation coincides with a period in which unemployment rose sharply. The increased economic uncertainty that most of these countries experienced during this period has been advanced as a potential explanation for these differences and for the acuteness in the decline of fertility in particular countries (Adsera 2005). Adverse employment conditions have been shown to inhibit the realization of desired fertility (see Adsera 2006a for Spain; Speder and Kapitany 2009 for Hungary).[13] Levels of support provided to women varied by welfare regime in Europe, either exacerbating or easing the trade-off women and their households faced between bearing children and entering the workforce (Esping-Andersen 1999; Gauthier 2007; Andersson, Kreyenfeld, and Mika 2009).

With regard to the extent of family cash and in-kind benefits provided by the government as a share of GDP, over the last three decades policies have become steadily more generous with the average share in the OECD moving from 1.54 percent in 1985 to 2.01 percent in 2005. However, even if gaps have narrowed somewhat, there are still extraordinary gaps among countries, with the Nordics the most generous and southern Europe, Japan, and the US the least.[14]

The differences are also large in employment. Female unemployment rates in Europe for 1998 ranged from 21.0 and 15.2 percent in Spain and Italy to 3 to 5 percent in Luxembourg, the United Kingdom, Holland, Austria, and Denmark, among others. During the same period, unemployment rates in the US, Australia, and Canada were also manifestly lower than the average in Europe. Overall in southern Europe, female unemployment rates rose above 15 percent in Greece and Italy and 20 percent in Spain by the mid-1990s, 7 to 12 points higher than for men (Azmat et al. 2006). During the late 1990s, fertility rates were lowest in southern Europe where the gap between female and male unemployment rates was greatest (Adsera 2005).[15]

In addition, European unemployment during this period was extremely persistent. By 1990, around 50 percent of the unemployed in the European Union had been out of work for over twelve months. Long-term unemployment may deter or delay household formation (and with it, childbearing). This seems clearest in European countries such as Italy or Spain (Aassve et al. 2001; Gutierrez-Domenech 2008). The threat that persistent unemployment poses to a woman's ability to combine childbearing and work can be eased if her current employer secures her return to her position after childbirth. Most government jobs in Europe offer such a guarantee in addition to generous parental leave, flexible work schedules, and often subsidized childcare. The public sector employs around 30 percent of workers in Nordic countries (and close to 25 percent in France) but only half that size in most other OECD countries.[16]

Conversely, temporary (or short term) contracts with meager provisions and high turnover do not offer any of those guarantees. Yet these are the jobs that expanded rapidly during the 1990s, particularly in southern Europe (Dolado et al. 2002). To what extent did restrictive labor market regulation dissuade employers from hiring new permanent workers? Might this have been one of the main factors driving an increase in unemployment in some European countries? This is still a hotly debated question (see Addison and Teixeira 2003 for a literature review on the subject).

Nonetheless there is some evidence that highly regulated markets were hostile environments for young workers. Bertola et al. (2002) note that countries with high employment protection have lower unemployment rates of men ages 25–54 compared to young and female workers. The strict regulation of permanent employment led to the expansion of temporary work as a means for people—particularly young southern Europeans—to deal with the paucity of full-time jobs (Booth et al. 2002; OECD 2004). Permanent jobs were the norm in European countries well into the early 1980s. However, precarious short-term contracts proliferated,[17] mainly in southern Europe, after several partial labor reforms were passed from the mid-1980s in an attempt to reduce unemployment.[18] Spain was the European country where temporary employment expanded the most, and in 1998 this category already accounted for a third of all employees. Figure 1.2 shows the dramatic, interrelated variation in fertility, unemployment, and temporary employment in Spain. Other countries with large shares of short-term contracts were Finland and Sweden, where these jobs were very cyclical, and France and several southern European countries—where they accounted for the majority of new jobs for young workers. Temporary employment also rose in Italy during the late 1980s and the 1990s as employers were searching for means to reduce non-wage costs and in many cases took the form of informal continuous agreements where employees would pay taxes as self-employed but would effectively work within a firm. Unfortunately some of these very precarious jobs are not accounted for by the Eurostat definition of short-term contracts and as such the frailty of the Italian labor market is understated in these data (as shown in Web Figure 1.3 on the book web site).

To understand the importance of different policies or labor market arrangements for fertility choices, some studies exploit sharp and relatively unexpected policy changes such as parental leave (Lutz and Büttner 1990 in Germany; Hoem 1993 in Sweden; Lalive and Zweimüller 2009 in Austria), financial incentives (Milligan 2005 in Canada), and US welfare reform (Joyce,

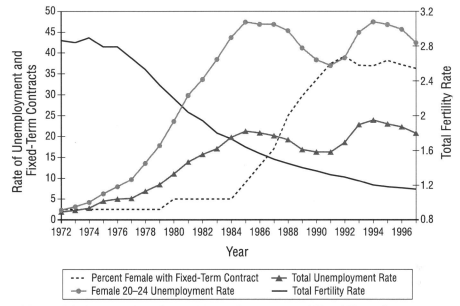

Figure 1.2 Total Fertility Rates, Unemployment, and Fixed-Term Contracts, Spain 1972–1997

Note: Spain was the European country where temporary employment expanded the most.
Source: Instituto Nacional de Estadistica (INE) of Spain (various years).

Kaestner, and Korenman 2004). Nonetheless these changes are rarely available and the inferences one can make are very limited to the particular context in which they occur.

Another strand of the literature has examined cross-country and within-country associations between fertility and economic/policy conditions. These studies have analyzed the differing degree of support available to women across welfare systems (Gauthier and Hatzius 1997; Esping-Andersen 1999; Pampel 2001; Adsera 2004); the degree of involvement of men in housework (Bettio and Villa 1998; Sevilla Sanz 2010; de Laat and Sevilla Sanz 2011); the availability of part-time working opportunities (Ariza, de la Rica, and Ungidos 2003); and access to childcare (Apps and Rees 2001; Del Boca 2002).

Similarly, I have examined the distinct fluctuations in unemployment rates across OECD countries during the 1980s and the 1990s and differences in countries' labor market arrangements to study how they affect fertility (Adsera 2004, 2005, 2011). Since the mid-1980s, countries with highly segmented markets and persistently high unemployment have had significantly lower fertility. This relationship holds even in the presence of family-friendly government policies, and it is obtained regardless of which measures of unemployment are used—total unemployment, male or female unemployment, youth unemployment or long-term unemployment (the proportion of jobless who have been out of work for more than one year), and so on. Plentiful public sector employment seems to reduce labor market uncertainty and provides women (and their spouses) access to stable jobs.

A legal and policy climate conducive to the creation of part-time employment, as exists in the Netherlands or the US, helps women progress more quickly to a second birth. Conversely, women with temporary contracts, mostly in southern Europe, are the least likely to give birth to a second child (Adsera 2011). The fact that the decrease in fertility was sharpest in OECD countries with traditionally low female participation indicates that the rapid feminization of the labor force collided with rigid labor market institutions geared toward prime-aged male workers. This resulted in both relatively high female unemployment and low fertility.

I use the 1994–2001 waves of the European Community Household Panel Survey to study around 48,000 women in thirteen European countries from when they turn sixteen until either the moment they bear their first child or the survey ends. In the statistical analysis I include the woman's education and place of birth and a set of variables indicating the aggregate labor market conditions prevalent in the country at the time this woman was making childbearing decisions. I also add information on family-friendly governmental policies. These were arguably more generous in countries with lower levels of unemployment over the past few decades.[19]

In particular, the model includes (1) an index of maternity benefits that measures weeks of leave multiplied by the percent of previous earnings received during the leave; (2) the number of children who are enrolled in pre-primary care, regardless of age, expressed as a percentage of those of eligible age; (3) the extent of family cash and in-kind benefits provided by the government as a share of GDP; and (4) as a measure of the tax benefits available to families, an index of disposable income that calculates the "additional disposable income (after taxes and cash transfers) of a one-earner-two-parent-two-child family as compared to the disposable income of a childless single earner, expressed as a percentage of the disposable income of the childless single earner" (Gauthier 2003).

The results of my analysis clearly indicate that women living in countries with more generous maternity leave and family benefits are more likely to become mothers earlier. A larger proportion of government employment is also associated with earlier first births in the country. Moreover, the coefficient on female unemployment rate is negative and statistically significant, indicating that, other things being equal, women postpone having children if they live in a country with high labor market uncertainty.

To get a sense of how important unemployment is in explaining cross-country differences in fertility, Table 1.4 includes simulations from my estimates of the percentage of women at different ages that would have either become mothers or already had a second or third child had conditions differed.[20] In countries where female unemployment rates stand at 5 percent, 81 percent of women are mothers by age 35. However, the latter percentage drops to 69 if the unemployment rate rises to 20 percent. The proportion of women that have had a second child eight years after the birth of their first is 79 and 71 percent correspondingly. In a rough approximation, the total fertility rate in both cases moves from 1.76 (on the upper end of European fertility) to 1.45 (slightly above southern European fertility). Note that in these simulations all other variables such as family benefits or provision of public jobs are held constant at the sample mean. Because in southern Europe public policies are less generous and the prevalence of full-time jobs (versus temporary employment) relatively low, we would anticipate that actual fertility would be even lower than that implied solely by their high and persistent unemployment.

Table 1.4 Predicted Proportion of Women Attaining First, Second, and Third Births When Their Country's Female Unemployment Rate Is Either 5% or 20%

Female Unemployment	*5%*	*20%*
First Birth		
By age 30	0.64	0.52
By age 35	0.81	0.69
By age 40	0.85	0.75
Second Birth		
5 years after 1st	0.67	0.57
8 years after 1st	0.79	0.71
Third Birth		
5 years after 2nd	0.25	0.24
8 years after 2nd	0.34	0.32
No. children—1	1.76	1.45
No. children—2	1.67	1.34

Note: All other variables set at the mean. No. children 1 and 2 are approximations. No. children—1 is calculated with the proportion of women who are mothers at age 40 and those who have had second and third births after 8 years from the previous. No. children—2 uses the proportion of mothers at age 35.

Source: Author's calculations based on Web Table 1.5 found on the book web site.

Work-Family Trade-Off Mediated
by Institutions and Religion?

From the discussions above I arrived at the conclusion that religious affiliation and, particularly, religiosity continue to be good predictors of ultimate family size. Even so, many families face real constraints in attaining their desired number of children stemming from labor market uncertainty and its negative impact on household income. Might the two factors interact? Do a woman's (or couple's) religious affiliation and their degree of religiosity affect how they respond to economic constraints? Do they shape the way they experience the trade-offs of work and family?

I employ two questions from the ISSP module Religion II (1998) survey to approach these issues. First, I consider the importance of religious affiliation, religious practice, and religiosity in predicting the answer to the statement "Family life suffers if mom works full time." Second, I estimate similar statistical models for the statement "A husband's job is to earn money and the wife's to look after the home." Respondents select an answer from a menu that goes from strong disagreement (1) to strong agreement (5). Note that both statements are far from equivalent. Whereas an unambiguous agreement with the second question signals a traditional view of gender roles, agreeing with the first statement may merely reflect the constraints that households face in making family and work compatible. Those barriers stem from the particular workings of the labor markets and welfare states in each country.

Results show that those individuals who are affiliated with a religion are more likely than the religiously unaffiliated to agree with both statements. However, the relative strength of this effect across denominations varies by question. Figure 1.3 presents the predicted difference in the answers across denominations compared to that given by an individual with no affiliation.[21] The difference is presented separately for those who consider themselves highly religious and for those who do not.

Catholics are most in agreement with the first question. Even after taking their religiosity into account, they significantly agree more that a child suffers if the mother works full time. However, the difference is smaller for Protestants and not even statistically relevant for conservatives of low religiosity once measures of religiosity are added to the analysis. Among practicing/religious individuals, Catholics are the most likely to agree that the children suffer if the mother works full time.[22] On the second statement, however, conservative Protestants are more likely to endorse traditional gender roles than liberals and Catholics. Individuals who claim to be somewhat or highly religious also

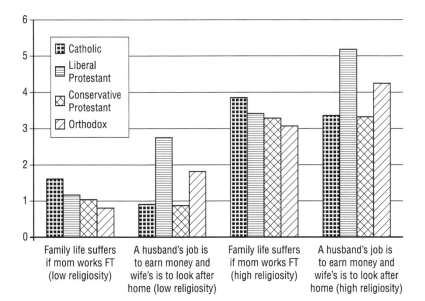

Figure 1.3 Views on Family-Career Tradeoff across Religious Denominations, OECD Countries in ISSP 1998, Module Religion II

Note: Predictions from an Ordinary Least Squares statistical model that uses data from the ISSP 1998 survey and also includes controls for age, education, marital status, and country of residence. Individuals in OECD countries are asked whether "Family life suffers if mom works full time" and whether "A husband's job is to earn money and wife's to look after home." Responses range from 1 (disagree) to 6 (agree). Self-reported religiosity is measured on a scale of seven options from extremely nonreligious to extremely religious. An individual is considered highly religious if she states herself to be somewhat religious to very religious.

endorse traditional gender roles. The response of non-practicing Catholics and liberals (obtained in a separate analysis that looks at frequency of church attendance) does not differ from the non-religious. These interdenominational differences are a function of both individual-level religious values and a country-level effect: the perception individuals have of the material feasibility of combining family and work where they live (e.g., in Catholic southern Europe). The view that a child suffers if a mother works full time may be related to the type of job that a young mother is expected to have access to, to her ability of temporarily moving out of the labor force and easily coming back after caring for the child, or to her opportunities to obtain flexible schedules or part-time employment while the child is young. To parse out these country-level effects, we use country indicators in the statistical analysis.

Individuals in OECD countries surveyed in the WVS-EVS were asked whether "Being a housewife is just as fulfilling" as full- or part-time work. This statement lies somewhere in between the previous two. On the one hand it is related to the notion of gender division within a household. On the other, the term *fulfillment* and the suggestion of other existing alternatives indicate an active choice on the part of the woman to remain in the house. Muslims and conservative Protestants are the most comfortable with the statement even after their practice is taken into account. Catholics and liberals are halfway between these groups and non-affiliated. For all groups, frequent practice is associated with more conformity with the statement.[23]

An interesting finding in this statistical analysis is the wide variation in the average position of individuals across countries once religion, religiosity, and other demographics have been taken into account.[24] In German-speaking and southern European countries those averages indicate large disagreement with the statement "Being a housewife is just as fulfilling." Recall that in these countries fertility has decreased the most, female participation in the labor market is relatively low, part-time or public sector jobs are hardest to obtain, and the ability to enter and exit the labor market without penalty (i.e., without decreasing your likelihood of finding a similar job again) is difficult. Conversely, in Anglo-Saxon and Nordic countries, which have more flexible labor markets, lower unemployment rates, and/or larger public employment sectors, the population is more apt to agree that being a housewife is a valid option. The discontent expressed by many southern European and German women probably derives from their perceiving that their national institutions are an obstacle to combining childbearing with a career at the same time.

Additional important constraints in the ability to "have it all" are the cost of caring for children and the availability of suitable educational institutions. Traditionally, religious institutions have played an important role in the provision of such services (as well as others such as health). Over time the public sector has been taking the lead role in the provision of such services, crowding out the private sector in some cases. In addition, the process of secularization has affected the provision of affordable labor (e.g., nuns as teachers) and the ability within denominations, particularly Catholicism, to provide quality but affordable services to their constituencies. Berman et al. (2005) argue that the increased scarcity of those services has constrained family fertility choices in countries such as Italy.

Conversely, Johnson et al. (2002) note that a quarter of the US population receives services from faith-based organizations annually. Berghammer (2009) writes that both the supply and demand of such church services are much lower in the Netherlands since the Dutch welfare system is among the most generous in western Europe. But the "free school" principle guarantees wide availability of religious education for those parents who choose it. Something similar happens in Belgium where effectively a voucher system is in place. In Nordic countries that task has been taken up by the state with wide provision of early childhood education. Therefore fertility is not constrained by the lack of religious services in these countries.

Conclusion

To predict future fertility trends we need to understand how work-family trade-offs are mediated by institutions and religion in each country. The literature reviewed and the new findings in this chapter show that fertility decline cannot be explained solely by culturalist or materialist theories. Both those who suggest a cultural explanation—the growth of more secular and individualistic values—and those who stress economic and institutional conditions hold part of the answer. As Frejka and Westoff (2008) note, fertility in western Europe would be substantially higher if its level of religiosity were equal to that of the US, but this would not suffice to bridge the fertility gap. Nor could it explain variation in total fertility rates across developed countries.

We can be more specific: it seems that cultural explanations are integral to explaining varying fertility ideals while material factors help us understand why people fail to attain those ideals. Importantly, the rising prevalence of individuals who do not *attain* their preferred number of children does not seem related to secularization but rather to new economic constraints. Whether this lower *realized* fertility will over time alter the *desired* family size of the next generation (toward smaller family sizes) remains to be seen. Cross-country differences in the answer to the question of whether being a housewife is as fulfilling as working indicate a degree of female frustration with the task of making work and family compatible. This seems especially marked in southern Europe. It is principally felt by members of mainstream religious groups such as Catholics or liberal Protestants, where traditional gender roles have eroded to a much larger extent than in the more conservative denominations and faith traditions. For the latter, by contrast, traditional gender norms are less problematic. This makes it easier for members to accept the limitations imposed by economic structures that impede women from combining work and family.

Notes

1. Only among some women in the US, particularly among the least educated, is the latter still an issue.

2. See studies for the United States by Lehrer and Chiswick (1993) and Lehrer (1996) that use a classification based on work by Kelley (1972) and Smith (1990).

3. See Web Table 1.1 on the book web site for graphical representation.

4. The International Social Survey Program (ISSP) is an ongoing program of cross-national collaboration formed in 1983. In the US the data is collected as part of the General Social Survey (GSS), conducted by NORC.

5. Self-reported religiosity is measured on a scale of seven options: extremely non-religious (0); very non-religious (1); somewhat non-religious (2); neither religious nor non-religious (3); somewhat religious (4); very religious (5); and extremely religious (6).

6. The data from the preceding discussion are presented in Web Table 1.1 on the book web site.

7. The results of this analysis may be viewed in Web Table 1.2 on the book web site.

8. To take into account that some common cultural, economic, or institutional features may jointly affect the fertility of individuals living in the same country, I include a dummy variable for each country and the errors are clustered at country level in all the models in Table 1.2.

9. The difference is calculated with respect to the 2.12 children (in the world sample) or 1.97 children (in the OECD sample) predicted for an employed man, aged 35–44, with no religious affiliation.

10. The reader can see these data in Web Figure 1.1, which is available on the book web site.

11. See Web Table 1.2 on the book web site.

12. See Web Figure 1.2 on the book web site.

13. For Spanish women in the 1985 and 1996 fertility surveys, for example, I find that even after controlling for religious affiliation, religious practice, and family planning, labor market circumstances (e.g., unemployment, temporary employment) explained a large part of the unfulfilled fertility desires of women.

14. Data for this paragraph are presented in Web Table 1.3 on the book web site.

15. Data for this paragraph are presented in Web Table 1.4 on the book web site.

16. Please see Web Table 1.4 on the book web site, column 5.

17. See Web Table 1.4 on the book web site for the percentage, according to Eurostat, of employees holding contracts of limited duration in 1998.

18. See Web Figure 1.3 on the book web site for the current prevalence of such contracts in the OECD.

19. The estimates of the statistical model discussed in this paragraph can be found in Web Table 1.5 on the book web site.

20. These simulations are based on the model in Web Table 1.5 on the book web site and similar models for the second and third birth. Estimates of the models of transition to the second and third child are available from the author.

21. All the statistical models include control variables such as age of the individual, number of children, marital status, and educational background, and those are kept constant in all the simulations in Figure 1.3.

22. I obtain the same ranking across religious groups analyzing a similar question from the WVS-EVS.

23. See Web Figure 1.4 on the book web site for the predicted difference across affiliations compared to an individual with no religion.

24. Numbers are available upon request.

References

Aassve, F. A., C. Billari, and F. Ongaro. 2001. The Impact of Income and Occupational Status on Leaving Home: Evidence from the Italian ECHP Sample. *Labour* 15 (3): 501–529.

Adam, P. 1996. Mothers in an Insider-Outsider Economy: The Puzzle of Spain. *Journal of Population Economics* 9: 301–323.

Addison, John T., and Paulino Teixeira. 2003. The Economics of Employment Protection. *Journal of Labor Research* 24 (1): 85–128.

Adsera, A. 2004. Changing Fertility Rates in Developed Markets: The Impact of Labor Market Institutions. *Journal of Population Economics* 17 (1): 17–43.

———. 2005. Vanishing Children: From High Unemployment to Low Fertility in Developed Countries. *American Economic Review Papers and Proceedings* 95 (2): 198–193.

———. 2006a. An Economic Analysis of the Gap between Desired and Actual Fertility: The Case of Spain. *Review of Economics of the Household* 4 (1, March): 75–95.

———. 2006b. Religion and Changes in Family-Size Norms in Developed Countries. *Review of Religious Research* 47 (3): 271–286.

———. 2006c. Marital Fertility and Religion in Spain. *Population Studies* 60 (2): 205–221.

———. 2007. Reply to the Note by Neuman: Is Fertility Indeed Related to Religiosity? *Population Studies* 61 (2): 225–230.

———. 2011. Where Are the Babies? Labor Market Conditions and Fertility in Europe. *European Journal of Population* 27 (1): 1–32.

Andersson, G., M. Kreyenfeld, and T. Mika. 2009. Welfare State Context, Female Earnings and Childbearing. Max Planck Institute for Demographic Research. (MPIDR Working Paper 2009-026).

Apps, Patricia, and Ray Rees. 2001. Household Production, Full Consumption and the Costs of Children. *Labour Economics* 8 (6): 621–648.

Ariza, A., S. de la Rica, and A. Ugidos. 2005. The Effect of Flexibility in Working Hours on Fertility: A Comparative Analysis of Selected European Countries. *Public Finance and Management* 5 (1).

Azmat, G., M. Guell, and A. Manning. 2006. Gender Gaps in Unemployment Rates in OECD Countries. *Journal of Labor Economics* 24 (1): 1–37.

Becker, G. 1960. An Economic Analysis of Fertility. *Demographic and Economic Change in Developed Countries*, NBER conference series 11: 209–231.

———. 1981. *A Treatise on the Family*. Cambridge, MA: Harvard University Press.

Becker, Gary S., Elisabeth M. Landes, and Robert T. Michael. 1977. An Economic Analysis of Marital Instability. *Journal of Political Economy* 85 (6): 1141–1187.

Becker, Gary S., and Kevin M. Murphy. 2001. *Social Economics: Market Behaviour in a Social Environment.* Cambridge, MA: Harvard University Press.

Becker, P. E., and H. Hofmeister. 2001. Work, Family and Religious Involvement for Men and Women. *Journal for the Scientific Study of Religion* 40 (4): 707–722.

Berghammer, C. 2009. Causality between Religiosity and Childbearing: Evidence from a Dutch Panel Study. Paper presented at the IUSSP conference, Marrakech.

Berman, E., L. Iannaccone, and G. Ragusa. 2005. From Empty Pews to Empty Cradles: Fertility Decline among European Catholics. Unpublished manuscript.

Bertola, G., F. Blau, and L. Kahn. 2002. Labor Market Institutions and Demographic Employment Patterns. Working Paper No. W9043, National Bureau of Economic Research, Cambridge, MA.

Bettio, F., and P. Villa. 1998. A Mediterranean Perspective on the Breakdown of the Relationship between Participation and Fertility. *Cambridge Journal of Economics* 22 (2): 137–171.

Bongaarts, J. 2002. The End of the Fertility Transition in the Developed World. *Population and Development Review* 28 (3): 419–443.

Booth, A. L., J. J. Dolado, and J. Frank. 2002. Symposium on Temporary Work: Introduction. *Economic Journal* 112 (480): F181–F188.

Brañas-Garza, Pablo, and Shoshana Neuman. 2006. Intergenerational Transmission of 'Religious Capital': Evidence from Spain. IZA (Bonn): Discussion Paper No. 2183.

Bruce, S. 2001. Christianity in Britain, R.I.P. *Sociology of Religion* 62: 191–203.

Bumpass, Larry. 1990. What's Happening to the Family? Interactions between Demographic and Institutional Change. *Demography* 27 (4): 483–498.

Butz, W., and M. Ward. 1979. The Emergence of Countercyclical U.S. Fertility. *American Economic Review* 69 (3): 318–328.

———. 1980. Completed Fertility and Its Timing. *Journal of Political Economy* 88: 917–940.

Colom, Maria Consuelo, Rosario Martinez, and Maria Cruz Moles. 2002. Un análisis de las decisiones de formación de hogar, tenencia y demanda de servicios de viviendas de los jóvenes españoles. *Moneda y Credito* 215: 199–223.

De Laat, Joost, and Almudena Sevilla Sanz. 2011. Working Women, Men's Home Time and the Positive Cross-Country Correlation between Fertility and Female Labor Force Participation. *Feminist Economics* 17 (2): 87–119.

Del Boca, D. 2002. The Effect of Child Care and Part Time Opportunities on Participation and Fertility Decisions. *Journal of Population Economics* 15 (3): 549–573.

Dolado, Juan Jose, Carlos García-Serrano, and Juan Francisco Jimeno. 2002. Drawing Lessons from the Boom of Temporary Jobs in Spain. *The Economic Journal* 112: 270–295.

Ermisch, J. 1988. Econometric Analysis of Birth Rate Dynamics in Britain. *The Journal of Human Resources* 23 (4): 563–576

Esping-Andersen, G. 1999. *Social Foundations of Postindustrial Economies.* Oxford: Oxford University Press.

Fahey, Tony, and Zsolt Speder. 2004. *Fertility and Family Issues in an Enlarged Europe.* Dublin: European Foundation for the Improvement of Living and Working Conditions.

Frejka, T., and C. F. Westoff. 2008. Religiousness and Fertility in the United States and in Europe. *European Journal of Population* 24 (1): 5–31.

Galor, O., and D. Weil. 1996. The Gender Gap, Fertility and Growth. *American Economic Review* 86: 374–387.

Gauthier, A. H. 2003. Comparative Family Benefits Database, Version 2 (University of Calgary). Online.

———. 2007. The Impact of Family Policies on Fertility in Industrialized Countries: A Review of the Literature. *Population Research and Policy Review* 26 (3): 323–346.

Gauthier, A. H., and J. Hatzius. 1997. Family Policy and Fertility: An Econometric Analysis. *Population Studies* 51: 295–306.

Goldin, C., and L. Katz. (2002). The Power of the Pill: Oral Contraceptives and Women's Career and Marriage Decisions. *Journal of Political Economy* 110: 730–770.

Goldscheider, Calvin, and William D. Mosher. 1991. Patterns of Contraceptive Use in the United States: The Importance of Religious Factors. *Studies in Family Planning* 22 (2): 102–115.

Goldscheider, Frances K., and Gayle Kaufman. 1996. Fertility and Commitment: Bringing Men Back In. *Population and Development Review* 22 (Suppl.): 87–99.

Goldstein, J. R., W. Lutz, and M. R. Testa. 2003. The Emergence of Sub-Replacement Family Size Ideals in Europe. *Population Research and Policy Review* 22: 479–496.

Gutierrez-Domenech, Maria. 2008. The Impact of the Labour Market on the Timing of Marriage and Births in Spain. *Journal of Population Economics* 21: 83–110.

Heaton, Tim B. 1986. How Does Religion Influence Fertility? The Case of the Mormons. *Journal for the Scientific Study of Religion* 25: 248–258.

Hoem, B. 2000. Entry into Motherhood: The Influence of Economic Factors on the Rise and Fall in Fertility, 1986–1997. *Demographic Research* 2 (4).

Hoem, B., and J. Hoem. 1989. The Impact of Women's Employment on Second and Third Births in Modern Sweden. *Population Studies* 43: 47–67.

Hoem. J. 1993. Public Policy as the Fuel of Fertility: Effects of a Policy Reform on the Pace of Childbearing in Sweden in the 1980s. *Acta Sociologica* 36 (1): 19–31.

Janssen, S., and R. Hauser. 1981. Religion, Socialization and Fertility. *Demography* 18 (4): 511–528.

Johnson, B., R. B. Tompkins, D. Webb. 2002. *Objective Hope: Assessing the Effectiveness of Faith-Based Organizations: A Review of the Literature.* Philadelphia: Center for Research on Religion and Urban Civil Society, University of Pennsylvania.

Joyce, T., R. Kaestner, S. Korenman, and S. Henshaw. 2004. Family Cap Provision and Changes in Births and Abortions. *Population Research and Policy Review* 23: 475–511.

Kaufmann, E. 2010. Sacralization by Stealth? The Religious Consequences of Low Fertility in Europe. Paper presented at the Social Trends Institute Conference, Barcelona.

Kelley, Dean M. 1972. *Why Conservative Churches Are Growing*. New York: Harper and Row.

Khawaja, Marwan. 2000. The Recent Rise in Palestinian Fertility: Permanent or Transient? *Population Studies* 54 (3): 331–346.

Kohler, H. P., F. Billari, and J. A. Ortega. 2002. The Emergence of Lowest-Low Fertility in Europe during the 1990s. *Population and Development Review* 28 (4): 599–639.

Krause, N., C. Ellison, B. Shaw, J. Marcum, and J. Boardman. 2001. Church Based Social Support and Religious Coping. *Journal for the Scientific Study of Religion* 40: 637–656.

Kravdal, O. 2001. The High Fertility of College Educated Women in Norway. *Demographic Research* 5 (6): 187–216.

———. 2002. The Impact of Individual and Aggregate Unemployment on Fertility in Norway. *Demographic Research* 6 (10): 263–294.

Lalive, R., and J. Zweimüller. 2009. Does Parental Leave Affect Fertility and Return-to-Work? Evidence from Two Natural Experiments. *The Quarterly Journal of Economics* 124 (3): 1363–1402.

Lehrer, Evelyn L. 1996. Religion as a Determinant of Marital Fertility. *Journal of Population Economics* 9 (2): 173–196.

———. 2004. Religion as a Determinant of Economic and Demographic Behavior in the United States. *Population and Development Review* 30 (4): 707–726.

Lehrer, Evelyn L., and Carmel U. Chiswick. 1993. Religion as a Determinant of Marital Stability. *Demography* 30 (3): 385–404.

Lesthaeghe, R., and G. Moors. 1996. Living Arrangements, Socio-economic Position and Values among Young Adults: A Pattern Description for Belgium, France, the Netherlands and West Germany 1990. In: D. Coleman (Ed.), *Europe's Population in the 1990s,* 163–221. Oxford: Oxford University Press.

Lesthaeghe, Ron, and Johan Surkyn. 1988. Cultural Dynamics and Economic Theories of Fertility Change. *Population and Development Review* 14 (1): 1–45.

Lutz, W., and T. Büttner . 1990. Estimating Fertility Responses to Policy Measures in the German Democratic Republic. *Population and Development Review* 16 (3): 539–555.

Marcum, J. P. 1988. Religious Affiliation, Participation and Fertility: A Cautionary Note. *Journal for the Scientific Study of Religion* 27 (4): 621–629.

McQuillan, Kevin. 2004. When Does Religion Influence Fertility? *Population and Development Review* 30 (1): 25–56.

Miller, A., and R. Stark. 2002. Gender and Religiousness: Can Socialization Explanations Be Saved? *American Journal of Sociology* 107 (6): 1399–1423.

Milligan, K. 2005. Subsidizing the Stork: New Evidence on Tax Incentives and Fertility. *Review of Economics and Statistics* 83 (3): 539–555.

Morgan, S. P. 2003. Low Fertility in the Twenty-First Century. *Demography* 40 (4): 589–603.

Morgan, S. Philip, and Heather Rackin. 2010. The Correspondence between Fertility Intentions and Behavior in the United States. *Population and Development Review* pp. 91–118.

Morgan, S. Philip, Sharon Stash, Hervert L. Smith, and Karen O. Mason. 2002. Muslim and Non-Muslim Differences in Female Autonomy and Fertility: Evidence from Four Asian Countries. *Population and Development Review* 28 (3, September): 515–537.

Mosher, William D., and Gerry E. Hendershot. 1984. Religion and Fertility: A Replication. *Demography* 21 (2): 185–191.

Mosher, W., L. Williams, and D. Johnson. 1992. Religion and Fertility in the United States: New Patterns. *Demography* 29 (2): 199–214.

———. (various years). *OECD Economic Outlook.* Paris: OECD.

———. 2004. Employment Protection Regulation and Labour Market Performance. In *OECD Employment Outlook,* chapter 2. Paris: OECD.

OECD. (various years). *Labour Force Statistics.* Paris: OECD.

O'Grada, Cormac, and Brendan Walsh. 1995. Fertility and Population in Ireland, North and South. *Population Studies* 49 (2): 259–279.

Pampel, F. 2001. *Institutional Context of Population Change. Patterns of Fertility and Mortaliy across High-Income Nations.* Chicago: The University of Chicago Press.

Pearce, L., and W. Axinn. 1988. The Impact of Family Religious Life on the Quality of Mother-Child Relations. *American Sociological Review* 63 (6): 810–828.

Petersen, Larry R., and Gregory V. Donnenwerth. 1997. Secularization and the Influence of Religion on Beliefs about Premarital Sex. *Social Forces* 75 (3): 1071–1089.

Philipov, D., and C. Berghammer. 2007. Religion and Fertility Ideals, Intentions and Behaviour: A Comparative Study of European Countries. *Vienna Yearbook of Population Research,* pp. 271–305.

Sander, William. 1992. Catholicism and the Economics of Fertility. *Population Studies* 46: 477–489.

Sevilla Sanz, Almudena. 2010. Household Division of Labor and Cross-Country Differences in Household Formation Rates. *Journal of Population Economics* 23 (1): 225.

Smith, T. W. 1990. Classifying Protestant Denominations. *Review of Religious Research* 31: 225–245.

Sobotka, T. 2004. Is Lowest-Low Fertility in Europe Explained by the Postponement of Childbearing? *Population and Development Review* 30 (2): 195–220.

Speder, Z., and B. Kapitany. 2009. How Are Time-Dependent Childbearing Intentions Realized? Realization, Postponement, Abandonment, Bringing Forward. *European Journal of Population* 25 (4): 503–523.

Stark, R. 1999. Secularization, R.I.P. *Sociology of Religion* 60: 249–273.

Stark, Rodney, and Laurence R. Iannaccone. 1994. A Supply-Side Reinterpretation of the Secularization of Europe. *Journal of the Scientific Study of Religion* 34 (1): 76–88.

Stolzenberg, R., M. Blair-Loy, and L. Waite. 1995. Religious Participation in Early

Adulthood: Age and Family Life-Cycle Effects on Church Membership. *American Sociological Review* 60 (1): 84–103.

Surkyn, Johan, and Ron Lesthaeghe. 2004. Value Orientations and the Second Demographic Transition (SDT) in Northern, Western and Southern Europe: An Update. *Demographic Research* S3 (3): 45–86.

Thornton, A. 1985. Reciprocal Influences of Family and Religion in a Changing World. *Journal of Marriage and the Family* 47 (4): 381–394.

United Nations. 2002. World Contraceptive Use 2001. New York: Population Division of the Department of Economic and Social Affairs of the United Nations Secretariat.

US Department of Health and Human Services. (various years). *Social Security Programs throughout the World.* Washington, DC.

Van de Kaa, Dirk. 1987. Europe's Second Demographic Transition. *Population Bulletin* 42 (1): 1–57.

———. 2004. Is the Second Demographic Transition a Useful Research Concept? Questions and Answers. In G. Feichtinger (ed.), *Vienna Yearbook of Population Research*: 4–10. Vienna: Institute of Demography.

Voas, D. 2007. Does Religion Belong in Population Studies? *Environment and Planning A* 39 (5): 1166–1180.

———. 2009. The Rise and Fall of Fuzzy Fidelity in Europe. *European Sociological Review* 25 (2): 155–168.

Voas, D., and A. Crockett. 2005. Religion in Britain: Neither Believing nor Belonging. *Sociology* 39 (1): 11–28.

Waite, Linda, and Evelyn Lehrer. 2003. The Benefits from Marriage and Religion in the United States: A Comparative Analysis. *Population and Development Review* 29 (2): 255–275.

Westoff, Charles F., and Elise F. Jones. 1979. The End of Catholic Fertility. *Demography* 16 (2): 209–217.

Westoff, C. F., and T. Frejka. 2007. Religiousness and Fertility among European Muslims. *Population and Development Review* 33.

Wilcox, W. B. 2004. *Soft Patriarchs, New Men: How Christianity Shapes Fathers and Husbands.* Chicago: University of Chicago Press.

Williams, Linda B., and Basil G. Zimmer. 1990. The Changing Influence of Religion on US Fertility: Evidence from Rhode Island. *Demography* 27 (3): 475–481.

Wolfinger, N., and W. B. Wilcox. 2008. Happily Ever After? Religion, Marital Status, Gender and Relationship Quality in Urban Families. *Social Forces* 86 (3): 1311–1337.

World Values Survey. (various years). Institute for Social Research of the University of Michigan, Ronald Inglehart, director. http://www.worldvaluessurvey.org/.

Chapter 2

The Social and Civic Consequences of Parenthood for Adults

David J. Eggebeen

The declines in fertility over the past few decades among developed nations to below replacement levels, and in some cases to well below replacement levels, are well known among demographers. European countries have been leading the charge. Recent data assembled by the Population Reference Bureau show that all forty-three European countries have below-replacement total fertility rates[1] as of 2005–2006 (Population Reference Bureau 2010). Furthermore, these rates have been stable; forty-two of these countries have been at below-replacement fertility rates since at least 1995. Ominously, eleven European countries, mainly concentrated in Eastern Europe, have extremely low total fertility rates—at or below 1.3. Demographers, as is their wont, have mainly focused on documenting and describing these trends and, to a lesser extent, explaining them (Kohler, Billari, and Ortega 2006). Comparatively little work, however, has focused on the implications of low fertility for the social, community, family, and individual lives of adults. The purpose of this chapter is to examine one possible consequence of low fertility—that citizen involvement in volunteer organizations or community life might be negatively affected. Put another way: is parenthood one of the mechanisms that propels investment in or attachment to one's community, and might the declining place of parenthood in the lives of adults threaten civic life?

A glance at comparative trends in civic engagement and fertility for seventeen European countries as well as the US in Table 2.1 suggests there might be a link. While there are exceptions, in general the countries with the lowest fertility rates also have the smallest fractions of adults actively involved in at least one volunteer organization. Could it be as Brooks observes, "The demographic implosion of Europe lies in some part behind its low charitable giving and volunteering rates" (2006, 132)? The question this chapter seeks to address is whether, beyond these aggregate relationships, there is evidence at the individual level that adults who have children are more likely to be actively involved in civic or volunteer organizations. The focus will be on five countries: Sweden, Britain, Spain, Poland, and the United States.

Civic participation has generated a fair amount of interest from scholars in recent years. In the 1980s Robert Bellah in his provocative book *Habits of the Heart* (1985) described the rise of what he called expressive individualism and argued that this trend was weakening civic participation. Fifteen years later Robert Putnam (1995, 2000) extended this line of thinking by providing a blizzard of data and statistics that showed that young Americans are significantly less civic minded than previous generations. Not everyone agrees with these conclusions. Some scholars dispute the statistics, offering studies that do not show declines in civic participation (Paxton 1999; Rotolo and Wilson 2004). Others contend that participation in traditional organizations may be declining but these declines are offset by shifts in involvement to new forms of associations—away from labor unions and churches to environmental and human rights groups, for example (Wuthnow 1998). In any event, whether one concludes that civic participation is declining or merely being transformed, there is broad consensus among all sides that civic participation is a desirable thing.

Table 2.1 Total Fertility Rates and the Percentage of Adults Active in Volunteer Organizations for Selected Countries

Country	Total Fertility Rate	Percent of Adults Actively Involved in at Least One Volunteer Organization
Ukraine	1.254	13.6
Poland	1.278	17.7
Moldova	1.306	23.6
Russia	1.312	11.6
Romania	1.312	9.5
Germany	1.340	40.4
Italy	1.352	36.1
Spain	1.370	21.0
Bulgaria	1.380	7.0
Switzerland	1.440	63.5
Serbia	1.452	13.5
Netherlands	1.730	55.4
Finland	1.840	41.4
Sweden	1.850	61.5
Britain	1.850	57.2
Norway	1.904	53.5
France	1.983	41.3
US	2.101	67.5

Sources: Total Fertility Rates are from 2005 or 2006 and are drawn from data assembled by the Population Reference Bureau (2010). Involvement in volunteer organizations is drawn from the 2005 wave of the World Values Surveys conducted in each European country, and the 1999 survey wave for the US.

Civic Engagement as a Social Good

There is good evidence that neighborhoods, communities, and nation-states benefit when individuals participate in community organizations or perform unpaid volunteer work. They also benefit economically from volunteering. When community members join volunteer fire companies or ambulance corps, tutor children in schools, help out in community health centers, start or supervise youth groups, or run soup kitchens, communities do not have to pay for these services. Precise estimates of the economic impact of volunteering are difficult given that governments do not measure the contribution of volunteering to their gross domestic product. Indirect estimates of the magnitude of the economic contributions of volunteering suggest it is probably considerable.

For example, a recent study of volunteering in the United States found that 61.8 million Americans contributed 8 billion hours of volunteer service worth an estimated $163 billion (Corporation for National and Community Service 2010). Communities also benefit from other forms of participation. Involvement in neighborhood associations, garden clubs, choral societies, and recreational soccer leagues builds healthy communities. They do this, according to Putnam (1993), for several reasons. First, civic engagement fosters norms of generalized reciprocity: "I will do this for you now, in the expectation that down the road you or someone else will reciprocate." Civic engagement also facilitates network ties that enhance communication and build trust. Finally, civic engagement, by fostering connections between individuals, builds the resources embedded in social relationships, what sociologists label "social capital."

Engagement in social groups also has positive consequences for individuals (Wilson 2000). For example, participating in community organizations can have a number of mental health benefits. Volunteering can boost self-esteem and self-confidence (Harlow and Cantor 1996). Volunteering can help convince people that they can make a difference, which can buffer against depression (Mirowsky and Ross 1989). Volunteering increases life satisfaction, especially among the elderly (Wheeler, Gorey, and Greenblatt 1998). Studies also show that active participation in community organizations is associated with better physical health (Stephan 1991), higher scores on functionality among the elderly (Moen, Dempster-McClain, and Williams 1992), and a lower risk of mortality (Musick, Herzog, and House 1999). Finally, there is some evidence of educational benefits for teenagers and young adults who volunteer or are involved in service learning projects (Wilson 2000).

Given the social importance of civic engagement for maintaining healthy and vital communities and nurturing good citizenship, it is important to determine what might influence civic engagement. Indeed there is a substantial literature that has developed over the past few decades that has focused on the role of such individual attributes as labor force participation, economic resources, family relationships, age and life stage (Wilson 2000), religiosity (Driskell, Lyon, and Embry 2008; Wilcox 2002), and gender (Hook 2004). Research has also examined the role of such contextual factors as birth cohort or nation-state differences in patterns of community involvement and civic participation (Anderson, Curtis, and Grabb 2006; Rotolo and Wilson 2004; Schofer and Fourcade-Gourinchas 2001). The role of parenthood, however, has not received much systematic attention.

Civic Engagement and Parenthood

How might parenthood affect civic engagement? A rational-choice perspective would suggest that children, especially young children, impose time and cost constraints on parents' ability to be involved in community groups or organizations (Hook 2004). Put another way, raising children takes a lot of time. Time outside of work that previously may have been devoted to volunteer work or participating in a recreational sports league may now be spent changing diapers and pushing a swing. The time costs of children may not diminish as children move through childhood. Changing diapers may be replaced by the demands of extracurricular activities that have become a common feature of parenting older children—especially among the middle class. In sum, a rational-choice perspective would argue that parenthood inhibits community involvement.

There is some evidence consistent with this perspective—at least for parents of very young children. Rotolo and Wilson (2007), using data drawn from the National Longitudinal Survey of Young Women, found that mothers of preschool-aged children were the least likely to be doing unpaid volunteer work relative to women with older children or childless women. This deterrence of young children, but not older children, on volunteering has also been found in other studies (Menchik and Weisbrod 1987; Schlozman, Burns, and Verba 1994; Vallancourt 1994).

An alternative possibility is that children present an opportunity for adults to increase their civic involvement. There are several possible mechanisms. Children provide a link or bridge to developing relationships with other parents in the neighborhood or community. This can happen informally when children and their parents congregate at the playground or when parents become acquainted with the parents of their child's friends in the neighborhood. Parenthood, then, potentially can enhance one's social capital, which may lead to other forms of social connections to one's community.

Parenthood can also draw adults into contact with institutions and organizations that serve their child (Wilson 2000). Adults may not have paid much attention to the neighborhood elementary school before they had children. It is a different matter once your child begins attending this school. As children become involved in school, as well as other child-oriented organizations like soccer teams, Boy or Girl Scouts, or church youth groups, parents are drawn into concern with, and involvement in, these organizations.

Sociologists would note that parenthood is a social role with socially agreed-upon expectations about how to behave in that role. When one has a child, one assumes the mantle and identity of mother or father and may begin to feel the pull of expectations and obligations attached to those identities. Thus, adults may become involved in churches, Scouts, or parent-teacher organizations not just because they want to but because they, as parents, are expected to be involved by friends, neighbors, and other family members (Eggebeen and Knoester 2001; Eggebeen, Dew, and Knoester 2010).

Finally, parenthood may initiate personal growth or transformation by challenging men and women to clarify values and set priorities (Palkovitz 2002; Snarey 1993). A number of scholars have asserted that fathering is generative (Hawkins and Dollahite 1997; Palkovitz 1996; Snarey 1993). That is, men, out of a strong desire to meet the needs of their children, become more caring human beings, more concerned about future generations, and thus more active in their communities.

A number of studies find an association between parenthood and community engagement. For example, Rotolo and Wilson (2006), using data drawn from the volunteer supplement of the 2002 Current Population Survey, found a positive relationship between the presence of a child aged 6–17 and the number of volunteer hours women reported contributing. Similarly a study based on the Baylor Religion Survey found that the number of children was positively correlated with the extent of civic engagement (Driskell, Lyon, and Embry 2008). Studies of the effects of fatherhood on men's lives find that becoming a father is positively associated with involvement in service organizations (Eggebeen and Knoester 2001; Knoester and Eggebeen 2006). Furthermore, there is evidence that this effect extends well into middle age when most men have launched their children into adulthood (Eggebeen, Dew, and Knoester 2010).

Most of the studies of civic engagement that have included parenthood variables have focused on the US. The few studies of other countries yield less consistent results. Hook (2004) found that parenthood positively predicted the number of minutes per week of volunteering among a representative sample of Australians, similar to patterns found with US data. However, a recent study of trends in civic association activity in Canada, Britain, the Netherlands, and the US using comparable time-use surveys found considerable variation in the link between parenthood and time spent in civic activities across these four countries (Anderson, Curtis, and Grabb 2006). In Canada, for instance, childless adults gave more time to civic activities than did parents. In Britain, no relationship between parenthood and civic involvement was found. Only in the United States and Canada did the data show that parenthood was positively associated with civic activities, but even then it was contingent on gender and labor force participation.

The Moderating Effects of Gender and Marital Status

Studies based on US data typically find that women have slightly higher rates of civic participation than men (Wilson 2000). Women's higher rates of civic participation may be because of a stronger correlation between parenthood and civic engagement. Given that full-time employment reduces the time available for other activities (Freeman 1997), and that fathers tend to be more attached to the labor force than mothers, we might expect that men become less involved as the demands of juggling work and fatherhood mount. There is evidence that with the transition to fatherhood, men cut back on informal social activities (Knoester and Eggebeen 2006). However, as children age, fathers, relative to men who are not fathers, tend to be more involved in community service organizations (Eggebeen and Knoester 2001). Other research shows that mothers of school-aged children increase their volunteering as well (Rotolo and Wilson 2007). However, studies that directly compare mothers and fathers across several countries tend to find complex and inconsistent results (Anderson, Curtis, and Grabb 2006).

Marital status may also moderate the relationship between parenthood and civic involvement. Studies show that married couples tend to be more involved in their communities than single adults (Wilson 2000). It is plausible, however, that the positive draw of parenthood into community life is strongest for those who are married. Married couples have more resources—time and money—than single parents to take on the added demands of civic participation. There is also some evidence that civic involvement, especially volunteering, is mutually reinforced within couples (Rotolo and Wilson 2006). Finally, at least in the United States, there is some evidence that cohabiting couples tend to be more socially isolated than married couples (Eggebeen 2005). All these factors suggest that we might expect to find that the positive effects of parenthood on civic engagement are only likely to be evident for those who are married.

Does Parenthood Lead to Involvement in Certain Types of Civic Organizations?

It is plausible that parenthood matters little for overall amount of civic engagement, but may shape where adults allocate their time. For example, parents may be less inclined to be involved in community garden clubs, choral societies, or sports teams and more interested in parent-teacher organizations, Scouts, churches, or youth organizations. There is limited evidence that this is the case.

A recent study by Knoester and Eggebeen (2006) shows that as men become fathers, they reduce their involvement in informal social groups and increase their church attendance and involvement in service organizations.

The link between parenthood and civic engagement will be explored using nationally representative surveys drawn from the World Values Surveys of four European countries—Britain, Spain, Sweden, and Poland—and the United States (see Table 2.2). Four hypotheses will be tested:

H1: Parenthood is positively associated with civic engagement.
H2: Gender will moderate the effect of parenthood on civic engagement.
H3: Marital status will moderate the effect of parenthood on civic engagement.
H4: The effect of parenthood will vary by type of civic involvement.

A series of three models for each country is estimated to examine the effect of parenthood on civic engagement.[2] The first models estimate the main effect of parenthood. The following two sets of models extend the analysis by examining interactions between parenthood and marital status and between

Table 2.2 Selected Fertility and Civic Engagement Indicators by Country

	Great Britain	Poland	Spain	Sweden	USA
TFR*	1.84	1.27	1.38	1.85	2.101
Percent active in volunteer organization	61.9	26.9	25.9	63.6	67.5
Average number of volunteer organizations actively involved	1.31	0.38	0.42	1.03	1.82
Percent active in Humanitarian	20.9	3.0	5.6	9.7	34.3
Church or religious organization	19.5	12.0	8.3	5.9	38.4
"Old order"	22.9	7.6	7.3	18.1	20.3
"New order"	9.1	2.0	2.0	3.9	16.2
Recreational	42.0	7.3	13.7	39.1	31.0

*TFR: Total Fertility Rate (2006 estimates).

Source: Population Reference Bureau. 2012. Fertility Rates for Low Birth Rate Countries, 1995 to Most Recent Year Available. http://www.prb.org/pdf12/TFR_Table2012_update.pdf, accessed June 11, 2012.

See text for definitions of civic groups.

gender and parenthood. Because the distribution of the dependent variable is a count of specific events, Poisson regression models are estimated (Long 1997).[3] Finally, we will explore how the effect of parenthood varies across specific types of civic engagement (Table 2.3). Given the dependent variables examined in Table 2.3 are binary, logistic regression models are estimated.

The World Values Surveys are designed to assess basic values, beliefs, and behavior of a representative sample of adults (World Values Survey 2010). The first wave of surveys was done on ten European countries in 1981. Since then there have been four additional waves of surveys and the number of countries surveyed has expanded to eighty countries. These data present several advantages for addressing the questions posed. First, they include a broad set of variables relating to participation in civic or voluntary organizations. Second, the standardized nature of the questions facilitates comparison across countries.

This analysis will use data from the 2005 surveys of Spain, Sweden, Britain, and Poland and the 1999 survey of the United States.[4] These five countries

Table 2.3 Logistic Regression Models of Effects of Parenthood on Active Involvement in Specific Civic Groups

	Recreation	Old Order	New Order	Humanitarian	Church/ Religious
Britain					
1–2 children	0.094	−0.016	0.208	−0.420+	−0.50*
3+ children	−0.233	−0.431	−0.426	−0.393	−0.078
Spain					
1–2 children	−0.132	0.099	0.562	−0.222	0.033
3+ children	−0.455	−0.145	−0.683	−0.292	0.032
Sweden					
1–2 children	−0.231	−0.330	0.469	−0.395	−0.410
3+ children	0.119	−0.667	−0.527	−0.242	−0.169
Poland					
1–2 children	−0.776+	0.116	0.774	−0.205	0.214
3+ children	0.102	−0.125	0.334	−0.233	0.269
USA					
1–2 children	0.012	−0.207	−0.166	0.246	0.289
3+ children	0.459*	−0.014	−0.132	0.595**	0.543**

Reference category: no children.

Significance level (*p*): +.10, *.05, **.01.

Other variables in models: age, gender, health, education, church attendance, and marital status.

Source: 2005 World Values Surveys for Spain, Sweden, Britain, and Poland, and the 1999 World Values Survey for the United States.

were chosen for several reasons. First, they are located in different regions with varying cultural and social value systems (Inglehart 1997). They also represent different institutionalized patterns of political sovereignty and organization, and these differences have been shown to account for a significant amount of the variation in voluntary association membership (Schofer and Fourcade-Gourinchas 2001). These national differences in patterns of civic engagement are clearly evident in Table 2.2 where we see that percentage of adults involved in at least one volunteer organization varies from a low of 26 percent among the Spanish to a high of nearly 68 percent of Americans. Perhaps there is something to the well-known characterization of America as a "nation of joiners" (Schofer and Fourcade-Gourinchas 2001). There is also considerable variation in the kinds of volunteering going on. A little more than a third of Americans are involved in humanitarian organizations compared to only 3 percent of adults from Poland. A larger percentage of British adults, 42 percent, participate in recreational organizations. In contrast this kind of involvement is rare for adults from Poland or Sweden.

These countries also have distinct fertility regimes. While all four European countries can be said to have low fertility, Poland and Spain have extremely low fertility. The US is somewhat of an anomaly among advanced industrialized countries, with a fertility rate hovering right around the replacement rate of 2.1. In short, these five countries present a fair range of social-cultural, family, and civic involvement differences.

Analyses are limited to respondents between the ages 20 to 70, leaving the following samples for analysis: Britain: $n = 844$, Sweden: $n = 859$, Spain: $n = 968$, Poland: $n = 824$, and the US: $n = 1,040$.

The dependent variable, *civic engagement,* was defined as a count of the number of organizations of which respondents indicated they were an "active member" (respondents from the four European countries) or "currently doing unpaid volunteer work" (the US respondents). This variable was drawn from a series of questions respondents for the European countries were asked about whether they were a member, an inactive member, or not a member of ten entities: churches or religious organizations; sports or recreation organizations; art, music, or education organizations; labor unions; political parties; environmental organizations; professional organizations; charitable or humanitarian organizations; consumer organizations; or "other" organizations.

The survey questions on volunteer organization involvement for the US sample differed slightly. Americans were asked about membership or involvement in fourteen different organizations. Ten of these were same entities asked of the Europeans. However, the American respondents were also asked about volunteer organizations concerned with health, the peace movement, women's groups, and youth work. The wording of questions about the nature of their association also differed from that of the European surveys. The American respondents were asked "… are you currently doing unpaid volunteer work?" for each of these organizations.

To test the hypothesis that effects of parenthood may lead to engagement in some types of organizations more than others, I took the list of ten distinct organizations in the European data (fourteen in the US data) and combined them into five types of volunteer organizations: *church or religious organizations*; *old order organizations* (political parties, unions, and professional organizations); *new order organizations* (consumer groups, environmental groups, women's groups, and peace groups); *humanitarian organizations* (human rights groups, charities, and youth organizations); and *recreational* (sports groups and arts, music, and educational organizations).

The key independent variable, parenthood status, is drawn from the question "Have you any children"? Responses could range from "no child" to "eight or more." I distinguish between one or two children and three or more with two dummy variables, "1–2" and "3+." The reference category is no children.

Previous explorations of the correlates of civic engagement suggest a number of factors that need to be included as controls: *age of respondent* (measured in years); *gender* (male = 1); *health status* ("All in all, how would you describe your health these days?"; range: 1 = very good, 4 = poor); *education* ("What is the highest educational level you have attended?"; range: 1 = no formal education, 9 = university level, with degree); *marital status* (currently married = 1, not currently married = 0); and *church attendance* ("Apart from weddings and funerals, about how often do you attend religious services these days?"; range: 1 = never or practically never; 7 = more than once a week).[5,6]

Model 1 for each of the five countries[7] shows the main effects of children on civic engagement. These models clearly show no main effects. Adults with children do not significantly differ from adults with no children in their patterns of active involvement in civic organizations.

Model 2 examines whether the effects of parenthood on civic engagement might be different for married individuals relative to those not currently married. We see some suggestive evidence that marriage conditions the effects of parenthood on civic involvement in Sweden, but not for any of the other four countries (Model 2). In Sweden, it appears that married individuals with one or two children are significantly more likely to be involved in volunteer organizations than either married adults without children or non-married adults (with or without children). I also explored the possibility that effects of merely being a parent (rather than a parent of 1 or 2 children or a parent of 3+ children) might differ by marital status. These models yielded patterns that suggest what effects parenthood has on civic engagement are mostly driven by the number of children rather than parenthood per se.

There is slightly more evidence that the effects of parenthood on involvement may differ between men and women. In Britain, women with three or more children are less involved than women with no children or only a few children. In contrast, parenthood appears to pull British men into civic engagement, although this is a statistically weak effect. The only other country showing evidence of gender by parenthood interactions is the US, where women with three or more children are less involved than women with smaller families.

In summary, there is only weak and scattered evidence that parenthood matters for the nature and extent of adults' overall involvement in volunteer organizations. In contrast to the relatively weak effects of parenthood are the effects for education and church attendance. Across all five countries, higher education and regular church attendance are strongly associated with higher levels of civic involvement.[8] Given the moderate correlation between marital status and church attendance, I tested models without controlling for church attendance. The results remained substantially the same.

Finally, there is some evidence that parenthood does matter for involvement in specific kinds of volunteer organizations—at least in some countries (Table 2.3). In Britain parents of one or two children are, surprisingly, *less* likely to be involved in humanitarian or religious organizations. It is unclear why this might be the case. Speculatively, this group of parents might be disproportionately made up of parents of very young children. There is some evidence—at least for American mothers—that preschool-age children are often an impediment to volunteer work (Rotolo and Wilson 2007). Regrettably, I am not able to test this hypothesis because these surveys do not have information on the ages of the children. In contrast, having three or more children for Americans is associated with involvement in humanitarian and religious organizations as well as recreational groups.

Conclusion

I started this analysis by noting a correspondence between fertility rates and levels of civic engagement across a range of European countries. Does this co-variation in macro trends indicate a linkage at the individual level? Both theory and previous work suggest we should expect a relationship: parenthood should be positively associated with participation in civic organizations. However, in my tests of this hypothesis I found no evidence that parenthood is directly related to civic engagement in any of the five countries. I also proposed that the effects of parenthood may be moderated by marital status and gender. I found only weak, scattered effects. In Sweden, married parents are more involved. In Britain, parenthood is positively, but weakly, associated with civic engagement for men, but negatively associated for mothers of three or more children. Similarly, in the United States, mothers of three or more children tend to be less involved than mothers of fewer children or than fathers. Finally, my exploration of the association between parenthood and specific types of civic involvement yielded only a few scattered significant effects. Only in the United States was there evidence that parenthood may be drawing adults into involvement in organizations that serve children. Unexpectedly, in Britain parents are less involved than non-parents in churches. In short these analyses show, at the individual level, only weak support for the idea that low fertility is associated with low levels of civic engagement.

Before we can be confident that low fertility is not a threat to civic life, several questions need to be addressed. First, as mentioned above, not having information on the ages of the children in the household prevented us from testing whether, as previous research suggests, there are opposite effects for preschool-aged children verses older children on parents' civic involvement. As a result, not taking into account the ages of children may have led to offsetting effects across families, weakening the observed relationships in our models.

Second, more work remains investigating the extent to which the effects of parenthood on civic engagement are moderated by gender and marital status. It is possible that the relationship between parenthood and civic engagement may be more complex and contingent than the two-way interactions tested in this analysis. For example, there is some evidence in my previous work that the positive effects of fatherhood for men on civic involvement may only be evident for married men (Eggebeen and Knoester 2001). Furthermore, other work suggests that mothers' involvement in volunteer work is somewhat constrained by their labor force participation (Hook 2004). However, while working may limit discretionary time available for engagement, work environments also present opportunities for developing social relationships and networks that can lead to involvement in various civic groups (Rotolo and Wilson 2007; Wilson 2000). I attempted to test some of these ideas with three-way interaction models. However, the small sample sizes either lead to models that failed to converge or had non-significant effects.

Two notable effects in the models presented in Table 2.2 are the large positive effects of church attendance and level of education on civic participation across all five countries. These patterns are consistent with most previous research. Studies using US data have generally found that religiosity, usually measured as attendance at religious services, is positively associated with civic engagement (Wilson 2000). However, there is also good evidence that both the religiosity of individuals as well as the national religious context both have a positive effect on volunteering in a wide range of countries (Ruiter and De Graaf 2006). Regular church attendance certainly increases engagement in church-related organizations and activities, but studies also show that religiosity "spills over" into engagement in other community activities and organizations (Ruiter and De Graaf 2006; Wuthnow 1999). Given the positive association between religiosity and fertility, is it possible that the positive effects of parenthood on civic engagement are most realized among the religious? Attempts to test for these interactions in these data yielded insignificant results. However, the relatively small fractions of adults who are frequent churchgoers in Sweden, Britain, and Spain may have reduced the power of these relationships.

Socioeconomic status, usually measured by level of education, is also generally found to be positively associated with participation in civic life in the United States (Wilson 2000). Studies of European countries find a similar positive correlation (Hooghe 2003; Ruiter and De Graaf 2006; Schofer and Fourcade Gourinchas 2001). It is plausible that highly educated parents may tend to be more engaged in civic life. For example, there is evidence of a growing class divide in parenting practices in the US. Lareau (2004) describes middle-class parents as engaging in "concerted cultivation" where their focus as parents is to "develop" the child using not only their personal resources but also by involving their child in a host of organized activities. Good middle-class parents by definition are engaged and involved in their communities. Exploratory analyses of these data yielded some suggestive findings. For the United States, parents with at least some college education were found to be more involved in civic organizations. However, the European countries did not follow this pattern. Highly educated parents in Britain and Spain were not more likely to be involved than non-parents. In contrast, highly educated parents in Sweden and Poland were less likely to be involved in civic organizations than non-parents. Again, small sample sizes render these estimates as tentative.

In conclusion, there is no evidence in these data that parenthood is directly associated with civic engagement. However, there are some telltale signs that parenthood may encourage civic involvement when it is nested in certain relationships or for certain types of parents. Clearly, more work on this needed before we can draw conclusions one way or the other about the consequences of low fertility for civic engagement.

Notes

1. Total fertility rate can be understood as the average number of children born to a woman if she were to experience the same rate of giving birth as women currently have (of each age group: 15–19, 20–24, and so on). In general, industrialized countries need a TFR of 2.1 to replace deaths if population equilibrium is to be maintained (assuming no immigration).

2. The model for this analysis may be found in Web Table 2.1 on the book web site.

3. Ordinary Least Squares regression models yielded essentially the same results.

4. The 1999 survey wave for the US was used because the 2005 survey wave did not ask respondents how many children they have.

5. This variable was reverse coded from the original scale.

6. This variable was reverse coded from the original scale.

7. See Web Table 2.1 on the book web site.

8. Church attendance is obviously highly correlated with active involvement in religious organizations (one of the ten activities in organizations making up civic involvement). However, further analyses show that church attendance remains a strong predictor of civic involvement even when church involvement is removed from the index of civic engagement.

References

Anderson, R., Curtis, J., and Grabb, E. 2006. Trends in civic association activity in four democracies: The special case of women in the United States. *American Sociological Review* 71: 376–400.

Bellah, Robert. 1985. *Habits of the Heart: Individualism and Commitment in American Life,* with Richard Madsen, William M. Sullivan, Ann Swidler, and Steven M. Tipton. Berkeley: University of California Press.

Brooks, A. C. 2006. *Who Really Cares? America's Charity Divide—Who Gives, Who Doesn't, and Why It Matters.* New York: Basic Books.

Corporation for National and Community Service. 2010. Volunteering in America: Research Highlights. http://www.volunteeringinamerica.gov/research-papers.cfm, accessed January 28, 2010.

Driskell, R. L., Lyon, L., and Embry, E. 2008. Civic engagement and religious activities: Examining the influence of religious tradition and participation. *Sociological Spectrum* 28: 578–601.

Eggebeen, D. J. 2005. Cohabitation and exchanges of support. *Social Forces* 83: 1097–1110.

Eggebeen, D. J., and Knoester, C. 2001. Does fatherhood matter for men? *Journal of Marriage and Family* 63: 381–393.

Eggebeen, D. J., Dew J., and Knoester, C. 2010. Fatherhood and men's lives at middle age. *Journal of Family Issues* 31: 113–130.

Freeman, R. 1997. Working for nothing: The supply of volunteer labor. *Journal of Labor Economics* 15: 140–167.

Harlow, R., and Cantor, N. 1996. Still participating after all these years. *Journal of Personality and Social Psychology* 71: 1235–1249.

Hawkins, A. J., and Dollahite, D. C. (Eds.). 1997. *Generative Fathering: Beyond Deficit Perspectives.* Thousand Oaks, CA: Sage.

Hooghe, M. 2003. Why should we be bowling alone? Results from a Belgian survey on civic participation. *Voluntas: International Journal of Voluntary and Nonprofit Organizations* 14: 41–59.

Hook, J. L. 2004. Reconsidering the division of household labor: Incorporating volunteer work and informal support. *Journal of Marriage and Family* 66: 101–117.

Inglehart, R. 1997. *Modernization and Post-Modernization: Cultural, Economic, and Political Change in 43 Countries.* Princeton, NJ: Princeton University Press.

Knoester, C., and Eggebeen, D. J. 2006. The effects of the transition to parenthood and subsequent children on men's well-being and social participation. *Journal of Family Issues* 27: 1532–1560.

Kohler, H. P., Billari, F. C., and Ortega, J. A. 2006. Low fertility in Europe: Causes, implications and policy options. In *The Baby Bust: Who Will Do the Work? Who Will Pay the Taxes?* ed. F. R. Harris, 48–109. Lanham, MD: Rowman and Littlefield.

Lareau, A. 2004. *Unequal Childhoods: Class, Race, and Family Life.* Berkeley: University of California Press.

Long, J. S. 1997. *Regression Models for Categorical and Limited Dependent Variables.* Thousand Oaks, CA: Sage.

Menchik, P., and Weisbrod, B. 1987. Volunteer labor supply. *Journal of Public Economics* 32: 159–183.

Mirowsky, J., and Ross, C. 1989. *Social Causes of Psychological Distress.* New York: Aldine de Gruyter.

Moen, P., Dempster-McClain, D., and Williams, R. 1992. Successful aging: A life course perspective on women's multiple roles and health. *American Journal of Sociology* 97: 1612–1632.

Musick, M., Herzog, A., and House, J. 1999. Volunteering and mortality among older adults: Findings from a national sample. *Journal of Gerontology* 54B: S173–S180.

Palkovitz, R. 1996. Parenting as a generator of adult development: Conceptual issues and implications. *Journal of Social and Personal Relationships* 13: 571–595.

———. 2002. *Involved Fathering and Men's Adult Development.* Mahwah, NJ: Lawrence Erlbaum.

Paxton, P. 1999. Is social capital declining in the United States? A multiple indicator assessment. *American Journal of Sociology* 105: 88–127.

Population Reference Bureau. 2010. Fertility rates for low birth-rate countries, 1995 to most recent year. http://www.prb.org/pdf08/TFRTable.pdf, accessed January 20, 2010.

Putnam, R. 1993. *Making Democracy Work: Civic Traditions in Modern Italy.* Princeton, NJ: Princeton University Press.

———. 1995. Bowling alone: America's declining social capital. *Journal of Democracy* 6: 65–78.

———. 2000. *Bowling Alone: The Collapse and Revival of American Community.* New York: Simon and Schuster.

Rotolo, T., and Wilson, J. 2004. What happened to the "long civic generation"? Explaining cohort differences in volunteerism. *Social Forces* 82: 1091–1121.

———. 2006. Substitute or complement? Spousal influence on volunteering. *Journal of Marriage and Family* 68: 305–319.

———. 2007. The effects of children and employment status on the volunteer work of American women. *Nonprofit and Voluntary Sector Quarterly* 36: 487–503.

Ruiter, S., and De Graaf, N. D. 2006. National context, religiosity, and volunteering: Results from 53 countries. *American Sociological Review* 71: 211–234.

Schlozman, K., Burns, N., and Verba, S. 1994. Gender and the pathways to participation: The role of resources. *Journal of Politics* 56: 963–990.

Schofer, E., and Fourcade-Gourinchas, M. 2001. The structural contexts of civic engagement: Voluntary association membership in comparative perspective. *American Sociological Review* 66: 806–828.

Snarey, J. 1993. *How Fathers Care for the Next Generation: A Four-Decade Study.* Cambridge, MA: Harvard University Press.

Stephan, P. 1991. Relationships among market work, work aspirations, and volunteering: The case of retired women. *Nonprofit and Voluntary Sector Quarterly* 20: 225–236.

Vallancourt, F. 1994. To volunteer or not: Canada, 1987. *Canadian Journal of Economics* 27: 813–826.

Wheeler, J., Gorey, K., and Greenblatt, B. 1998. The beneficial effects of volunteering for older adults and the people they serve. *International Journal of Aging and Human Development* 47: 69–80.

Wilcox, W. B. 2002. Religion, convention, and paternal involvement. *Journal of Marriage and Family* 64: 780–792.

Wilson, J. 2000. Volunteering. *Annual Review of Sociology* 26: 215–240.

World Values Survey. 2010. http://www.worldvaluessurvey.org/.

Wuthnow, R. 1998. *Loose Connections.* Cambridge, MA: Harvard University Press.

———. 1999. Mobilizing civic engagement: The changing context of religious involvement. In *Civic Engagement in American Democracy,* ed. T. Skocpol and M. P. Fiorina, 331–363. Washington, DC: Brookings Institution Press and Russell Sage Foundation.

Chapter Three

Do Children Bring Happiness and Purpose in Life?

Hans-Peter Kohler

Conventional wisdom arguably suggests that parenting is satisfying for parents: individuals in early to mid-adulthood often claim to look forward to entering parenthood and having children. Even in contexts of highly developed societies where childbearing has become financially expensive and is associated often with considerable trade-offs in terms of professional careers and pursuing other goals in life, childbearing has remained an important aspect of most adult lives. An overwhelming majority of high school seniors in the US, for example, believe that motherhood and fatherhood will be fulfilling, and this number increased throughout the 1970s, 1980s, and 1990s (Thornton and Young-DeMarco 2001). Mothers also report intense emotions evoked by their children (Preston and Hartnett 2008), and parents often feel "madly in love" with their children and report high levels of agreement with statements such as "I have an overwhelming love for my children unlike anything I feel for anyone else" (Erickson and Aird 2005). fMRI studies have shown that pictures of one's own—but not others'—children activate regions of the brain rich in oxytocin and vasopressin receptors—receptors and neurohormones associated with pair-bonding and happiness (Bartels and Zeki 2004). Moreover, despite declines of fertility rates to below-replacement levels in virtually all developed countries, and to lowest-low fertility levels in many southern and central/eastern European countries during the 1990s, childlessness remains relatively low and often below 20 percent (Kohler et al. 2002; Sobotka 2004). Parenthood remains a widespread experience, even when contraceptive control is easily accessible and lifestyle options other than parenthood are widely accepted in highly developed countries. It does not appear as if this pattern is fundamentally changing in advanced societies. For example, Myrskylä et al. (2009) document a fundamental change in the well-established negative relationship between fertility and development as the global population entered the twenty-first century. While development continues to promote fertility decline at low and medium levels of the human development index (HDI), Myrskylä et al.'s analyses show that at advanced HDI levels, further development can reverse the declining trend in fertility. The previously negative development–fertility relationship has therefore become J-shaped, with HDI being positively associated with fertility among highly developed countries (for related analyses, see Goldstein et al. 2009). Interpreting these trends in light of the second demographic transition theory—a leading theoretical framework for explaining low fertility that emphasizes the emergence of self-fulfillment as an increasingly important goal of life in the most developed societies (Van de Kaa 1987)—these trends would seem to confirm the conventional wisdom that parenthood is rewarding for individuals and that having children would tend to increase individuals' satisfaction with life and possibly their social relationships.

In sharp contrast to the conventional wisdom about parenthood and happiness, and potentially puzzling in light of the second demographic transition theory and recent trends in fertility, several recent articles in the popular press have questioned the notion that children and childrearing increase the subjective well-being of their parents. In a recent *New York* magazine article, Senior (2010) summarized the relationship between parenthood and happiness as "All Joy and No Fun: Why Parents Hate Parenting," pointing to the fact that children often "expose the gulf between our fantasies about family and its spikier realities; [they] mean parting with an old way of life, one with more freewheeling rhythms and richer opportunities for romance." In a related *Time* magazine article on "The Only Child: Debunking the Myths," Sandler (2010) discusses the pros and cons of progressing to the second child, writing, "Talk to parents and you'll often hear that they opt to have another because they think it will be better for the child they already have. Not many say they do it for themselves, no matter how much they may love the experience of parenting." In both cases, the authors suggest that parenting may be much less rewarding in terms of subjective well-being than is suggested by the conventional wisdom about parenthood and happiness.

How can we reconcile these different viewpoints and perspectives? In trying to answer this question about whether children bring happiness—and perhaps purpose—in life, this paper reverses the most often asked question about contemporary fertility trends in developed countries. In particular, while much of the existing literature on low fertility focuses on the questions of why fertility is low or lowest-low in many European countries, this chapter turns this question around: Why isn't fertility even lower? And, perhaps related, a question asked by Golini (1998) more than a decade ago: "How low can fertility be?"

Fertility and Happiness

The two leading theoretical frameworks explaining contemporary fertility trends in the rich world, with numerous variations, are the economic theory based on Becker's seminal work (e.g., Becker 1991) and the second demographic transition (SDT) framework proposed by Lesthaeghe and Van de Kaa (Lesthaeghe and Van de Kaa 1986; Lesthaeghe and Neidert 2006; Van de Kaa 1987). In the economic theory framework, individuals or couples maximize life-cycle well-being by considering the quantity and quality of children in the context of various other possible allocations of scarce resources such as time and money. According to the "cultural perspective" in the SDT framework, self-fulfillment is the main goal of life, and childbearing is predicted to occupy an increasingly less central role in the lives of individuals and couples. As such, childbearing and marriage are often postponed until other goals in life—such as completing education and establishing oneself in the labor market—are fulfilled. A third, re-emerging area, related to both the mentioned approaches, is the "value of children" approach (Friedman et al. 1994; Hoffman et al. 1978; Nauck 2007; Nauck and Klaus 2007).

To explain continued childbearing and partnership formation in low fertility contexts, most economic and rational-choice approaches to fertility and union formation assume that individuals derive "utility" from having children or being in unions (e.g., Becker 1991). Decisions about fertility and union formation are based on the utility gains attained by having children and/or being in unions as compared to the utility gains that are incurred from alternative allocations of resources, like income or time, that are required to raise children and maintain partnerships. The basic implication of this conceptual framework—that individuals engage in partnerships or have children because this increases their utility and makes them better off—can be empirically investigated. In particular, several recent studies suggest that utility can be measured using information about subjective well-being or "happiness" (e.g., Frey and Stutzer 2002; Layard 2005). If individuals (1) do not have systematic misconceptions about the benefits of children and partnerships, and (2) make conscious and informed choices about the formation of partnerships and their level of fertility, one would expect that the relation "Partner + Children = Happiness" holds: individuals form unions or have children because these decisions increase their subjective well-being or happiness.

In sharp contrast, however, as Easterlin (2003, 2005) notes, a growing number of psychologists have argued for a "setpoint theory" of happiness, in which happiness is primarily determined by personality traits and other genetic factors and is highly stable over the life course. In this view, significant life events, such as the formation or dissolution of unions and the birth of children, only transitorily change an individual's happiness from a setpoint given by personality and other genetic traits. Easterlin (2005) provides a number of quotations from the psychological literature that encapsulate this theory: "Each individual may be on a personal treadmill that tends to restore well-being to a predetermined setpoint after each change of circumstances" (Kahneman 1999, p. 14). "Chance events like personal tragedies, illness, or sudden strokes of good fortune may drastically affect the level of happiness, but apparently these effects do not last long" (Csikszentmihalyi and Jeremy 2003, pp. 185–186). "Objective circumstances appear to be limited in the magnitude, scope, and particularly duration of their effects on psychological well-being, which, in the long run, is likely to reflect instead stable characteristics of the individual" (Costa et al. 1987, p. 54). Setpoint theory thus predicts that a substantial fraction of variation in well-being is due to social or biological endowments that are unobserved in social science data sets. Several empirical studies support this prediction. For example, Lykken and Tellegen (1996) report that variation in the well-being component of the Multidimensional Personality Questionnaire (MPQ) for twins in the Minnesota Twin Register in the 1980s is primarily associated with genetic variation: genetic effects account for about

50 percent of the variation in one-time survey reports of well-being, and up to 80 percent of the variance in happiness indicators obtained by averaging repeated measures of well-being. Moreover, neither socioeconomic status, schooling, family income, marital status, nor religious commitment account for more than 3 percent of the variance in these averaged measures of well-being. In addition to these behavior genetic studies, there is also an emerging literature linking specific genes to variation in well-being. Using data from the National Longitudinal Study of Adolescent Health, for example, De Neve et al. (2010) show that individuals with a transcriptionally more efficient version of the serotonin transporter gene (5HTT) are significantly more likely to report higher levels of life satisfaction. Having one or two alleles of the more efficient type raises the average likelihood of being very satisfied with one's life by 8.5 percent and 17.3 percent, respectively. In light of this evidence, therefore, the economic models of fertility would seem to have it wrong. Changing the nature of partnerships or having children would only have temporary effects on happiness. In the now-famous metaphor of Brickman and Campbell (1971), each individual would seem to be on a "hedonic treadmill."

After decades of research on the determinants of fertility decline (e.g., see Bulatao and Casterline 2001), an increasing number of studies have started to address the question "Why do individuals in developed countries continue to form unions and have children?" (Foster 2000; Hakim 2003; Morgan and King 2001; Schoen et al. 1997). This recent research in part builds on the value-of-children approach of the 1970s that argues that children (and also marriage) contribute to individuals' well-being (e.g., Billari 2009; Fawcett 1988; Friedman et al. 1994; Hoffman and Manis 1979; Hoffman et al. 1978; Jones and Brayfield 1997; Margolis and Myrskylä 2011). For instance, Morgan and King (2001) relate the motivations to have children in contemporary societies to three areas: biological predispositions, social coercion, and rational choice. They conclude that humans are likely to have evolved preferences for children, and Morgan and King emphasize the opportunity that evolutionary theories and behavioral genetics provide for improving our understanding of human preferences for children. The arguments in Morgan and King are thus closely related to other work that has tried to interpret the preferences for children and related behaviors, such as sexual intercourse and changing fertility rates, in an evolutionary perspective. For instance, Foster (2000) draws on evidence from evolutionary biology, ethnology, quantitative genetics, developmental psychobiology, and psychology and argues that humans' evolved biological predisposition is toward nurturing behaviors, rather than having children per se. In her view, humans also have the unique ability to be aware of such biological predispositions and translate them into conscious, but nevertheless biologically based, fertility motivation or preferences for children. Consistent with these findings, Kohler et al. (1999) and Rodgers et al. (2001) have interpreted their findings of heritability patterns in fertility and fertility precursors as evidence for systematic genetic influences on fertility motivations and preferences. Several other studies also have proposed relations between evolved dispositions/preferences and desires for children. On one hand, Carey and Lopreato (1995) suggest a "two-child psychology" that implies a strong desire for two surviving children. Hakim (2003), on the other hand, stresses the heterogeneity in women's desires for children and proposes three idealized preference categories: home centered (about 20 percent of women), work centered (about 20 percent), and adaptive (a combination of work and home, about 60 percent). Hakim (2003) also argues that, after the contraceptive revolution, women are happy if they can achieve their preferred lifestyle, that is, a lifestyle that is a good match between their preferences regarding being with/without a job and with/without children. In contrast to the above literature that emphasizes preferences for children, Potts (1997) emphasizes humans' evolved desire to have sexual relations, rather than children per se. In contemporary modern societies with effective contraception, Potts claims, these inherited predispositions mix with unconscious physiological mechanisms working toward optimal birth spacing to make modern humans seek personal wealth and health rather than large families.

Reproduction is also at the core of many evolutionary explanations for marriage or long-term unions (for recent reviews, see for instance Daly and Wilson 2000; Gangestad 2003; Hrdy 1999; Kaplan and Lancaster 2003; Lawson and Mace 2010). In the context of sexual reproduction, however, evolutionary models also predict marked male-female differences in fertility behavior and motivations to engage in partnerships. A husband is seen as gaining sexual access to his wife and the ability to sire her children, while women obtain support in raising their children. As a consequence, youth and the ability to reproduce are often associated with increased value of women in the marriage market, while social status and wealth enhance the desirability of males. Conflicts over reproduction and resource allocation to children are hence seen as one of the prime causes of tensions within marriage and divorce. For instance, men are profoundly concerned that the children in whose welfare they invest are their own, and infertility is frequently a reason to divorce. Sexual jealousy is also found to be different, with male jealousy more focused on the sexual act and female jealousy focused on the alienation of the partner's attention and material resources. From an evolutionary perspective, these dissimilarities between males and females are rooted in the asymmetrical efforts of males and females in producing egg and sperm cells, and they result in different short- and long-term mating strategies, differences in attachment to children, and willingness to invest in offspring. For instance, females commonly invest vastly more time and energy in nurturing each offspring than do males, who can "disappear" after conception and still gain the evolutionary fitness benefit from a success-fully raised biological child. This often stronger attachment of women to their offspring puts women at the risk of being "prisoners of love" (England and Folbre 2002): men can exploit the stronger maternal attachment to children in bargaining within the household or in divorce settlements because mothers are likely to take care of their common children even if their mates withdraw resources from the partner or child.

Despite the strong evolutionary arguments linking the motivation for chil-dren and partnerships to evolved preferences and associated levels of subjective well-being, with possibly important differences across gender, studies of the contribution of children and partnerships to happiness are few. For instance, several studies on subjective well-being—including some by a leading economic demographer—often do not address the contributions of fertility to well-being in detail (e.g., Argyle 2001; Diener et al. 1999; Easterlin 2001, 2003; Kahneman et al. 1999; Layard 2005; Myers 1993). Exceptions include McLanahan and Ad-ams (1987) who conclude that adults with children at home often report lower levels of happiness and life satisfaction than other groups, and these reports of lower happiness are associated with increased worries and higher levels of anxiety and depression. In a similar vein, Nomaguchi and Milkie (2003) find that becoming a parent is both detrimental and rewarding; unmarried parents tend to report lower self-efficacy and higher depression than their childless counterparts; and married mothers' lives are marked by more housework and more marital conflict but less depression than their childless counterparts. Angeles (2009) documents an effect of children on life satisfaction that is posi-tive, large, and increasing in the number of children. This effect in Angeles (2009), however, is contingent on individual characteristics, with children making married people better off, while most unmarried individuals appear to be worse off with children. Aassve et al. (2008) and Margolis and Myrskylä (2011) also document important country differences in the association be-tween happiness and childbearing, and particularly point to the fact that the association between fertility and happiness is strongest in social democratic countries. Hakim (2003) also reports findings that women's general happiness and satisfaction with life display a U-shaped trend among people who have children. Contrary to the popular stereotype, Hakim concludes from these studies, children seem to seriously depress satisfaction levels in the middle years of marriage; marital satisfaction seems to decline from the time children are born up to the teenage years, then rises again to former levels after children leave home. Consistent with this observation, Margolis and Myrskylä (2011) find that the negative association between happiness and number of children decreases with age, and changes to positive above 40, suggesting that small children may have a negative effect on well-being, but as children grow older, the positive aspects of parenthood dominate.

In contrast to the effects of children on women's satisfaction levels, parental status has been found to have little influence on the lives of married men (Nomaguchi and Milkie 2003). Some of these results, however, change once unobserved factors are taken into account. Clark and Oswald (2002), for instance, find that children are not associated with well-being in longitudinal analyses with controls for individual longitudinal fixed effects, except for third or higher-order children that have a negative effect. Using longitudinal data, Clark et al. (2008), moreover, show that the anticipation of a birth in the near future leads to increases in subjective well-being for women (but not for men), an effect that turns negative two to three years after the birth of the child. Clark et al. (2008) thus summarize their findings as "the birth of a child provides a larger satisfaction boost to women than to men when it happens but four years later both sexes are equally unhappy." No data on the long-term effects of children on well-being are available in this study. Stanca (2009) argues that the negative effect of parenthood on well-being is explained by a large adverse impact on financial satisfaction, which on average dominates the positive impact on non-financial satisfaction. Powdthavee (2009) speculates if current and prospective parents accept a "comfortable illusion" because of necessity to cope with the difficulties of childrearing, the findings of a negative effect of having children on happiness "are, of course, extremely depressing. Yet perhaps they represent something we know deep down to be true: Raising children is probably the toughest and the dullest job in the world. But what if we do not give in to this comfortable illusion? What if all of us decided one day—for the sake of our own personal happiness—not to have children anymore? Then chances are that the future will stop at our generation, which is perhaps worse beyond our comprehension."

Recent psychological studies also provide a rich—albeit not necessarily consistent—set of findings about the contribution of children to well-being. Rogers and White (1998), for instance, find that one's biological children give more satisfaction with parenting than adopted children; Buss (2000) argues that humans have evolved mechanisms for mating bonds and close kinship that produce "deep sources of happiness" (see also Miller and Rodgers 2001); and Hilleras et al. (2001) show that having children contributes to the well-being and happiness of the elderly (see also Pinquart and Sörensen 2000). In addition to these studies on overall well-being, there has been active research on associations between having children and marital satisfaction (e.g., Bradbury et al. 2000; McLanahan and Adams 1987; Mizell and Steelman 2000; Russell and Wells 1994), associations that are at times positive and at times negative. In a recent study focusing on Italy and France, for example, Coppola et al. (2009) study the short-term effect of the first marriage and of the first childbearing satisfaction with the financial situation and with the amount of leisure time. The results show that the first marriage positively affects the satisfaction with the financial situation, while the first childbirth has no significant impact on it. In contrast, both events negatively affect the satisfaction with the amount of leisure time, showing that these transitions are in conflict with the need for determining one's autonomy. Moreover, differences across countries show that in contexts characterized by a higher gender equity and by a stronger welfare state's support, the stressing impact of these events is weakened. Consistent with these findings, a recent review of the (small) economic literature on subjective well-being states that "The evidence with regard to the well-being effects of having children is mixed and differs across measure and country" (Dolan et al. 2008, p. 107). This might be due to the difficulty of taking into account potential unobserved factors that affect the number of children and that are likely to bias the effect of the number of children on happiness.

In understanding the possible contributions of children to well-being, however, it is also important to highlight the possibly two-way relationship between happiness and fertility/partnerships. For example, Jokela et al. (2009) argue that there is a two-way relationship between personality traits—which are also closely linked to happiness and life satisfaction—and having children. On the one hand, high emotionality among Finnish respondents who are longitudinally followed decreased the probability of having children, whereas high sociability and, in men, high activity increased this probability; similarly, Parr (2010) found among Australian male and female respondents a strong positive relationship between prior satisfaction with life and fertility two years later. On the other hand, having children seems to affect personality characteristics, and as we will show below also happiness, and in Jokela et al.'s (2009) study, predicted increasing emotionality, particularly in respondents with high baseline emotionality and two or more children. Moreover, the personality characteristics of children (which might be inherited from the parents) have been shown to affect future childbearing. Jokela (2010), for example, has shown that a child's cognitive ability, adaptability to novelty, and pro-social behavior may be relevant to parents' future childbearing.

At older ages, the evidence about the relationship between having had children and well-being is also mixed. For example, Dykstra and Keizer (2009) investigate whether there are variations in well-being by parenthood status among forty- to fifty-nine-year-old men in the Netherlands and find that, in terms of psychological well-being, men's partner history counts, not their parenthood status: being single contributes to low levels of psychological well-being. In a Norwegian sample of men and women at midlife to old age, Hansen et al. (2009) find that childless women report significantly lower life satisfaction and self-esteem than both mothers with residential children and empty nest mothers, while motherhood is inconsequential for affective well-being. Similar to the findings for the Netherlands, parental status is unrelated to any of the well-being aspects among men.

Expected Change in Happiness Due to Having a Child

In summary, the review of the literature provides a mixed picture about the relationship of having children with subjective well-being. While parents report being in love with their children and perceiving children as extremely valuable in their lives, studies of happiness and children often find small or even no effect of having children on subjective well-being. If positive associations between well-being and fertility exist, they have mostly been shown for first children—or the entry into parenthood—while for second and higher-order children the associations with happiness that have been documented in the literature are at best mixed.

To perhaps better integrate these divergent findings, we investigate in this chapter the ex-ante anticipated changes in well-being that individuals expect from entering parenthood or having an additional child and compare them with the ex-post realization of happiness changes that occur after individuals had children. We begin our discussion of the relationship between happiness and childbearing by focusing on the (arguably) conventional wisdom that parenthood on average is perceived as desirable by young adults. In this section we therefore accept a forward-looking perspective and ask, Do individuals, and in particular, prospective parents, expect that having children and entering parenthood will increase their subjective well-being? And do these expected happiness gains vary across countries and institutional contexts in ways that are consistent with observed fertility patterns?

Our discussion in this section draws primarily on Billari and Kohler (2009), who analyzed the relationship between fertility and its effect of future well-being using data from the Generations and Gender Survey (GGS). GGS is a comparative cross-country and individual-level survey effort (Vikat et al. 2007), and the analyses in Billari and Kohler (2009) draw on six countries (Bulgaria, France, Georgia, Germany, Hungary, and Russia) for which data were available at the time of the analyses. In all these countries surveys have taken place between 2004 and 2006, and sample design guidelines and survey documentation are found in UNECE and UNFPA (2002).

The GGS targeted a representative sample of the adult population (ages 18 and over) and collected data about a broad range of subjects, including retrospective reconstructions of event histories, current assessment of the situation, values and attitudes, and prospective evaluations (Vikat et al. 2007). A measure of predicted happiness from childbearing is included in the fertility section of the Wave 1 GGS standard questionnaire. This is seen specifically in Billari and Kohler's (2009) focus on the responses to the following question: "Now, suppose that during the next 3 years you were to have a/another child. I would like you to tell me what effect you think this would have on various aspects of your life." Part f of this question pertains to the "joy and satisfaction" that the respondent gets from life, with possibly answers ranging from "much better," "better," "neither better nor worse," "worse," and "much worse." Recoding the responses as –2 ("much worse") to +2 ("much better"), with 0 being "neither better nor worse," results in a measure that reflects the extent to which individuals—and most importantly, also prospective parents—associate fertility and childrearing with increases in their subjective well-being or happiness. Across the six countries included in the analyses, this information on the expected changes of having a child on well-being is available for a total of 11,609 men and 14,305 women.

Figure 3.1 reports for each country the average expected change in subjective well-being resulting from having a first, second, or third child for both men and women. The key finding of this graph is that for both men and women, and for the progression to the first and second child, the average expected change in happiness is positive across the seven countries with very different socioeconomic and demographic contexts. So, on average, this graph is consistent with the conventional wisdom that childless adults on average look forward to entering parenthood and that parents with one child on average perceive that they would be happier if they had a second child. It is important to note, however, that there is considerable variation in this pattern: First, cross-country differences show a simple link between expected happiness from having a/another child and actual fertility (Billari 2009) (see the TFR levels included in Figure 3.1), with happiness gains being highest in France and Georgia and lowest in Bulgaria, Germany, Hungary, and Russia, corresponding roughly to the ranking of current fertility levels in these countries. Second, the expected happiness gains decline substantially with the number of children an individual already has. Specifically, in all but one case, first children are perceived as making larger contributions to the subjective well-being of individuals than second children. The gaps between the happiness gains for first and second children are usually larger for women and, for women, are often large in countries that are characterized by relatively low parity progression probabilities from the first to the second child (including, for example, Bulgaria, Georgia, Hungary, and Russia). The progression to the third child is perceived with considerably smaller gains in subjective well-being, particularly for women, and in Bulgaria and Russia, the average perception among women even seems to be that having a third child would lead to reductions in subjective well-being.

In addition to the variation among first, second, and third children, it is important to ask if entering parenthood—which arguably is the most important fertility decision individuals make—is perceived as desirable at particular ages, and if entering parenthood at ages other than the "optimal age range" would be perceived with lower gains in happiness from having a child. To shed some light on this issue, even if selectivity for the individuals who remain childless at older ages cannot be controlled for, Billari and Kohler (2009) also investigate the age pattern in the perceived gains in happiness by having a/another child during the next three years. In our discussion here we focus on childless women and the age pattern of the expected happiness gains from having a child by entering parenthood in the near future (for further analyses, see Billari and Kohler 2009). In general, one would expect these age profiles of expected happiness gains from having a first child to correspond to the well-known shape of the fertility-age relationships: happiness gains increase as fertility rates rise at relatively young adult ages, and happiness gains from children decline as fertility rates decrease at later childbearing ages. In all six countries the pattern is as expected.[1] With the exception of Russia, childless women associate the largest happiness gains from entering parenthood during the late twenties and early to mid-thirties; especially in France, Germany, and Hungary, entering parenthood at earlier or older ages is perceived as resulting in much smaller gains in subjective well-being. As already mentioned, there is important country variation in the level of these happiness gains, with Germany standing out as expecting particularly small gains in happiness from entering parenthood.

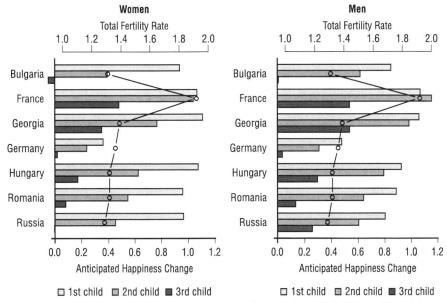

Figure 3.1 Average Expected Change in Subjective Well-Being Resulting from Having a First, Second, or Third Child

Note: TFR shown by superimposed line/points. Respondents are ages 18–40 years old; based on GGS question: "Now, suppose that during the next 3 years you were to have a/ another child. I would like you to tell me what effect you think this would have on [the joy and satisfaction you get from life]." Answers are coded as "much better" (= +2), "better" (= +1), "neither better nor worse" (= 0), "worse" (= –1), "much worse" (= –2). All estimates are significantly positive according to a *t*-test, except Bulgaria (men, 2 children; women, 2 children), Germany (men, 2 children; women, 2 children), Russia (women, 2 children). Adjusting for different age-structures populations at risk of having first, second, or third children across countries does not change the overall pattern of this graph.

Source: Adapted from Billari and Kohler (2009).

In Russia, consistent with a generally earlier pattern of childbearing, the peak happiness gains from entering parenthood occur relatively earlier during the early to mid-twenties.

In summary, the above analyses based on Billari and Kohler (2009) suggest that, in the low fertility context studied prevailing in Bulgaria, France, Georgia, Germany, Hungary, and Russia, predicted happiness from having a(nother) child is generally positive, but it diminishes with the number of children an individual already has, with important differences across countries, following a pattern that approximately mirrors observed parity progression ratios in these countries. Second, the anticipated changes in subjective well-being from having a first birth approximately follow the observed age pattern of fertility in all countries. Hence, consistent with the conventional wisdom about parenthood discussed in the introduction of this chapter, entering parenthood, in the low fertility countries included in the analyses, is perceived as providing increases in subjective well-being on average, and these expected gains in happiness are particularly pronounced if birth of the first child occurs at the "right age," which in the countries studied here is often in the late twenties and early thirties. Germany, a country that has a long tradition of relatively low fertility (with TFR around 1.3–1.4 for more than two decades) stands out as a country in which entering parenthood and progressing to the second child is associated with the smallest gains in happiness among adults. Additional analyses in Billari and Kohler (2009) also show that several macro-level variables reflecting institutional contexts and local cultures are importantly related to the anticipated well-being changes from having a(nother) child, although the direction is not always as hypothesized and the interpretation of these interactions between institutional contexts and socioeconomic conditions and expected happiness gains from having a/another child remains somewhat poorly understood.

Partner + Children = Happiness?

A natural question to ask after the previous discussion is, Are expected gains in happiness fulfilled after individuals have children? Our review of the literature above has already indicated that the answer to this question may not be as clear-cut as one might expect—many studies have documented no or only small gains in happiness as a result of children. However, many of the existing studies have been able to identify associations between fertility and happiness, which might be different from the causal contributions of children on well-being if unobserved factors—such as personality traits, ability, preferences, and attractiveness—affect both an individual's fertility outcomes as well as his or her subjective well-being. For example, Jokela et al. (2009) assessed whether three personality traits—sociability, emotionality, and activity—predicted the probability of having children and whether having children predicted personality change. They documented that high emotionality decreased the probability of having children, whereas high sociability and, in men, high activity increased this probability. Similarly, behavioral genetic analyses of the Danish twin data (Rodgers and Kohler 2008) reveal for males ages twenty-five to forty-five a systematic positive association between the genetic components of variation in subjective well-being and of variation in fertility/ partnership behaviors: genetic dispositions that tend to increase subjective well-being—say, dispositions toward a "happy personality"—are associated with a higher number of partnerships, a higher probability of being currently in a partnership, and a larger number of children. For females ages twenty-five to forty-five, the relationships are similar, except that dispositions toward a "happy personality" tend to be associated with increased partnership stability rather than a higher number of partnerships.

In order to better understand how having children may affect well-being, we present in this section results from Kohler et al. (2005) on the contribution of children and partnership to subjective well-being. In particular, in contrast to the majority of studies on this topic, the estimates in Kohler et al. (2005) are based on monozygotic (MZ), or identical, twins, and it can be argued that these estimates better reflect the causal impact (rather than just the associations) of fertility on subjective happiness through the first estimates of such effects that use a sample of MZ twins to control for unobserved endowments that influence subjective well-being. For example, an important caveat of the findings in Billari and Kohler (2009) is that the analyses do not necessarily indicate causal relationships as the cross-sectional data are subject to important endogeneity concerns—for example, due to the fact that happier persons might be more likely to have children. Kohler et al. (2005) overcome these estimation problems because MZ twins share the same genetic endowment as well as the same parental background and various social or economic endowments related to parental households (e.g., neighborhoods, schools). The analyses can therefore use fixed-effect analyses within MZ twins in order to control for a wide range of unobserved factors.

The data used for these analyses are based on the Danish Twin Registry that was established in 1954 as the first nationwide twin registry in the world (see Hauge 1981; Hauge et al. 1968; Kyvik et al. 1995, 1996; Skytthe et al. 2002). In 2002, the Danish Twin Register conducted a Twin-Omnibus Survey of all registered male and female twins born in 1931–1982, resulting in a total of 34,944 completed questionnaires (a response rate of 75.4 percent). This 2002 survey included a measure of subjective well-being, or "happiness," that was obtained through the question "How satisfied are you with your life, all things considered?" with responses ranging from very satisfied to not satisfied at all. In contrast to other investigations focusing on satisfaction with some particular aspects of life such as marriage or work, this survey question attempts to elicit overall well-being. Descriptive statistics for this measure of well-being are reported in Table 3.1. In the analyses below, subjective well-being is represented through a "happiness indicator" that is obtained from the twins' responses to the question "How satisfied are you with your life, all things considered?" where 0 = not satisfied or not particularly satisfied, 1 = rather satisfied, and 2 = very satisfied.

We focus here on the results for men and women during their primary ages of childbearing (ages twenty-five to forty-five), an age range that matches those for our previous analyses of anticipated changes in well-being.[2] The specification of the model allows for a possibly non-linear effect where the effect of the first child (boy or girl) on subjective well-being may differ from that of higher-order children. These initial analyses do not control for partnership status of the respondents; that is, they reflect the overall effect of having children on happiness including those that might operate through the fact that individuals who have children are much more likely to be in a partnership.

Table 3.1 Subjective Well-Being in Danish MZ (Identical) Twins

	Females	Males
Ages 25–45		
Not particularly satisfied/not satisfied	4.9%	4.8%
Rather satisfied	44.4%	43.7%
Very satisfied	49.7%	50.1%
n/a	1.0%	1.5%
Mean	1.45	1.46
Overall std. dev.	(0.59)	(0.59)
Within-twin pair std. dev.	(0.52)	(0.52)
Within-twin pair correlation	0.21	0.21
N	2,114	1,314
Ages 50–70		
Not particularly satisfied/not satisfied	3.7%	2.6%
Rather satisfied	46.0%	43.1%
Very satisfied	48.8%	53.3%
n/a	1.5%	0.9%
Mean	1.46	1.51
Overall std. dev.	(0.57)	(0.55)
Within-twin pair std. dev.	(0.49)	(0.48)
Within-twin pair correlation	0.25	0.24
N	1,112	874

Notes: Means, standard deviations, and within-twin pair correlations are calculated by converting the responses into a single happiness indicator using 0 = not satisfied or not particularly satisfied, 1 = rather satisfied, and 2 = very satisfied. Within-twin pair standard deviation is estimated using a one-way analysis of variance (ANOVA) of this happiness indicator.

Source: Kohler, H.-P., Behrman, J. R., and Skytthe, A. (2005). Partner + children = happiness? An assessment of the effect of fertility and partnerships on subjective well-being in Danish twins. *Population and Development Review* 31 (3): 407–445.

The key finding of these analyses is that the first-born child—independent of its sex—has a large positive effect on subjective well-being: having at least one child improves happiness by .20–.23, which is equivalent to 35–39 percent of one standard deviation (and 39–44 percent of one within-twin pair standard deviation). In contrast to the large positive effect of the first child on well-being, additional children beyond the first child are not associated with higher levels of happiness; instead, the within-MZ results reveal that additional children beyond the first tend to be associated with lower levels of happiness for females. Each child beyond the first decreases the happiness indicator by 13 percent of one standard deviation for females, and three additional children almost completely compensate for the positive effect resulting from the first child.

The corresponding analyses for males result in a strikingly different pattern. First, there is an important sex difference associated with the happiness gains resulting from a first child: first-born boys have an effect on happiness equal to .172 (29 percent of one standard deviation of well-being), almost 75 percent larger than that of a first-born girl (.099 or 17 percent of one standard deviation). Hence, male children not only tend to increase marital stability (Dahl and Moretti 2004; Morgan et al. 1988) and cause fathers to work longer hours at higher wages (Lundberg and Rose 2002), first-born sons also make fathers happier than first-born daughters. This effect is important since there is no revealed sex preference in parity progression probabilities: the probability of having a second child and the overall number of children do not significantly differ between male twins having a boy or girl as their first child. While males therefore enjoy greater happiness from a first-born son than a first-born daughter, this does not translate into higher levels of fertility. Second, additional children beyond the first child have virtually no effect on subjective well-being. Males therefore do not suffer the same declines in happiness with additional children that females do, but they also do not gain from additional children in terms of their subjective well-being.

These findings are consistent with evidence from earlier studies of the costs and satisfactions associated with childbearing (e.g., Bulatao 1981; Fawcett 1983) and some recent studies of happiness and fertility in a global and/or comparative context (Aassve et al. 2008; Margolis and Myrskylä 2011). In particular, respondents' motivations for the first child emphasize family status, role, and emotional rewards for the parent, while the values motivating second births are strongly associated with providing companionship for the first child. Consistent with the focus on emotional rewards and family status, first children are associated with significant increases in parents' well-being, with males enjoying higher happiness gains from first-born boys than first-born girls. The differential motivations for higher-order children, however, are also reflected in the results. For females, additional children beyond the first decrease well-being, and for males the effect of additional children is not distinguishable from zero. Further analyses that include a control for current partnership status, which are not reported here in detail, show an important sex difference in the effect of fertility on well-being. For females, the effect of children on subjective well-being remains strong and significant even after the current partnership status is included. Similar to our earlier analyses, the first child has a strong positive effect, independent of its sex, and additional children have a negative effect on happiness. For males, however, the effect of children on happiness vanishes once the current partnership status is included. The happiness of males increases strongly if they are in a partnership, but after controlling for the current partnership status, children no longer significantly affect subjective well-being. The coefficients for first-born boys and first-born girls are of opposite sign, consistent with our earlier discussion about the influence of the first child on happiness, but neither of the coefficients is significant.

In summary, these additional results reveal a striking male-female difference with respect to the impact of children on well-being after controlling for the current partnership. Females ages twenty-five to forty-five derive happiness gains from children even after controlling for the current partnership status. The happiness of males, however, depends primarily on the partnership status; once the current partnership status is controlled, men's happiness does not vary systematically with fertility. These findings suggest a somewhat provocative interpretation about the motivations of men and women to engage in partnerships: in particular, the results can be interpreted to suggest that women are in partnerships, among other reasons, in order to have children that increase their subjective well-being. Males in the same age range, on the other hand, have children in order to remain in the partnerships that strongly affect their happiness. The male preference for boys may in this context be the result of the higher divorce probabilities of couples who have a first-born daughter as compared to a first-born son (Dahl and Moretti 2004; Morgan et al. 1988).

Additional analyses in Kohler et al. (2005) also investigate the effects of having had children and partnerships on well-being at post-reproductive years at ages fifty to seventy. One of the important findings of these analyses is that the effects of having had children on subjective well-being are relatively small—if they exist at all—for men and women at this age range. The number of children does not have a large or significant effect, nor is there a strong positive effect due to "at least one child." If the current partnership is included, a current partner is strongly associated with increases in subjective well-being, while the number of children does not affect happiness at ages fifty to seventy.

These findings are surprising because children are often thought to be a source of social contacts and support at older ages. The results, however, suggest that the effect of having children on happiness is quite small for both males and females in this age range, similar to what has been found in some related studies (Dykstra and Keizer 2009; Hansen et al. 2009). In part, this small effect of children on well-being found by Kohler et al. (2005) may be due to the fact that respondents ages fifty to seventy years are not yet old enough to encounter widespread health problems that may be associated with an increased demand for care and support provided by children.

Conclusion

In some general sense, the above results are consistent with evolutionary psychological and biological theories that claim to provide an evolutionary rationale for the motivation to have children and form long-term partnerships. In particular, besides establishing the basic contribution of children and partnerships to well-being that is predicted by these theories, the analyses discussed above show that (1) adults in childbearing ages generally seem to expect increases in their subjective well-being as a result of having a/another child, with these effects being particularly strong for childless men and women in the primary ages of childbearing; and (2) the expected happiness gains from children differ importantly by institutional contexts, especially at higher parities. The perceived conventional wisdom may therefore be correct: on average, individuals expect gains in their subjective well-being from entering parenthood, especially if this occurs during a "desirable age window," and the progression to the second child is mostly seen as adding to the happiness of parents. In the low fertility contexts studied here, having a third child is not generally expected to increase parental happiness to a relevant extent. However, the ex-post experience of individuals after they had entered parenthood and/or had an additional child can importantly differ from the anticipated changes in well-being. While this is expected on an individual basis due to idiosyncratic influences on the satisfaction derived from parenting, it is important to observe that this may also be the case for the experience on average—especially higher-order children. In particular, in terms of the contributions of children and partnerships to subjective well-being, the analyses by Kohler et al. (2005) provide a number of important results about the demographic determinants of happiness: First, the estimates raise questions about the almost complete dominance of endowments in affecting happiness, as suggested by the setpoint theory of happiness. To the contrary, the analyses suggest that some dimensions of partnership formation and childbearing have persistent effects on happiness. Second, it is primarily the first-born children who are an important source of happiness at ages twenty-five to forty-five for females, and also for males if we do not condition on partnership status. Additional children reduce the subjective well-being of females while leaving the well-being of males unaffected. Moreover, the estimates for respondents in this age range reveal that (1) men, but not women, experience larger happiness gains from a first-born son than a first-born daughter; (2) children directly contribute to happiness for women, but only indirectly through increasing the probability of a current partnership for men; and (3) children have no indirect effect on well-being by increasing the happiness gains obtained from a current partnership.

Considering the fact that it is primarily first children who increase an individual's subjective well-being, which is broadly consistent with the anticipated happiness change for entering parenthood, the contributions of second children often seem to fall short of their expected impact on parental happiness. This finding raises important questions about the motivations for having a second child; motivations other than subjective well-being may be underlying the progression to additional children after the first child. After experiencing the positive happiness gains after the first child, men and, even more so, women may under-predict the additional work implied by a second child or over-predict the increases in happiness. The latter possibility is suggested by recent psychological research on projection biases or impact biases in the evaluation of future well-being (Gilbert et al. 2002; Loewenstein et al. 2003), showing that people tend to overestimate the enduring impact—positive as well as negative—of important life events on their future emotional well-being. Gilbert et al. (2002, p. 117), for instance, claim that persons "predictably mispredict" how novel events, like having another child, will unfold. An alternative explanation is that parents who get a good draw in endowments for their first child have higher than warranted expectations about the endowments that their subsequent children are likely to have; therefore they decide to have more children, but are often disappointed with the outcome.

Happiness in life is of course distinct from the "purpose" of life, and some studies have argued that children may be important for individuals' purpose in life, even if happiness—narrowly defined—may not increase. For example, in the US a vast majority of mothers continues to agree with the statement that "being a mother is the most important thing that I do" (Erickson and Aird 2005). Religion might be an important factor influencing the extent to which children are seen as important aspects of an individual's purpose in life. For example, recent studies have consistently documented higher fertility among more religiously active women across denominations (Hayford and Morgan 2008), an effect that might be due to a different meaning of children for religious individuals, increased social support through religious institutions, and/or a selection of more child-oriented individuals toward religiosity. While disentangling these aspects is beyond the scope of this chapter, it is important to note that religiosity may modify the extent to which considerations about individual happiness and subjective well-being will affect fertility decisions.

In some general sense, the results about the interrelations between happiness and children that were discussed here are consistent with evolutionary psychological and biological theories. In particular, besides establishing the basic contributions of children and partnerships to well-being that are predicted by these theories, our analyses additionally show that important sex differences exist between women and men with respect to the influence on well-being of the number of children, stepchildren, the timing of fertility, and the role of current partnerships. Despite this general agreement with biosocial predictions, however, the support for evolutionary perspectives is much less strong in terms of specifics. For example, once there is control for current partnerships, past partnerships do not increase happiness significantly more for males than for females, as would seem to be suggested by the evolutionary approach; nor do our analyses provide evidence that males benefit in terms of well-being from a large number of children. Nevertheless, the differential effect of additional children on well-being is consistent with the evolutionary argument that females and males invest differentially in children and that females may therefore have a lower "optimal fertility" in terms of subjective well-being than men. However, gender specialization in childcare also could lead to this result if, as a result of this specialization, women bear most of the costs in raising children.

In addition to these interpretations in terms of the evolutionary basis for the motivations for childbearing and union formation, the analyses in this chapter are relevant because they provide empirical support for recent speculations about the limits to low fertility and related patterns of union formation. In particular, the substantial happiness gains associated with first children may limit the extent to which present and future fertility declines are driven by reductions in first-birth childbearing. Our discussion suggests that women may be willing to have at least one child even if this child is associated with considerable costs to them. The first child seems to provide an important part of women's fulfillment in life, even if they are in partnerships, and childlessness may remain relatively low even in contemporary industrialized countries with low or lowest-low fertility. This corroborates the relatively low estimates of childlessness in lowest-low fertility countries with total fertility rates below 1.3 after distortions in the data have been removed (e.g., Kohler et al. 2002).

Since happiness gains are primarily associated with the first child and not with additional children, however, women's and couples' motivations to have additional children may be weaker and thus more responsive to altered socioeconomic conditions, family policies, social norms, or ideational contexts. While this study suggests a potential lower limit to low fertility due to the strong happiness gains associated with first children, our analysis does not suggest that the individual motivation in terms of subjective well-being for second or third children is sufficiently strong to result in a fertility level close to replacement level. The emergence of stated sub-replacement fertility preferences found in recent analyses of Eurobarometer surveys (Goldstein et al. 2003) may be an indication that levels of desired fertility decline as they become increasingly motivated by individualistic considerations focused on self-fulfillment and subjective well-being. In addition, our results about the contributions of additional children to happiness suggest that changes in family or related policies aimed toward increasing fertility, motivated for instance by the substantial positive externalities associated with childbearing in low fertility contexts (e.g., see Lee 2001), may not necessarily result in increases in subjective well-being for parents. This may make broad support for such policies in a democratic decision process unlikely.

It is important to realize that the relationship between anticipated and/or realized happiness changes and fertility differs across countries and institutional contexts. Our discussion in this context has primarily focused on the variation in the extent to which individuals in different countries associated the entry into parenthood with differential changes in subjective well-being. Other studies have shown that the realized changes in happiness vary across countries (Aassve et al. 2008), with happiness gains being largest in countries with a fairly generous welfare state; the financial stress and trade-off that children imply for parents may be lowest in these contexts (Aassve et al. 2005). Given the heterogeneity of institutional, cultural, and policy contexts across developed countries, further research is required to investigate the different mechanisms that may underlie these heterogeneous implications of children for well-being. An improved understanding of how labor market flexibility, social security and individual welfare, gender and economic equality, human capital, and social/family policies can facilitate a relatively high satisfaction with parenthood in advanced societies is needed (Brewster and Rindfuss 2000; Kohler et al. 2002; McDonald 2000; Neyer and Andersson 2008). For instance, analyses on Europe show that nowadays a positive relationship is observed between fertility and indicators of innovation in family behavior or female labor force participation (Billari and Kohler 2004). Also, at advanced levels of development, governments might explicitly address fertility decline by implementing policies that improve gender equality or the compatibility between economic success, including labor force participation, and family life (Balter 2006; McDonald 2000; Neyer and Andersson 2008). In addition to government policies, religious and other formal or informal institutions can possibly help balance the tensions between parenthood and other domains that seem to underlie the low happiness gains from parenting in some contexts. Failure to answer to the challenges of parenthood in advanced societies with institutions that facilitate work-family balance and gender equality might explain the exceptional pattern for rich countries in which parenthood is—ex-ante and/or ex-post—not associated with high levels of individual satisfaction.

Notes

1. See Web Figure 3.1 on the book web site.
2. See the top panel of Web Figure 3.2 on the book web site for the effect of the number of biological children on subjective well-being.

References

Aassve, A., Goisis, A., Ruggeri, C., and Sironi, M. (2008). Childbearing and happiness across Europe. Bocconi University, Dondena Centre for Research on Social Dynamics, Working Paper No. 10, http://www.dondena.unibocconi.it/wp10.

Aassve, A., Mazzucu, S. and Mencarini, L. (2005). Childbearing and well-being: A comparative analysis of European welfare regimes. *Journal of European Social Policy* 15 (4): 283–299.

Angeles, L. (2009). Children and life satisfaction. *Journal of Happiness Studies* Pre-print Epublication. http://dx.doi.org/10.1007/s10902-009-9168-z.

Argyle, M. (2001). *The Psychology of Happiness.* 2nd ed. London: Routledge.

Balter, M. (2006). The baby deficit. *Science* 312 (5782): 1894–1897.

Bartels, A., and Zeki, S. (2004). The neural correlates of maternal and romantic love. *Neuroimage* 21 (3): 1155–1166.

Becker, G. S. (1991). *A Treatise on the Family.* 2nd ed. Cambridge, MA: Harvard University Press.

Billari, F. C. (2009). The happiness commonality: Fertility decisions in low-fertility settings. In: UNECE (ed.). *How Generations and Gender Shape Demographic Change.*

Unpublished manuscript prepared for the UN-ECE (Population Activities Unit). New York: United Nations, 7–38.

Billari, F. C., and Kohler, H.-P. (2004). Patterns of low and lowest-low fertility in Europe. *Population Studies* 58 (2): 161–176. doi:10.1080/0032472042000213695.

———. (2009). Fertility and happiness in the XXI century: Institutions, preferences, and their interactions. Paper presented at the Annual Meeting of the Population Association of America, Detroit, MI, April 30–May 2.

Bradbury, T. N., Fincham, F. D., and Beach, S. R. H. (2000). Research on the nature and determinants of marital satisfaction: A decade in review. *Journal of Marriage and the Family* 62 (4): 964–980.

Brewster, K. L., and Rindfuss, R. R. (2000). Fertility and women's employment in industrialized nations. *Annual Review of Sociology* 26: 271–296.

Brickman, P., and Campbell, D. T. (1971). Hedonic relativism and planning the good society. In: Appley, M. H. (ed.). *Adaptation Level Theory: A Symposium*, 287–305. London: Academic Press.

Bulatao, R. A. (1981). Values and disvalues of children in successive childbearing decisions. *Demography* 18 (1): 1–25.

Bulatao, R. A., and Casterline, J. B. (eds.) (2001). Global Fertility Transition. Supplement to *Population and Development Review* 27.

Buss, D. M. (2000). The evolution of happiness. *American Psychologist* 55 (1): 15–23.

Carey, A. D., and Lopreato, J. (1995). The evolutionary demography of the fertility-mortality quasi-equilibrium. *Population and Development Review* 21 (3): 613–630.

Clark, A. E., Diener, E., Georgellis, Y., and Lucas, R. E. (2008). Lags and leads in life satisfaction: A test of the baseline hypothesis. *The Economic Journal* 118 (529): F222–F243.

Clark, A. E., and Oswald, A. J. (2002). Well-being in panels. Unpublished working paper, University of Warwick, United Kingdom. http://en.scientificcommons.org/43256748.

Coppola, L., Mazzuco, S., and Michiclin, F. (2009). Do demographic events affect the quality of life? Unpublished manuscript, Italian National Institute of Statistics (ISTAT).

Costa, P. T., Zonderman, A. B., Mccrae, R. R., Cornoni Huntley, J., Locke, B. Z., and Barbano, H. E. (1987). Longitudinal analyses of psychological well-being in a national sample—stability of mean levels. *Journal of Gerontology* 42 (1): 50–55.

Csikszentmihalyi, M., and Jeremy, H. (2003). Happiness in everyday life: The uses of experience sampling. *Journal of Happiness* 4 (2): 185–189.

Dahl, G. B., and Moretti, E. (2004). The demand for sons: Evidence from divorce, fertility, and shotgun marriage. NBER Working Paper No. 10281. http://www.nber.org/papers/w10281.

Daly, M., and Wilson, M. I. (2000). The evolutionary psychology of marriage and divorce. In: Waite, L. J., Bachrach, C., Hindin, M., Thomson, E., and Thornton, A. (eds.). *Ties That Bind: Perspectives on Marriage and Cohabitation*. New York: Aldine de Gruyter, 91–110.

De Neve, J.-F., Fowler, J. H., and Frey, B. S. (2010). Genes, economics, and happiness. CESifo Working Paper Series No. 2946. http://ssrn.com/paper=1553633.

Diener, E., Suh, E. M., Lucas, R. E., and Smith, H. L. (1999). Subjective well-being: Three decades of progress. *Psychological Bulletin* 125: 276–303.

Dolan, P., Peasgood, T., and White, M. (2008). Do we really know what makes us happy? A review of the economic literature on the factors associated with subjective well-being. *Journal of Economic Psychology* 29 (1): 94–122. doi:10.1016/j.joep.2007.09.001.

Dykstra, P. A., and Keizer, R. (2009). The wellbeing of childless men and fathers in mid-life. *Ageing and Society* 29 (Special Issue 08): 1227–1242. doi:10.1017/S0144686X08008374.

Easterlin, R. A. (2001). Income and happiness: Towards a unified theory. *Economic Journal* 111 (473): 465–484.

———. (2003). Explaining happiness. *Proceedings of the National Academy of Sciences of the United States of America* 100 (19): 11176–11183.

———. (2005). Is there an "iron law of happiness? Unpublished working paper, Department of Economics, University of Southern California.

England, P., and Folbre, N. (2002). Involving dads: Parental bargaining and family well-being. In: Tamis-LeMonda, C. S., and Cabrera, N. (eds.). *Handbook of Father Involvement: Multidisciplinary Perspectives*. Mahwah, NJ: Erlbaum Associates, 387–408.

Erickson, M. F., and Aird, E. G. (2005). The motherhood study: Fresh insights on mothers' attitudes and concerns. *Research Report, Motherhood Project and the Mothers' Council of the Institute for American Values*. http://www.motherhoodproject.org.

Fawcett, J. T. (1983). Perceptions of the value of children: Satisfactions and costs. In: Bulatao, R. A. and Lee, R. D. (eds.). *Determinants of Fertility in Developing Countries: Supply and Demand for Children*. New York: Academic Press, 429–457.

———. (1988). The value of children and the transition to parenthood. *Marriage and Family Review* 12 (3–4): 11–34.

Foster, C. (2000). The limits to low fertility: A biosocial approach. *Population and Development Review* 26 (2): 209–234.

Frey, B. S., and Stutzer, A. (2002). What can economists learn from happiness research? *Journal of Economic Literature* 40 (2): 402–434.

Friedman, D., Hechter, M., and Kanazawa, S. (1994). A theory of the value of children. *Demography* 31 (3): 375–401.

Gangestad, S. W. (2003). Sexually antagonistic coevolution: Theory, evidence, and implications for patterns of human mating and fertility. In: Wachter, K. W. and Bulatao, R. A. (eds.). *Offspring: Human Fertility Behavior in Biodemographic Perspective*. Washington, DC: The National Academies Press, 224–259.

Gilbert, D. T., Driver-Linn, E., and Wilson, T. D. (2002). The trouble with Vronsky: Impact bias in the forecasting of future affective state. In: Barrett, L. F., and Salovey, P. (eds.). *The Wisdom in Feeling: Psychological Processes in Emotional Intelligence*. New York: Guilford, 114–143.

Goldstein, J. R., Lutz, W., and Testa, M. R. (2003). The emergence of sub-replacement family size ideals in Europe. *Population Research and Policy Review* 22 (5–6): 479–496.

Goldstein, J. R., Sobotka, T., and Jasilioniene, A. (2009). The end of lowest-low fertility. *Population and Development Review* 35 (4): 663–699. doi:10.1111/j.1728 -4457.2009.00304.x.

Golini, A. (1998). How low can fertility be? An empirical exploration. *Population and Development Review* 24 (1): 59–73.

Hakim, C. (2003). A new approach to explaining fertility patterns: Preference theory. *Population and Development Review* 29 (3): 349–374.

Hansen, T., Slagsvold, B., and Moum, T. (2009). Childlessness and psychological well-being in midlife and old age: An examination of parental status effects across a range of outcomes. *Social Indicators Research* 94 (2): 343–362. doi:10.1007/s11205-008-9426-1.

Hauge, M. (1981). The Danish twin register. In: Mednich, S. A., Baert, A. E., and Bauchmann, B. P. (eds.). *Prospective Longitudinal Research: An Empirical Basis for the Primary Prevention of Psychological Disorders.* Oxford: Oxford University Press, 217–221.

Hauge, M., Harvald, B., Fischer, M., Gotlieb-Jensen, K., Juel-Nielsen, N., Raebild, I., Shapiro, R., and Videbech, T. (1968). The Danish twin registers. *Acta Geneticae Medicae et Gemellologiae* 2: 315–331.

Hayford, S. R., and Morgan, S. P. (2008). Religiosity and fertility in the United States: The role of fertility intentions. *Social Forces* 86 (3): 1163–1188. doi:10.1353/sof.0.0000.

Hilleras, P. K., Aguero-Torres, H., and Winblad, B. (2001). Factors influencing well-being in the elderly. *Current Opinion in Psychiatry* 14 (4): 361–365.

Hoffman, L. W., and Manis, J. D. (1979). The value of children to parents in the United States: A new approach to the study of fertility. *Journal of Marriage and the Family* 41: 583–596.

Hoffman, L. W., Thornton, A., and Manis, J. D. (1978). The value of children to parents in the United States. *Journal of Population Studies* 1: 91–131.

Hrdy, S. B. (1999). *Mother Nature: Maternal Instincts and How They Shape the Human Species.* New York: Ballantine Books.

Jokela, M. (2010). Characteristics of the first child predict the parents' probability of having another child. *Developmental Psychology* 46 (4): 915.

Jokela, M., Kivimaeki, M., Elovainio, M., and Keltikangas-Jaervinen, L. (2009). Personality and having children: A two-way relationship. *Journal of Personality and Social Psychology* 96 (1): 218–230. doi:10.1037/a0014058.

Jones, R. K., and Brayfield, A. (1997). Life's greatest joy? European attitudes toward the centrality of children. *Social Forces* 75 (4): 1239–1269.

Kahneman, D. (1999). Objective wellbeing. In: Kahneman, D., Diener, E., and Schwarz, N. (eds.). *Well-Being: The Foundations of Hedonic Psychology.* New York: Russell Sage Foundation, 3–25.

Kahneman, D., Diener, E., and Schwarz, N. (eds.) (1999). *Well-Being: The Foundations of Hedonic Psychology.* New York: Russell Sage Foundation.

Kaplan, H., and Lancaster, J. (2003). An evolutionary and ecological analysis of human fertility, mating patterns, and parental investment. In: Wachter, K. W., and Bulatao, R. A. (eds.). *Offspring: Human Fertility Behavior in Biodemographic Perspective.* Washington, DC: The National Academies Press, 170–223.

Kohler, H.-P., Behrman, J. R., and Skytthe, A. (2005). Partner + children = happiness? An assessment of the effect of fertility and partnerships on subjective well-being in Danish twins. *Population and Development Review* 31 (3): 407–445. doi:10.1111/j.1728-4457.2005.00078.x.

Kohler, H.-P., Billari, F. C., and Ortega, J. A. (2002). The emergence of lowest-low fertility in Europe during the 1990s. *Population and Development Review* 28 (4): 641–681. http://www.jstor.org/stable/3092783.

Kohler, H.-P., Rodgers, J. L., and Christensen, K. (1999). Is fertility behavior in our genes? Findings from a Danish twin study. *Population and Development Review* 25 (2): 253–288. http://www.jstor.org/stable/172425.

Kyvik, K. O., Christensen, K., Skytthe, A., Harvald, B., and Holm, N. V. (1996). The Danish twin register. *Danish Medical Bulletin* 43 (5): 465–470.

Kyvik, K. O., Green, A., and Beck-Nielsen, H. (1995). The new Danish twin register: Establishment and analysis of twinning rates. *International Journal of Epidemiology* 24: 589–596.

Lawson, D., and Mace, R. (2010). Optimizing modern family size. *Human Nature* 21 (1): 39–61. doi:10.1007/s12110-010-9080-6.

Layard, P. R. G. (2005). *Happiness: Lessons from a New Science.* New York: Penguin Press.

Lee, R. D. (2001). Externalities of childbearing. In: Smelser, N. J., and Baltes, P. B. (eds.). *International Encyclopedia of the Social and Behavioral Sciences.* Amsterdam: Elsevier Science, 1686–1689.

Lesthaeghe, R., and Van de Kaa, D. (1986). Twee demografische transities? In: Lesthaeghe, R., and Van de Kaa, D. (eds.). *Bevolking: Groei en Krimp.* Deventer: Van Loghum Slaterus, 9–24.

Lesthaeghe, R. J., and Neidert, L. (2006). The second demographic transition in the United States: Exception or textbook example? *Population and Development Review* 32 (4): 669–698.

Loewenstein, G., O'Donoghue, T., and Rabin, M. (2003). Projection bias in predicting future utility. *Quarterly Journal of Economics* 118 (4): 1209–1248.

Lundberg, S., and Rose, E. (2002). The effects of sons and daughters on men's labor supply and wages. *Review of Economic Statistics* 84 (2): 251–268.

Lykken, D. T., and Tellegen, A. (1996). Happiness is a stochastic phenomenon. *Psychological Science* 7 (3): 186–189.

Margolis, R., and Myrskylä, M. (2011). A Global Perspective on Happiness and Fertility. *Population and Development Review* 37 (1): 29–56.

McDonald, P. (2000). Gender equity in theories of fertility transition. *Population and Development Review* 26 (3): 427–440.

McLanahan, S., and Adams, J. (1987). Parenthood and psychological well-being. *Annual Review of Sociology* 13: 237–257.

Miller, W. B., and Rodgers, J. L. (2001). *The Ontogeny of Human Bonding Systems: Evolutionary Origins, Neural Bases, and Psychological Manifestations.* Boston: Kluwer Academic Publishers.

Mizell, C. A., and Steelman, L. C. (2000). All my children: The consequences of sibling group characteristics on the marital happiness of young mothers. *Journal of Family Issues* 21 (7): 858–887.

Morgan, S. P., and King, R. B. (2001). Why have children in the 21st century? Biological predispositions, social coercion, rational choice. *European Journal of Population* 17 (1): 3–20.

Morgan, S. P., Lye, D. N., and Condran, G. A. (1988). Sons, daughters, and the risk of marital disruption. *American Journal of Sociology* 94 (1): 110–129.

Myers, D. G. (1993). *The Pursuit of Happiness.* London: Aquarian.

Myrskylä, M., Kohler, H.-P., and Billari, F. C. (2009). Advances in development reverse fertility declines. *Nature* 460 (7256): 741–743. doi:10.1038/nature08230.

Nauck, B. (2007). Value of children and the framing of fertility: Results from a cross-cultural comparative survey in 10 societies. *European Sociological Review* 23 (5): 615–629.

Nauck, B., and Klaus, D. (2007). The varying value of children: Empirical results from eleven societies in Asia, Africa and Europe. *Current Sociology* 55 (4): 487–503. doi:10.1177/ 0011392107077634.

Neyer, G., and Andersson, G. (2008). Consequences of family policies on childbearing behavior: Effects or artifacts? *Population and Development Review* 34 (4): 699–724.

Nomaguchi, K. M., and Milkie, M. A. (2003). Costs and rewards of children: The effects of becoming a parent on adults' lives. *Journal of Marriage and the Family* 65 (2): 356–374.

Parr, N. (2010). Satisfaction with life as an antecedent of fertility: Partner + happiness = children? *Demographic Research* 22 (21). doi:10.4054/DemRes.2010.22.21.

Pinquart, M., and Sörensen, S. (2000). Influences of socioeconomic status, social network, and competence on subjective well-being in later life: A meta-analysis. *Psychology and Aging* 15 (2): 187–224.

Potts, M. (1997). Sex and the birth rate: Human biology, demographic change and access to fertility-regulation methods. *Population and Development Review* 23 (1): 1–39.

Powdthavee, N. (2009). Think having children will make you happy? *The Psychologist* 22 (April): 308–311.

Preston, S. H., and Hartnett, C. S. (2008). The future of American fertility. NBER Working Paper 14498. http://www.nber.org/papers/w14498.

Rodgers, J. L., and Kohler, H.-P. (2008). Subjective well-being, fertility and partnerships: A biodemographic perspective. Unpublished manuscript, Population Studies Center, University of Pennsylvania, Philadelphia.

Rodgers, J. L., Kohler, H.-P., Kyvik, K., and Christensen, K. (2001). Behavior genetic modeling of human fertility: Findings from a contemporary Danish twin study. *Demography* 38 (1): 29–42. doi:10.1353/dem.2001.0009.

Rogers, S. J., and White, L. K. (1998). Satisfaction with parenting: The role of marital happiness, family structure, and parents' gender. *Journal of Marriage and the Family* 60 (2): 293–308.

Russell, R. J. H., and Wells, P. A. (1994). Predictors of happiness in married couples. *Personality and Individual Differences* 17 (3): 313–321.

Sandler, L. (2010). The only child: Debunking the myths. *Time* 176 (3), July 8. http://www.time.com/time/nation/article/0,8599,2002382,00.html.

Schoen, R., Kim, Y. J., Nathanson, C. A., Fields, J., and Astone, N. M. (1997). Why do Americans want children? *Population and Development Review* 23 (2): 333–358.

Senior, J. (2010). All joy and no fun: Why parents hate parenting. *New York Magazine*, July 4. http://nymag.com/news/features/67024/.

Skytthe, A., Kyvik, K., Holm, N. V., Vaupel, J. W., and Christensen, K. (2002). The Danish twin registry: 127 birth cohorts of twins. *Twin Research* 5 (5): 352–357.

Sobotka, T. (2004). *Postponement of Childbearing in Europe.* Amsterdam: Dutch University Press, Population Studies Series.

Stanca, L. (2009). Suffer the little children: Measuring the effects of parenthood on well-being worldwide. Department Of Economics, University of Milan Bicocca, Working Paper No. 173. http://fromgdptowellbeing.univpm.it/doc/papers/GDP2WB_092.pdf.

Thornton, A., and Young-DeMarco, L. (2001). Four decades of trends in attitudes toward family issues in the united states: The 1960s through the 1990s. *Journal of Marriage and Family* 63 (4): 1009–1037. doi:10.1111/j.1741-3737.2001.01009.x.

UNECE and UNFPA (2002). *Generations and Gender Programme: Survey Instruments.* New York: United Nations.

Van de Kaa, D. J. (1987). Europe's second demographic transition. *Population Bulletin* 42 (1): 1–59.

Vikat, A., Spéder, Z., Beets, G., Billari, F. C., Bühler, C., Desesquelles, A., Fokkema, T., Hoem, J. M., MacDonald, A., Neyer, G., Pailhé, A., Pinnelli, A., and Solaz, A. (2007). Generations and Gender Survey (GGS): Towards a better understanding of relationships and processes in the life course. *Demographic Research* 17 (14): 389–440. doi:10.4054/DemRes.2007.17.14.

Chapter 4

Gift or Commodity

How Ought We to Think about Children?

Elizabeth Marquardt

Children are a gift. It rolls off the tongue, a sentiment easily affirmed by anyone who has ever loved a child. For mothers and fathers the deep, sense-experience, jolting awareness of this gift can strike at any time: when your baby smiles at you; when your five-year-old, eyes wide, asks a question both innocent and profound; when your seven-year-old picks up a restaurant menu, sits tall and with complete confidence reads the choices aloud, as if she's been doing this all her life. As parents we witness in a whoosh of time this new life go from a twinge of morning sickness, to a tiny, floppy infant, to a young person completely unique, unlike any who has ever lived before, vulnerable, full of light, wholly beautiful. A gift indeed.

The world's great religious traditions have affirmed this gift. In the Hebrew Bible children are not only a gift but a command: "Be fruitful and multiply," God says, twice, in Genesis. The book of Psalms declares that children are "a heritage from the Lord" (Psalm 127:3). In Isaiah, God is called the one who "opens the womb" (Isaiah 66:9). The religions of the book can be seen as responding to cultures in which they arose, which marginalized or abused children. "Let the little children come unto me," said Jesus, who gave voice to the most vulnerable, among them children. The Qur'an affirms the sanctity of children and forbids infanticide of female as well as male children, in contrast to an Arab society of the time that viewed children as property (Giladi 2009).[1] The Psalmist sings to God, "it was you who formed my inward parts; you knit me together in my mother's womb" (Psalm 139:13). Children—people, creation—are God's gifts to the world, the prophets tell us.

But there are tensions as well. In Judaism, procreation is a command, but Hebrew Bible women (and generations after them) sometimes agonize in seeking to fulfill this command, with children being a gift seemingly withheld by God. The Qur'an is rich with references to God as the Creator who gives the blessed gift of children—"He gives to whom He will females, and He gives to whom He will males" (Sura 42:49–50); "It is He who created you out of one living soul" (Sura 7:189)—but children also are depicted as earthly or material attachments that detract from a spiritual focus: "Wealth and sons are the adornment of the present world" (Sura 18:46). The Christian tradition has scriptural support for this view as well: "Anyone who loves his son or daughter more than me is not worthy of me," said Jesus (Matthew 10:37). Children are a gift but they are also a distraction, leading to tensions between visions of the spiritual life and visions of family life.

Even if we accept that children are a gift, humanity clearly has not always been content simply to receive this gift and, like a flower, to watch its unfolding. Long before the world heard of IVF or designer babies, women and men hoped that having sexual relations in a certain way, consuming certain foods, avoiding certain emotions, or any number of other actions initiated or avoided by the would-be parents would make for a better, more acceptable gift of a child (Epstein 2010). Because we can sometimes see ourselves in the gift, we mistake it as something of our own making. Sometimes we do not want the gift. Or sometimes we desperately desire the gift and it does not come. When it does come, quite often we want sympathy and support for how hard it can be to honor this gift, to do it justice, to raise it right, even as we willingly affirm that we are extraordinarily, embarrassingly blessed to have this new life in our lives at all. Like the gift of faith, or the gift of our own lives, the gift of children is not one that simply brings ease and joy. It calls us, it makes demands, it can be uncomfortable, it can lead to suffering, and sometimes tremendously so. Children are a gift—it smacks of a saccharine sentiment, a Hallmark card filed in the "inspiration" section, but those four small words could be the seedbed for much of the theological corpus, the kind of blessing and contradiction and calling that has led generations of restless thinkers to try to name and understand God and God's reasons and the purpose of life itself.

The language of gift can be tied up in the injustice humans do to one another. For women, the language of the child as a gift can have problems, especially in cultures that sought and seek to control the bestowal of this gift by controlling women's role in the public sphere or by rigidly, even brutally, sanctioning women's sexuality and other activity in private life. For some young people who are adopted or conceived through sperm or egg donation, the language of the child as gift incites anger. The phrase makes them feel objectified and dismissed when it is used by others to imply that children can be gifted from one person to another and that the children in question should be both silent and grateful. And while the world's great religious traditions affirm the notion of the child as a gift, the material demands of human life have often encouraged other, less exalted ways of thinking about children: as field workers, household help, pawns to negotiate in marriage contracts, insurance for their parents' old age, child laborers, property. Further, most parents can relate to the tension between seeing *my* child as a gift but *your* child as a burden, threat, or, at best, useful accessory in my child's life.

The idea of the child as a gift—a gift from God—is paramount in our traditions, but the concept retains its power in part because it is a difficult idea, one in tension with other visions of the spiritual life, and in tension with human urges to control life, to have power, to see one's glory reflected in another, to will away uncertainty and with it the prospect of loss and suffering and despair.

Today, given advances and developments in the hard sciences, law, and culture, the concept of the child as gift continues to be challenged, arguably in newer and even more fundamental ways.

Artificial Reproductive Technologies and the Commodification of Children

Histories of artificial reproductive technologies (ARTs) tend to begin in 1978, with the introduction of in vitro fertilization by Robert Edwards, in Britain. In fact, conceiving children with sperm donation—a fairly low-tech procedure if the woman herself is not infertile—has a much longer track record. The first documented case in the US was in the 1890s, in Philadelphia. Britain experienced its first major public debate about the ethics of sperm donation in the 1950s, with a flurry of media coverage, medical journal articles, protests by the Roman Catholic church, and eerie film footage produced showing scores of wriggling infants looking like they'd just rolled off an assembly line. By 1978, scientists had figured out how to unite egg and sperm in a petri dish, implant the embryo in a woman's uterus, and bring it to term. In the 1980s, surrogacy gained quasi-legal status in at least some jurisdictions. (Surrogacy—that is, paying or forcing a woman to bear a child on behalf of another couple who typically has more money or social power than the surrogate mother—is not a new idea either.) By 1985, scientists were conceiving children with one woman's egg and implanting them in another woman's womb. With that development a new language of egg donation and "gestational" surrogacy (that is, when a woman carries a fetus that was not conceived with her own egg) was born.

These technological developments took place in tandem with notable trends in marriage, fertility, and social attitudes. In the United States, for example, the average age of first marriage is now about age twenty-five for women and age twenty-seven for men. The average age of first birth is now twenty-four years of age for women in the US. Younger women are more likely to say that their pregnancy was unintended. If one measures only intended first births, the average age of the first-time mother is still higher.

Reasons for these delays are many. The sexual revolution reinforced attitudes that separated sex from marriage, with one consequence being a greater tolerance for premarital sex and delays in first marriage. The availability of widespread contraception and legal abortion were part and parcel of these changes. A greater emphasis on women accessing higher education and economic pressures for both members of a couple to be income earners have also increased pressures that young women feel to complete their education and get established in the labor market before marrying or having children. Also, in a less child-centered society, more newly married couples embrace the idea of delaying a first birth for at least a few years so that they can have time together for just themselves. More recently, the US and other nations are seeing greater acceptance of out-of-wedlock childbearing, with couples who have a baby on the way not necessarily feeling the need to marry.

The result is that, especially among more affluent and higher-educated adults, these societies are seeing a postponement of marriage and parenthood. But amid the social and demographic sea changes of recent decades, one factor that has not changed much is women's fertility and, to a lesser extent, men's.

Women's fertility begins naturally to drop off after age twenty-five and can begin a serious drop after age thirty. To a lesser extent, men's fertility can also be impacted during the delay before childbearing, for reasons that will be discussed below. Today, couples who marry and feel ready to have children may discover that getting pregnant is harder than they thought. Some of them turn to technological solutions for answers.

Reproductive technologies are not only sought out by the affluent. *Washington Post* reporter Liza Mundy, in her book *Everything Conceivable,* makes the case that infertility is actually more a problem of the less affluent than those with more resources (Mundy 2007). Among those who are poor or struggling economically, rates of infertility, even at younger ages, can be higher because of less access to the health care system for the treatment of sexually transmitted diseases and other ailments that affect fertility; poorer nutrition and higher incidences of chronic disease; and greater likelihood of working in jobs that have higher exposures to chemicals or other agents that may affect fertility (such as toxic chemicals used in cleaning solutions, in farming, or on industrial sites). Poorer couples, like everyone else, feel the pain of infertility deeply and may seek whatever treatments they can. Mundy explains that higher-order multiple births (that is, triplets or greater) are more often seen among less-affluent couples because doctors may treat the woman with ovulation stimulating drugs (which have a much higher risk of producing multiple embryos) rather than with more expensive treatments such as IVF that better control how many embryos are placed in the womb. If male infertility is the factor, getting pregnant through use of sperm donation may be presented as a much more affordable option than accessing treatments that might improve the man's fertility.

Whatever the reasons behind the trends, one thing is clear: today, sperm donation, egg donation, IVF, and surrogacy are old news. These days a woman can acquire embryos on ice, left over from another couple's IVF treatments, to carry in her own womb and raise as her own child—variously called embryo donation, embryo transfer, or embryo adoption (the latter is a misnomer, for these transfers take place with none of the child-centered legal protections in place for adoptions). Children have been conceived with the DNA of three adults—the mitochondrial DNA of one woman's egg, the nuclear DNA of another woman's egg, and the sperm of a man. Scientists in New Zealand and Australia are seeking to create offspring with two same-sex parents; scientists in Japan have succeeded in creating a mouse with two mothers and no father. Reproductive cloning is now embraced by notable international scientists and bioethicists, including Robert Edwards, the father of IVF, and James

Watson, the co-discoverer of the structure of DNA, as well as by 10 percent of US fertility clinic directors. British scientists have received state permission to develop hybrid embryos that contain some human cells and some animal cells, for research purposes. A scientist who conducted her research in Israel and now practices maternal and child health in Missouri has retrieved eggs from aborted female fetuses for use in stem cell research. Sex selection through pre-implantation genetic diagnosis (PIGD) (or through ultrasound and abortion) is common in India and China and in some ethnic groups in the US and Canada. The list goes on.

In recent decades, countless opinion pieces in scientific journals and mainstream media have been written on all this, variously celebrating or agonizing over the brave new world that is already upon us. Some hard research on the children's well-being has been conducted, particularly on outcomes for children conceived from IVF who, it now appears, suffer birth defects at about twice the rate of those naturally conceived. Yet, astonishingly, given that the whole field is about the conception of children, very little attention overall has been given to how the children fare—physically and emotionally, in the short term and the long haul.

The research faces at least two serious challenges. The first is that much of the field has developed in secrecy. Sperm donation occurred for generations with doctors insisting that patients tell no one, especially the child, how the child was conceived. The US and many other nations still do not require reporting of pregnancies achieved through sperm donation. Experts estimate that perhaps between 30,000 and 60,000 children are conceived through sperm donation in the US each year—with about one million sperm donor–conceived young people alive in the world today—but really it is anyone's guess.[2] In the US reporting *is* required for pregnancies achieved through egg donation and embryo transfer, and other nations, particularly those with national health care systems, seem to do a better job of at least keeping track of the numbers, if not studying the long-term results. But in the US and most countries, anonymous donation of sperm and eggs remains the standard.[3] Most donor offspring are not told the truth by their parents about their origins[4] and if and when they do find out, they have little hope of identifying their biological father or mother.

The researchers face a second major challenge as well: the ART baby-making business, $1.3 billion a year in the US alone, is now a global one. The largest sperm bank in the world, Cryos, is located in Denmark and ships three-quarters of its sperm overseas. Women in nations such as Britain, which not long ago banned anonymous donation of sperm and eggs, get their eggs from Spain,

Eastern Europe, or Russia. Most Canadian clinics use sperm from US sperm banks. Couples in wealthy developed nations now pay village women in India to be the surrogate carrier of their child; her services cost much less (and most of the fee goes to the broker, not the surrogate), she doesn't put up a fuss, and there is little to no chance of her being involved in the child's life. Sperm banks in Australia ran an ad campaign urging young male college students from abroad to visit Australia for a subsidized spring break and deposit some sperm before they went home. Gay couples from around the world visit the largely unregulated clinics of California to purchase eggs, rent wombs, and go home with a baby (or twins, or triplets). South Africa bills itself as a one-stop "fertility tourism" destination for would-be parents who can take advantage of high-quality clinics, visit beautiful beaches, and go home pregnant, all for less than the cost of one clinic visit back home.

Thus, the global scope as well as the secrecy present serious challenges for researchers. One of the very few researchers on the question of child outcomes is Susan Golombok, of Cambridge University, who has conducted small studies of convenience samples of young children conceived through sperm or egg donation, and concludes they are doing well.

But the main reason there is so little research on the well-being of the children is this: It's not really about the children. The ART market, tacitly or outright supported by the state, exists for adults who want to be parents. The language of ARTs is about adult rights to have children. Its supporters routinely draw upon legitimate public sympathies for people struggling with infertility, even though an increasing proportion of the clientele are not persons with medical infertility. They invoke a language of reproductive rights, arguing that there is or should be a legal or moral right to have a child and for the state and society to help if necessary. They invoke this language even though the concept of reproductive rights was developed in international human rights law to address the evil of states or authorities denying individuals or couples their natural fertility and was developed in US law to address the plight of women who wish not to reproduce. When critics raise concerns about the well-being of children born of ARTs they are quickly reassured. The kids are fine, supporters say. After all, their parents went to great lengths to have them. The children are 100 percent wanted. For a child, what could be better?

My colleagues and I decided to learn more. I teamed up with Norval Glenn, professor of sociology at the University of Texas at Austin, and Karen Clark, an author and person conceived via sperm donation who lives in the New York City area, to design a survey instrument with the goal of studying the identity, kinship, well-being, and social justice experiences of donor-conceived adults.

Through this method we assembled a representative sample of 485 adults between the ages of eighteen and forty-five years old who said their mother used a sperm donor to conceive them. We also assembled comparison groups of 562 young adults who were adopted as infants and 563 young adults who were raised by their biological parents.

We found that, on average, young adults conceived through sperm donation are hurting more, are more confused, and feel more isolated from their families (Marquardt et al. 2010). They fare worse than their peers raised by biological parents on important outcomes such as depression, delinquency, and substance abuse. Nearly two-thirds agree, "My sperm donor is half of who I am." Nearly half are disturbed that money was involved in their conception. More than half say that when they see someone who resembles them they wonder if they are related. Almost as many say they have feared being attracted to or having sexual relations with someone to whom they are unknowingly related. Approximately two-thirds affirm the right of donor offspring to know the truth about their origins. And about half of donor offspring have concerns about or serious objections to donor conception itself, even when parents tell their children the truth.

In the study, the family relationships of persons conceived this way were more often characterized by confusion, tension, or loss. More than half (53 percent) agree, "I have worried that if I try to get more information about or have a relationship with my sperm donor, my mother and/or the father who raised me would feel angry or hurt." Seventy percent agree, "I find myself wondering what my sperm donor's family is like." And 69 percent agree, "I sometimes wonder if my sperm donor's parents would want to know me."

Nearly half of donor offspring (48 percent) compared to about a fifth of adopted adults (19 percent) agree, "When I see friends with their biological fathers and mothers, it makes me feel sad." Similarly, more than half of donor offspring (53 percent, compared to 29 percent of the adopted adults) agree, "It hurts when I hear other people talk about their genealogical background."

Forty-three percent of donor offspring, compared with 15 percent of adopted persons and 6 percent of those raised by their biological parents, agree, "I feel confused about who is a member of my family and who is not."

Almost half of donor offspring (47 percent) agree, "I worry that my mother might have lied to me about important matters when I was growing up," compared with 27 percent of the adopted and 18 percent raised by their biological parents. Similarly, 43 percent of donor offspring, compared to 22 percent and 15 percent, respectively, of those raised by adoptive or biological parents, agree,

"I worry that my father might have lied to me about important matters when I was growing up."

When they grow up, well over half (57 percent) of donor offspring agree, "I feel that I can depend on my friends more than my family"—about twice as many as those who grew up with their biological parents.

Donor offspring also told us that they more often worry about the implications of interacting with—and possibly having intimate relationships with—unknown, blood-related family members. Well over half of donor offspring—58 percent—agree, "When I see someone who resembles me I often wonder if we are related," compared to 45 percent of adopted adults and 14 percent raised by their biological parents.

Nearly half—46 percent—of donor offspring, but just 17 percent of adopted adults and 6 percent of those raised by their biological parents, agree, "When I'm romantically attracted to someone I have worried that we could be unknowingly related." Similarly, 43 percent of adult donor offspring, and just 16 percent of adopted adults and 9 percent of those raised by their biological parents, agree, "I have feared having sexual relations unknowingly with someone I am related to."

We also found that donor offspring are far more likely to have experienced divorce or multiple family transitions in their families of origin. The married heterosexual parents of the donor offspring are unusually likely to have divorced, with 27 percent of donor offspring reporting that their parents divorced before the respondent was age sixteen, compared to 14 percent of those who were adopted and 25 percent of those raised by their biological parents. (The comparison between the parents of donor offspring and those of the adopted is apt, because in both cases the parents would likely have turned to donor conception or adoption later in their marriages, when marriages on the whole are more stable.) Overall, 44 percent of donor offspring experienced one or more "family transitions" between their birth and age sixteen, compared to 22 percent of the adopted, and 35 percent of those raised by their biological parents.[5]

Perhaps most importantly, in the study donor offspring are significantly more likely than those raised by their biological parents to struggle with serious, negative outcomes such as delinquency, substance abuse, and depression, even when controlling for socioeconomic and other factors. As illustrated in Figure 4.1, donor offspring and those who were adopted are twice as likely as those raised by biological parents to report problems with the law before age twenty-five. Donor offspring are more than twice as likely as those raised by biological parents to report substance abuse problems (with the adopted falling between the two groups). Donor offspring are about 1.5 times more likely than those raised by their biological parents to report mental health problems, with the adopted being closer to twice as likely as those raised by biological parents to report the same thing.

The study also affirmed that donor offspring as a group broadly support the right to know about their origins. Depending on which question is asked, approximately two-thirds of grown donor offspring support the right of offspring to have non-identifying information about the sperm donor biological father, to know his identity, to have the opportunity to form some kind of relationship with him, to know about the existence and number of half-siblings conceived with the same donor, to know the identity of half-siblings conceived with the same donor, and to have the opportunity as children to form some kind of relationship with half-siblings conceived with the same donor.

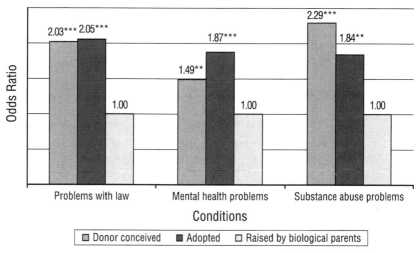

Figure 4.1 The Relationship between Biological Origin and Well-Being
Notes: Odds ratios predicting three conditions, by biological origin, controlling for age, gender, race, subjective family income at age 16, and mother's education.
Reference Group: Raised by biological parents
** Significantly different from raised by biological parents at p< .01 (two-tailed tests)
*** Significantly different from raised by biological parents at p< .001 (two-tailed tests)
Source: Marquardt, Elizabeth, Norval D. Glenn, and Karen Clark. 2010. *My Daddy's Name Is Donor: A New Representative Study of Young Adults Conceived through Sperm Donation.* New York: Institute for American Values.

Other themes arise as well when speaking with young adults who were conceived this way. Some donor offspring say they feel isolated and disturbingly unusual, conceived in a way that is just not "normal," and not understood by virtually anyone around them. Christine Whipp of the UK tells of finding out, at age forty-one, that her mother had used a sperm donor to get pregnant with her, after a lifetime of painful, emotional tumult and powerful feelings of being rejected by her mother:

> My ancestral home was a glass sample jar, and my [biological] parents never knew one another in either the personal or the biblical sense. I couldn't name a single person who shared this strange, science-fiction style background, and found myself feeling more alone and completely separate from the rest of the human race than I had ever felt before. (Whipp 2006)

When Adam Rose of the UK found out the truth about his origins, he says, "I felt like a freak, because no one else in my perception had been conceived in that way and it was something that nobody had heard of. It was very shocking" (Rose 2000). Another donor offspring reports she has long struggled with feelings of shame "for being conceived in such an unusual way."[6]

In a *Washington Post* essay, Katrina Clark of the US, then barely twenty years old, told her story. She was born to a single mother who was always open with Katrina about the facts of her conception. She has a close, loving relationship with her mother. Still, as Katrina got older and began to wrestle with the identity issues that confronted her, she looked around at friends who had both their parents and wrote, "That was when the emptiness came over me. I realized that I am, in a sense, a freak. I really, truly would never have a dad. I finally understood what it meant to be donor-conceived, and I hated it" (Clark 2006).

Lindsay Greenawalt's mother, who had her as a single mom, also informed Lindsay about the truth of her origins. At the same time, Lindsay recalls, her mother did not ever raise the subject or encourage discussion about it. Lindsay writes, "I had wondered about my biological father most of my life.... I usually saw myself as a 'freak of nature.'"[7]

Twenty-three-year-old Alana reports what happened the first time she tried to confide in a friend: "In junior high I told my best friend about my conception," she said. "Then we had a fight. She told the entire school that I was a 'test tube baby,' essentially a freak of science." She adds, "I would like more Donor Kid stories to be publicized and shared without the 'freak' connotation."

In our study, we asked donor-conceived persons the questions "At age fifteen, what feelings best describe how you felt about being donor conceived?"

and "At the age you are now, how do you feel about being a donor-conceived person?" (The first question was asked only of those who knew at age fifteen that they were donor conceived.) Each question offered a list of positive, negative, or neutral terms; respondents could select as many of the terms as they wished. From that list, 11 percent chose the powerfully negative term "freak of nature," and 14 percent chose the equally disturbing phrase "lab experiment."

For some donor offspring, their deep discomfort about their origins appears to lie, at least in part, in their feeling of being a product made to suit their parents' wishes—of being made, not born.

Lynne Spencer is a nurse and donor-conceived adult who interviewed eight other adult donor offspring for a master's thesis (Spencer 2007). Spencer writes of finding out, as an adult, that her married parents had conceived her with donor sperm. The profound question with which she struggled was this: "If my life is for other people's purposes, and not my own, then what is the purpose of my life?" In a later exchange she expanded on this thought:

> I think one of the most unusual aspects of being a donor offspring is the feeling of being inanimate, or that I didn't exist in part. The whole sense that I don't matter, who I am doesn't matter and needs to be repressed. It's only what I represent that matters ... that I am someone's child, but I'm not a person in my own right.

Another participant in Spencer's study said this:

> I had always been very scared of dying, because I couldn't really come to terms with my nonexistence in the world. I think part of that was to do with the fact that in some sense I didn't feel like I existed in the world, because I didn't know what half of me originated from. It was almost like that part of me had been seriously denied because of the secrecy. Nobody had spoken about it for me ... it's almost like I had come into the world by magic.

Christine Whipp reports that she has long felt that "having bought and paid for me ... my mother view[ed] me more as her personal property [rather] than seeing my existence as a serendipitous piece of good fortune."

Several years ago, a then-thirty-nine-year-old Japanese woman whose mother used donor insemination to conceive her told a reporter that she struggles with this overwhelming feeling: "I feel that I came into this world for the sake of my mother. After she died, I started wondering if I had a reason to exist anymore" (Otake 2005).

These young people tell us what it is like to know that the parts to make you were bought and sold, that your biological mother and father never even met one another, that your birth story is one of doctors in lab coats, catheters, and contracts.

Gift or Commodity:
How Ought We to Think about Children?

Today, if you wish to have a child and don't wish to have a father involved, your options are many. Among the simplest is to visit the Internet and start surfing online catalogs of sperm donors. Much like shopping for a new sofa or a car, you can assess and compare various traits, such as heights, weights, and eye color; education levels; and athletic accomplishments. You can read essays or listen to audio recordings in which the sperm donor waxes about the meaning of life and why sperm donation appeals to him. To remove some of the guess work, some sperm banks recently began marketing "celebrity look-alike" sperm. This potential father favors Brad Pitt. That one, a taller George Clooney. Handsome men not available to most women on the dating market are allegedly available at the sperm bank.

The sperm banks also allege, as a marketing tool, that their sperm is the best quality—carefully screened, disease-free, and really a much better gamble than a personal relationship would provide. Would-be mothers are led to believe that going with a sperm bank will take the uncertainty out of childbearing. You'll get a healthy, disease-free child with a smart, handsome father who won't interfere in your parenting decisions. In fact, online message boards populated by mothers who've used anonymous donor insemination are full of chatter that tells a different story. Some mothers blame their child's autism on the donor. Some, their child's anger management issue. One woman's children are excessively short and she is suing the sperm bank. One woman wrote to an advice columnist that her donor-conceived daughter had developed type 1 diabetes. "Maybe I chose the wrong donor," said the mother.

In other words, if the commodification of children—and a global trade in the parts to make them—is not enough to get our attention, let's keep in mind that in this system adults become commodities, too. The children grow up to become people, people who were bought and sold through largely anonymous contracts in which they had no say. Men are reduced to genetic stock, rated and bartered on the Internet. When the sperm of a popular donor runs dry, would-be mothers post messages online seeking to purchase unused vials of his sperm that might be available from another mother.

Young egg donors are even more precious commodities. Eggs are far more difficult to retrieve than sperm and thus far more expensive to buy. In order to pay college tuition or credit card bills, some young women subject themselves to months of shots and a painful surgical extraction of some of their eggs, typically for around $5,000, at an unknown risk to their own health or future fertility, and at the price of selling what will be their future children's half-brothers and sisters. Other women become surrogate mothers, seeing it as a way to earn an income while staying at home with their kids. Wealthier couples pay US surrogates around $25,000–$30,000 for nine months' use of their body to carry and give birth to a child, again with possible grave, lasting consequences to the woman's health. The surrogates' own children see the babies disappear to be raised in another family. In India, village women are paid far less.[8] Knowing that their neighbors might frown on their decision to participate in surrogacy, at least one village woman told a newspaper reporter that after the baby is born she simply tells her neighbors that the baby died.

The upshot is this: When we commodify children, we commodify ourselves. When our emerging cultural story is that people are made by humans, birthed through the will of their mothers, it is not just a few children on the margins who are conceived by ARTs who are affected. We all are.

Conclusion

What ought we to do? I offer the following recommendations:[9]

- End anonymous donation. A number of European nations—including Britain, Sweden, Norway, the Netherlands, and Switzerland—have ended the practice of anonymous donation of sperm and eggs. Other nations in the West and around the world should follow their lead.
- Recognize that reproductive technologies create people, not just babies. The offspring created by reproductive technologies grow up to be mature adults and full citizens just like every other person. Their perspective on these technologies is just as important as, and perhaps more important than, the views of doctors, parents, and would-be parents who use these technologies.

- Pediatricians and other health professionals must confront the implications of treating children conceived through anonymous donations and other artificial reproductive technologies. The genetic, heritable basis of disease is increasingly important in the practice of medicine. What is the position of pediatricians and other health professionals on the practice of anonymous donation, conceiving children who will have dozens or hundreds of unknown half-siblings, parents not telling their children or their children's doctors the truth about the child's biological origins, and sperm and egg banks not being required to track the health of donors and keep parents informed about genetic diseases that donors might develop in the future? Regarding IVF, what is their stand on a procedure that appears to result in birth defects at about twice the rate of children resulting from natural conception? These questions and more can no longer be in the domain solely of fertility doctors and ethicists. It is time for pediatricians and other health professionals to confront, wrestle with, and take a firm stand on these issues of urgent importance to a generation of young people.
- In line with Canadian bioethicist Margaret Somerville's recommendation, the right of children to be born from one identified, untampered-with sperm and one identified, untampered-with egg should be legally affirmed.
- Retrieve and lift up the religious and ethical story of children as a gift, while also recognizing that honoring that gift requires attention to men's sexual behavior as well as women's. Be clear that children are gifts from beyond, not gifts from one person to another.
- Some faith traditions have addressed the complexities of ARTs in the modern world. Most have not. Those religious traditions that reject, ignore, accept, or welcome ARTs must grapple with emerging evidence about the impact of ARTs on young people and the broader culture, and with the presence of donor-conceived persons in the pews. One intriguing finding in our study was that significant numbers of donor offspring were raised in faith traditions and identify with faith traditions today. They are in the churches and they are hurting. What do the churches have to say?[10]
- Resist the trend in family law to focus on the conception of "intentional parenthood" or identifying the legal parent as the adult who intended to be the parent.[11] Offer up the strong body of social science evidence that suggests that being raised by one's own married mother and father

is powerfully correlated with positive child outcomes, with adoption as a vitally important, child-centered complimentary institution. Give greater attention in law and policy to the institutions—such as marriage and adoption—that demonstrably foster improved child outcomes.

Overall, social leaders must seek to affirm for the *next* generation of young people that no matter the circumstances of their conception and birth, no matter their parents' intentions when sperm met egg and a new life formed, they are all, on the most important, even transcendent level, part of a plan, welcomed, and thoroughly wanted.

Notes

1. Avner Giladi, "Islam," in Don Browning and Marcia Bunge, eds., *Children and Childhood in the World's Religious Traditions* (New Brunswick, NJ: Rutgers University Press, 2009), p. 166. This entire volume represents a treasure trove of scholarly essays and primary texts on the question of how the world's religious traditions treat children and childhood.

2. See Wendy Kramer, "A Call by the Donor Sibling Registry to Stop Using the Figures of 30,000–60,000 US Sperm Donor Births," *BioNews,* May 8, 2012. http://www.bionews.org .uk/ page.asp?obj_id=2567#BMS_RESULT, accessed June 11, 2012.

3. The nations that allow only non-anonymous donation include Britain, Sweden, Norway, the Netherlands, Switzerland, New Zealand, and some parts of Australia. In May 2011, a judge in British Columbia, Canada said that anonymous donation could no longer occur in that province.

4. "Since its initiation in the early twentieth century, DI [donor insemination] has been considered a very private process which should be kept secret, even 'forgotten.' According to some authors (e.g. Turner & Coyle, 2000), this view was strongly encouraged by clinicians, who recommended that parents should not disclose to their children the processes by which they were created. If it became necessary to acknowledge a lack of biological connection, it has been claimed that parents were advised to tell their children that they were adopted (Rowland, 1985). The shameful association of sperm donation with masturbation and marital unfaithfulness remains an undercurrent in attitudes to donor insemination (Kirkman, 2004b)." From Infertility Treatment Authority of Australia, Parents Disclosing Donor Conception to Their Children: What Does the Literature Tell Us? January 2006, p. 2. Report available online.

5. See Web Figure 4.1 on the book web site.

6. Quotations from donor offspring that are not otherwise cited come from journalistic interviews that Marquardt conducted with donor offspring. Some of these persons asked Marquardt to use their full first and last name, some their first name only, and some a pseudonym.

7. http://cryokidconfessions.blogspot.com/p/about-this-blog.html, accessed June 11, 2012.

8. See Shekhar Bhatia, "'Baby Factory' Proliferation Worries Indian Government," *Vancouver Sun*, June 9, 2012. http://www.vancouversun.com/health/Baby+factory+proliferation +worries +Indian+government/6756902/story.html, accessed June 11, 2012.

9. Most, but not all, of these recommendations are drawn from my co-investigated report, *My Daddy's Name Is Donor: A New Representative Study of Young Adults Conceived through Sperm Donation.*

10. One of the more interesting findings to come to light in this survey is how many of today's adult donor offspring (who were 18 to 45 years old in the year 2008) were raised Catholic and are still Catholic today. We asked all survey respondents, "What religion if any were you raised in?" and "What is your religious preference today?" A surprising 36 percent of donor offspring said they were raised Catholic, compared with 23 percent from adoptive families and 28 percent raised by their biological parents. (By contrast, persons from adoptive or biological families were much more likely to say they had been raised in a Protestant denomination.) This finding is especially startling given that Catholic teaching does not support the use of donor insemination. As adults, donor offspring are also much more likely to say they are Catholic today. Nearly a third of donor offspring—31 percent—say Catholicism is their religious preference today. By contrast, their Catholic-raised peers from adoptive families or raised by their biological parents appear more often to have left the Catholic church. As adults, 15 percent of those from adoptive families and 20 percent of those raised by their biological parents say that Catholicism is their religion today. Finally, more than a third—34 percent—of donor offspring say that they are Protestant today, and about one-quarter of all three groups say their religious preference today is "none." (About 6 percent of donor offspring say they are Jewish.) So while a minority of donor offspring do embrace a secular belief system, the majority of them are religious and they are surprisingly over-represented in the Catholic church.

11. See Elizabeth Marquardt, "One Parent or Five: A Global Look at Today's New Intentional Families" (New York: Institute for American Values, 2011). Report available online at FamilyScholars.org.

References

Clark, Katrina. 2006. "My Father Was an Anonymous Sperm Donor." *Washington Post,* December 17, 2006.

Epstein, Randi Hutter. 2010. *Get Me Out: A History of Childbirth from the Garden of Eden to the Sperm Bank.* New York: W. W. Norton.

Giladi, Avner. 2009. "Islam." In Don Browning and Marcia Bunge (eds.), *Children and Childhood in the World's Religious Traditions,* 166. New Brunswick, NJ: Rutgers University Press.

Marquardt, Elizabeth, Norval D. Glenn, and Karen Clark. 2010. *My Daddy's Name Is Donor: A New Representative Study of Young Adults Conceived through Sperm Donation.* New York: Institute for American Values.

Mundy, Liza. 2007. *Everything Conceivable: How Assisted Reproduction Is Changing Our World.* New York: Knopf.

Otake, Tomoko. 2005. "Lives in Limbo." *The Japan Times Online,* August 28, 2005. http://www.japantimes.co.jp/text/fl20050828x1.html. Accessed June 11, 2012.

Rose, Adam. 2000. "'Faceless Fathers' May Be Identified." *The Independent,* April 24, 2000.

Spencer, Lynne W. 2007. *Sperm Donor Offspring: Identity and Other Experiences.* Charleston, SC: Self-published, available from Booksurge.

Whipp, Christine. 2006. "Worrying the Wound: The Hidden Scars of Donor Conception." In Alexina McWhinnie (ed.), *Who Am I: Experiences of Donor Conception.* Warwickshire, UK: Idreos Education Trust.

Chapter 5

Little Emperors?

Growing Up in China after the One-Child Policy

Susan E. Short, Hongwei Xu, and Ying Liu

China's one-child policy, a state population-reduction initiative, is among the most fascinating family experiments of the twentieth century. The policy, first instituted in late 1979, came at a time when China's total fertility rate was estimated at 2.7 births, dramatically lower than the total fertility rate of 6.0 only a decade earlier (Tien 1991). However, with a large cohort of women soon to enter their childbearing years, policy-makers sought to reign in fertility further so as to enhance China's economic development efforts. China's fertility today is well below replacement level, estimated around 1.5 children per woman of reproductive age (Retherford et al. 2005). Although factors other than the one-child policy shape fertility, the state, through regulating births, remade the Chinese family.

More than thirty years have passed since the one child policy was introduced. How have the children born under the policy fared? Popular images of childhood in China range from "spoiled little emperors" indulged by parents and grandparents to "unwanted and abandoned baby girls." Although these are starkly different images, both suggest concern over the well-being of children. Indeed, scholars have pondered the implications of a society filled with only children (Fong 2004; Shen and Yuan 1999). Would such children grow up morally underdeveloped, selfish, socially deficient, and anxious from the pressure to succeed they would feel under the watchful eyes of their parents and grandparents? Early studies suggested concern was warranted (Jiao et al. 1986; Tseng et al. 1988).

Co-existent with this narrative of social demise, however, is another narrative. One way the Chinese state persuaded couples to reduce family size was by promoting the idea that having fewer "quality" children was modern, desirable, and good for the state and the family. They urged couples to choose "quality" over "quantity." Among scholars, the quality-quantity trade-off and its connection to fertility was a common theme. Economist Gary Becker popularized the application of economic principles to understand family processes, including quality-quantity trade-offs in children (Becker and Lewis 1973). Judith Blake (1981) wrote about family size in the US and suggested that children with many siblings were disadvantaged in educational attainment relative to children with fewer siblings, although the extent to which this relationship is causal at the individual level has been debated (e.g., Downey 1995; Guo and VanWey 1999), with some suggesting that there is little evidence for a quantity-quality trade-off (Angrist et al. 2010). In the case of China, findings are mixed. Social scientists have suggested both that smaller families might lead to greater investment in children, which would advantage children, not disadvantage them (Li et al. 2008), and that family size has a positive effect on school enrollment for some children (Qian 2009).

In this chapter we revisit these themes. Although considerable scholarly attention on the one-child policy has focused on the effects of the policy on fertility and related reproductive outcomes, such as sex-selective abortion, much less attention has been paid to the implications of the policy for the children who are born under it. One reason is that this question poses a methodological challenge. The policy is a national policy with implementation that has varied over time and across geographies. Thus, the policy itself has varied at the local level (Short and Zhai 1998), a level at which we rarely have the detailed data we need to make desired inferences regarding policy effects.

Moreover, the one-child policy is but one policy affecting the social fabric of Chinese society. At about the same time the one-child policy was introduced, China undertook expansive economic reforms that included policies to encourage marketization and a shift away from the state-sponsored socialist economy. Coincident with these changes have been rapid economic growth and a decentralization of the health system that have led to a decrease in the accessibility of preventive services, at least for an intermediate period. Thus, over the past thirty years families have been reshaped and children's lives affected by social change in numerous dimensions. One consequence is that it is challenging to draw conclusions about policy implications by looking at children's lives before and after policy introduction.

Accordingly, though the one-child policy motivates and informs our work, the goal of this chapter is to describe what it is like to be a child growing up in contemporary China. We pay particular attention to the "onlies" experience by contrasting it to the experience of other children. We begin by describing previous research focused on the one-child policy, or China's low fertility regime, and children's well-being. Subsequently, we turn to data from a survey of over 4,000 households that includes more than 1,500 children ages 6–18 years collected by the China Health and Nutrition Survey in 2004 (Popkin et al. 2010). With these data we ask whether empirical evidence exists to support the idea that children in single-child families differ from children in sibling families in their experiences growing up. We examine multiple dimensions with our data: participation in school, participation in extra-school activities, child life priorities, parental supervision, and health-related outcomes.

We have two working hypotheses. The first is that differences in child outcomes associated with the number of siblings will be minimal once basic family and individual characteristics are controlled. Perceptions that such differences exist derive from direct experience with only children and sibling children. However, anecdotal evidence is similar to "unadjusted" data so that the differences in child attributes associated with number of siblings appear marked when not taking into account underlying factors that shape family composition. Our second working hypothesis is that differences that remain after adjustment will vary based on the dimension explored. For example, we think it possible that only children will be more likely to be involved in extra-school activities, experience higher levels of parental supervision, or express concern about achievement or other markers of success in the new economy. We think it less likely we will see differences in school participation or health-related outcomes, as these activities are more likely subsidized by the government for all children and are considered more fundamental to child welfare.

Background on the One-Child Policy

Instituted in late 1979, the one-child policy encourages couples of Han ethnicity, over 90 percent of the population, to give birth to only one child, allowing exceptions based on personal circumstances, including place of residence (Scharping 2003). Differences in policy across provinces and across administrative classifications in regard to urbanization are marked (Short and Zhai 1998). In cities, a stricter version of the policy holds most couples to one child. As one moves away from cities, exceptions that allow a second birth grow more lenient. They are most lenient in the least developed provinces and most rural areas. Exceptions, which are many, include an allowance for a second child if the first child is disabled, if both parents are only children, if parents are not of the majority Han ethnicity, and if the first child is a girl (Scharping 2003). Exceptions are usually implemented by and negotiated with local cadres (Greenhalgh 1993). The girl exception, most common in parts of rural China, is particularly important to family composition (Short et al. 2001). As a result of this exception, in combination with individual-level preference, more one-child families will include boys.

Child gender merits careful consideration in describing child experiences across one-child and sibling children families. Both within and beyond China, researchers and policy-makers are concerned that the one-child policy may exacerbate discrimination against girls. Patterns of abortion, mortality, and abandonment indicate that, in the aggregate, girls have been less welcome family members (Coale and Banister 1994; Johansson and Nygren 1991; Johnson 1993). Yet, once they become part of a family, it is less clear that their experiences growing up differ from those of boys in ways that are detrimental. Indeed, due to selective forces in play in regard to family formation, the girls who become part of a family may be particularly wanted. Moreover, in one-child families, girls may fare similarly to boys because families may invest fully in their one child regardless of gender (Short et al. 2001; Fong 2002). At the same time, childhood activities and experiences differ by gender around the world. Thus, we fully expect gender difference, especially in time use, for children in China.

Previous Research on One-Child and Sibling Children in China

Numerous scholars have argued that number of siblings is negatively related to child outcomes, especially educational attainment (Blake 1981, 1989; Mare 1995). The usual argument is that more children dilute the investment parents can make in any one child. Also, it has been suggested that intellectual stimulation in the family declines with a new birth (Zajonc and Markus 1975). More generally, time use in families with many children may be different than in families with few. For example, Hofferth and Sandberg (2001) show that American children in large families spend more time in sports and playing with their siblings than those in small families. Time use in childhood has been shown to be correlated with later life emotional, cognitive, and health outcomes (see Xu and Minca 2008 for a review). Much of the literature on family size and child quality focuses on cognitive or educational outcomes. Health outcomes, including psychosocial outcomes, are less frequently examined empirically.

In the case of China, early research, based on two surveys conducted in Beijing and Jilin Province in the 1980s, suggested that only children enjoyed an advantage in school achievement, but only in urban areas (Falbo et al. 1989). This study also assessed children's personality. It did not find evidence that only children had undesirable personalities, or "less virtue" as assessed by Chinese standards, than children with siblings as judged by teachers or mothers. Falbo and Poston assessed personality in other studies, and each time reported that they could find no difference between only children and others (Falbo and Poston 1993; Poston and Falbo 1990). Similarly, an assessment of self-concept, sociability as reported on by peers, and behavior as reported on by teachers, in children from sixth grade classrooms in urban and rural China, did not indicate difference by family size (Meredith et al. 1992). However, urban children and boys scored higher on self-concept. Yang and colleagues (1995), however, in a design that compared urban adolescents born before, during, and after implementation of the one-child policy found that children with siblings had higher levels of fear and anxiety than only children across all three policy periods. They also found that adolescents who had siblings born during or after implementation of the one-child policy had higher levels of depression than only children.

The finding that children with siblings had higher levels of depression when siblings were born during the one-child policy period, although a tentative finding, is provocative. It suggests that societal context may condition differences in outcomes experienced by only children and sibling children. Conceptually and empirically, this idea has been represented in recent work that focuses on economic contexts and educational outcomes across only children and sibling children in China. Lu and Treiman (2008) demonstrate differences in educational outcomes across only and sibling children by examining the relationship across periods when competition for educational resources changed due to shifts in policies. Recent research has also found that family size is negatively correlated with educational attainment, but more so in rural areas (Li et al. 2008). Far less research has considered ideological context and its implications for children. As Yang and colleagues suggest, being an only child may well advantage children in a setting where couples are encouraged to have one child for the good of the nation. In some cases, having more children means violating the policy, a behavior akin to breaking the law, and is punishable with a fine. Indeed, in their paper they suggest that this context may be relevant to children's interactions, such that only children can make disparaging remarks to children with siblings *because* they are from sibling families. We might expect such factors to be more relevant for children of higher birth order.

Other research on behavioral characteristics shows a mixed pattern of results. In one study only children were rated by their peers as more uncooperative and selfish than sibling children (Jiao et al. 1986). Another study found differences between only children and sibling children among boys but not among girls (Tseng et al. 1988). Still others found no behavioral differences (Chen et al. 1994; Poston and Yu 1985). Finally, in a study of the values of adolescents in Beijing and Shanghai, researchers found no evidence of difference between only children and sibling children and concluded that the stereotype of only children as spoiled was not supported by the data (Shen and Yuan 1999).

Lastly, research on only children versus sibling children families has assessed health. In a study based on a cross-sectional survey of 4,197 adolescents in Zhejiang Province, children ages 12–16 years were assessed on nutritional indicators, health-seeking behaviors, risk behaviors such as smoking and drinking, psychological indicators, and social indicators. After controlling for background characteristics, only children and sibling children fared similarly on most measures. Psychological indicators related to self-esteem, anxiety, and depression showed no evidence of difference. However, in terms of social differences, sibling children were more likely to be bullied and were less likely to confide in parents or other relatives. This study concluded no detrimental effects of being an only child based on the measures assessed.

The research we reviewed above is diverse in approach. Not surprisingly, results vary based on the particular samples, methods, and outcomes examined. Much of the previous research is based on specialized samples collected in one, two, or a few schools or communities. When it is not (e.g., Li et al. use 1990 census data), one outcome, such as educational attainment, is usually examined. Our goal is to extend this literature by drawing on an unusually diverse sample of children and adolescents from rural and urban areas across nine provinces in China. Further, rather than focus on one outcome, we review the multiple domains available in our data. In so doing, we provide one of the most comprehensive descriptive analyses to date of differences in the lives of only children and sibling children in China.

This analysis draws on data from the 2004 China Health and Nutrition Survey (CHNS). The CHNS is a survey conducted jointly by the Chinese Academy of Preventive Medicine, Beijing, and the University of North Carolina at Chapel Hill every few years since 1989. The survey has been conducted in nine provinces including, from northeast to southwest, Heilongjiang, Liaoning, Henan, Shangdong, Jiangsu, Hubei, Hunan, Guizhou, and Guangxi. The sample is not nationally representative, but the surveyed areas reflect substantial demographic and socioeconomic variation. Moreover, the rural villages and urban neighborhoods are located in coastal, central, and mountainous provinces that are home to approximately one-third of China's mainland population.

The CHNS sampling strategy is a multistage, random cluster process. Counties in the nine provinces are stratified by income (high, middle, and low), and four counties in each province are randomly selected using a weighted sampling scheme. In addition, the provincial capital and a lower income city are selected. Villages and townships within the counties, urban and suburban neighborhoods within the cities, and households within the neighborhoods are selected randomly.

From the 2004 CHNS we draw on a sample of 1,523 children and adolescents ages 6–18 from 1,260 households across urban and rural China. We analyze information regarding school enrollment, time spent in extra-school activities, nutritional status, and use of health care. We also analyze child self-reports of priorities in life and child reports of parents' encouragement regarding diet and activity. In addition to data collected for each child, we detail mothers' reports on household practices regarding their oldest child's TV watching based on questions answered by mothers with children ages 6–18 in their household.

In all analyses we distinguish between children from one-child families and children from sibling families on the dimensions of interest. However, as detailed in Table 5.1, children in one-child families differ from children in sibling families on numerous background characteristics. Children in one-child families are more likely to live in urban areas, be male, and live in households with parents who have achieved a higher level of formal education compared with children in sibling families. They also live in wealthier households.[1] Consequently, in all analyses we compare children from one-child families with those from sibling families by showing two sets of odds ratios: unadjusted odds ratios that we presume inform anecdotal reports; and adjusted odds ratios, or odds ratios that adjust for differences due to place of residence, gender, parental education, and household wealth. In addition, standard errors are adjusted for multiple children per household.

Table 5.1 Sociodemographic Differences between Children Living in One-Child and Sibling Children Families

	1 Child	2+ Children	P-value
Total (*n* = 1523)	809[a] (53.12[b])	714 (46.88)	*
Area			
Rural (*n* = 1153)	523 (64.65)	630 (88.24)	**
Urban (*n* = 370)	286 (35.35)	84 (11.76)	
Sex			
Male (*n* = 810)	454 (56.12)	356 (49.86)	*
Female (*n* = 713)	355 (43.88)	358 (50.14)	
Parents' highest education			
No or primary school (*n* = 260)	106 (13.10)	154 (21.57)	**
Junior high school (*n* = 751)	374 (46.23)	377 (52.80)	
Senior high school or above (*n* = 512)	329 (40.67)	183 (25.63)	
Wealth quartiles			
1st (poorest; *n* = 387)	169 (20.89)	218 (30.53)	**
2nd (*n* = 370)	177 (21.88)	193 (27.03)	
3rd (*n* = 450)	244 (30.16)	206 (28.85)	
4th (richest; *n* = 316)	219 (27.07)	97 (13.59)	

[a]Frequency.
[b]Percentage.
Note: *p* < 0.05; **p* < 0.001.
Source: China Health and Nutrition Survey (CHNS), 2004.

Children's Participation in School and Extra-School Activities

Rates of participation in school are high with approximately 90 percent of all children reporting school attendance in this sample. Although only children are slightly more likely to be in enrolled in school, adjusting for background characteristics suggests that differences in school enrollment among children in this sample have more to do with these characteristics than with having a sibling. On the other hand, participation in extra-school activities is associated with family composition. Only children are more likely to engage in homework and extra-curricular reading, writing, and drawing. They are also more likely to engage in organized physical exercise and play with toys. After controlling for background characteristics there is little difference in use of computers, including video games.[2]

Children's Reports of Priorities

In the CHNS children ages 7–18 were asked to report on how often they cared about the following four priorities: being praised by parents, being liked by friends, looking modern, and getting good grades. The percentage of children reporting that they "always" or "often" cared about a given priority was similar among only children and those with siblings.[3]

Parent-Child Interaction in Regard to Diet, Physical Activity, and TV

The CHNS data provide insight on three dimensions of interaction—diet, physical activity, and TV. Although these are a select subset of activities, these are activities that nearly all children engage in at home every day. Further, previous research suggests that when differences are found between only children and children with siblings, they are often due to parent-child interaction (Mellor 1990).

Children ages 7–18 were asked about parental encouragement in regard to diet and physical activity. One way that parents lavish attention on children is by preparing them food and encouraging them to eat. Once adjusted for background characteristics, only children and children with siblings report similar encouragement from parents to eat more food, with about one-third of children reporting that their parents encourage them to eat more food. However, differences emerge in regard to type of food. Only children experience more encouragement to eat fruits and vegetables. These foods can be more expensive than staple foods of rice and wheat and may well indicate that only children receive more attention to their diet or that they have greater access to such foods in their families. Or it could be that only children need more encouragement than children with siblings to eat fruits and vegetables due to the "culture" of snacking that some report disproportionately affects only children (Chee 2000). Such differences may also reflect differences in household wealth, place of residence, or parental education not captured by our background controls. Only children also report more encouragement to engage in physical activity by their parents. These patterns are consistent with those indicated by reports on children's actual time spent in physical activity.[4] Thus, on balance, it does seem that parents may well be encouraging more healthful behaviors in one-child families.[5]

Finally, after adjustment for background characteristics, children in only-child and sibling households appear just as likely to be told not to imitate things on TV, to experience monitoring of the content of their TV viewing, and to have limits on total time spent watching TV.[6]

Overall, these results suggest that although only children and children with siblings report a similar desire to be praised by parents, the day-to-day interaction between parents and children who are in only-child and sibling families may well differ and merits further investigation.

Child Health

Given anecdotal reports that only children are indulged—including with excessive food and higher fat foods, nutritional status provides a window into whether such observations are reflected in children's height and weight (World Health Organization [WHO] 2006). Using anthropometric data we consider four measures related to child growth, both overweight and underweight. Using the WHO reference population, we calculate the percentage of children whose z-score on BMI falls more than one (overweight) or two (obese) standard deviations above the average of the reference population based on age and sex. Similarly, we calculate the percentage of children whose z-score falls two standard deviations below the appropriate reference population based on age and sex for weight-for-age (underweight) and height-for-age (stunted).

Earlier, we showed that only children and children with siblings reported similarly on their parents' encouragements to eat more food. Only children reported more encouragement to eat fruits and vegetables, but this difference, if reflected in actual differences in dietary intake, would not suggest greater obesity among only children. Indeed, although a higher percentage of only children in China are overweight or obese, once background characteristics are controlled, there is little evidence that such differences are due to being an only child per se. However, only children are much less likely to be underweight or stunted. This difference holds after taking into account selected background characteristics.[7] These results are consistent with the narrative that children from one-child families may be advantaged in their access to material resources, including food, because household resources need not be spread across multiple children. We note, however, that other interpretations are possible as well. Nutritional status, and undernutrition in particular, can reflect a constellation of factors, not all of which can be fully accounted for with these data. Given extensive poverty in parts of China, circumstances such as lack of clean water, for example, could lead to diarrhea, which could slow child growth. Thus, while undernutrition may be associated with number of children, other unobserved factors may well be correlated with both number of children and healthy growth.

Lastly, we consider differences in the use of health care among only children and children with siblings. The CHNS includes information on whether each child was covered by health insurance, sick or injured over the past four weeks, immunized in the past year (for children 6–12 years), and received any preventive health service in the past four weeks. If parents are more attentive to, or better able to provide for, the health and well-being of only children, we might expect to see differences across one-child and sibling children families. There is no indication of significant difference ($p < .05$) in the use of health care based on the unadjusted or adjusted odds ratios on any of these dimensions. Thus, to the extent that only children and children with siblings grow up differently, use of health care seems similar. It is, of course, still possible that the health care they receive is qualitatively different, but it seems more likely that such differences would reflect background characteristics rather than only-child or sibling family status.

Gender in One-Child and Sibling Families

Thus far we have controlled for gender as a background characteristic in comparing children's experiences across one-child and sibling families. Controlling for gender enhances our ability to compare across one-child and sibling families, taking into account that children in one-child families are more likely to be boys. It is possible to look more closely at gender by comparing girls' and boys' experiences *within* each family type.[8] We see little indication of difference by gender in nutritional status and use of health care. Further, our results suggest that girls and boys are just as likely to be in school within one-child and sibling families. Given that sex preference is strongly indicated in family formation behavior, including our own data, little evidence of gender difference in these outcomes is noteworthy. Differences emerge, however, in participation in extra-school activities. Regardless of one-child or sibling family status, boys are more likely to participate in leisure activities, including video games and other games. They are also more likely to use computers and, in one-child families, to watch TV, videotapes, and DVDs. Across both types of families, boys are more likely to engage in formal physical activities. In sibling families, girls are more likely than boys to do extracurricular reading, writing, and drawing, a difference that remains after adjustment ($p < .05$). In one-child and sibling families, girls are more likely than boys to do household chores.[9]

Experiences within family type by gender suggest difference in children's reporting on life priorities. In both one-child and sibling families, girls indicate that being liked by friends is more important than do boys. In addition, in sibling families, girls indicate a stronger interest in praise from parents and getting good grades than do boys. In addition, we note a difference in children's reporting on parental encouragement regarding diet. Boys in one-child families report that parents encourage them to eat more rice or wheat and meat than do girls. Finally, in one-child families, boys are more likely to be overweight and to have been taken for a preventive health service in the past four weeks.

Conclusion

As fertility around the world declines and more couples choose small family size, we can speculate about the implications of such declines for children's experiences. In this chapter we inform such speculation by describing children's lives in one-child and sibling families in China, where a one-child population policy has been in place for three decades. We emphasize that our analysis does not report on trends in children's well-being over time. Nor does it make causal arguments. Rather, we report on similarities and differences among children between 6 and 18 years of age in 2004 across family types.

At the outset our working hypothesis was that anecdotal impressions captured by newspaper headlines reflected real, but unadjusted, differences in the lives of children across one-child and sibling families. Our results suggest a more complicated picture. After adjustment for place of residence, family wealth, parental education, child age, and sex, results suggest that while on most dimensions only children and sibling children are similar, only children may indeed have day-to-day experiences different than their peers with siblings. Children in only-child families are more likely to participate in formal extra-school activities. They also have a lower likelihood of undernutrition and are more likely to indicate that parents encourage them to eat fruits and vegetables and engage in physical exercise.

Gender patterns are similar in one-child and sibling families. Boys are more likely to participate in leisure activities, and girls are more likely to do housework. Notably, although there is little average difference in the desire of only children and sibling children to be praised by parents or get good grades, within sibling families, girls are more likely than boys to indicate that these priorities are always or often important to them. Consistent with this reporting, girls in sibling families are more likely to report that they spend time outside of school doing reading, writing, or drawing than are boys in sibling families.

A contribution of this study is its review of multiple dimensions of child experience across urban and rural areas in nine provinces. Although the analysis is broader than most, it nonetheless is limited to schooling, extra-school activities, and physical health. Social and emotional correlates are little addressed. The lack of information on social and emotional aspects of children's lives in these data is unfortunate. To the extent popular concern exists about the well-being of only children, it is most often in regard to social skills or emotional health, especially as a result of excessive parental attention, indulgence of children's desires, and pressure placed upon only children to succeed.

In recent years, as intergenerational factors receive heightened scrutiny in China, concern about only children is resurgent. Such sentiments are captured in discussions regarding the "second-generation only child," an only child born to a mother and a father who are both only children. The headline of a 2010 article published in the *People's Daily Online,* "China's Second Generation of Only-Child Have More Severe Personality Problems," represents a popular view. The reported problematic personality characteristics associated with growing up as an only child, including apathy and selfishness, are suggested to result from a lack of family. Second-generation children lack not only brothers and sisters but also aunts, uncles, and cousins, intensifying the problem. As explained in an article in the *China Daily* (Cheng 2010) the personality problem is perceived to stem from excessive attention. "Compared with their parents, the second-generation only child enjoys more care. Usually, a child will get help in every possible way from six people—the father, mother, father's parents, and mother's parents."

The combination of great economic opportunity, expensive housing, and extremely competitive entrance requirements for top universities promotes investment in a child who represents the family's future and fortune. It also can result, at least in cities, in a highly scheduled child who is anxious about school and success (Fong 2002; Hesketh et al. 2010). Further, popular reports suggest that the emphasis on achievement may lead to stressed and unrealistic adults (Yu 2010) and that the singleton experience more generally may undermine marriage satisfaction (Du 2007). Du (2007) reports that divorce among the recently married has become more frequent in Beijing, a phenomenon labeled "flash divorce." While the article reviews many factors that may contribute to this rise, singleton status is prominent among them. Because singletons generally marry other singletons, and singletons are used to being taken care of by their parents, negotiating financial independence and care of a home can create tension and unhappiness for the newly married couple. Furthermore, daughters, many of whom are only daughters, are elevated and empowered and may be less flexible in these negotiations with their husbands. Taken together, despite current studies within China that suggest more singleton advantage than disadvantage on psychological outcomes (Dai et al. 2005; Liu et al. 2010; Zhang 2001), popular media portrayals of the social and psychological costs of a one-child society persist.

In closing, we consider whether this analysis in China should inform our understanding of what it is like to grow up in a small family elsewhere. Many of the other settings with low fertility differ substantially from China. In mainland China, although times are changing, childbearing is near universal. In addition, the structure of institutions that shape everyday life, including education, religion, family, and labor market, differs significantly from many other low-fertility settings. Women's labor force participation rates in China are relatively high, further shaping childhood experiences and the expectations of young people. Also, societal context in regard to fertility and local ideas about family compositions that are normative and desirable likely have implications for the children born into small and large families. Thus, the rewards that derive from having one child in a society with an explicit one-child policy should not be expected to transfer to other low-fertility settings, many with pro-natalist policies. On balance, it seems unlikely that the Chinese experience applies elsewhere.

At the same time, we observe that if lowest-low fertility around the world is accompanied by increases in intensive parenting, concern about the well-being of singletons and other children may well arise in other settings, too. Wang and Fong (2009) remind us that such concern is common when fertility first declines. When cultural shifts in parenting "catch up," concerns diminish and new childrearing expectations replace the old. Certainly, critiques today of intensive parenting and overscheduled children are familiar in many places outside China.

Finally, we emphasize that concern about the indulgence of only children in China is largely focused on urban settings. It is also a narrative that plays out in a time of rapid economic growth, new wealth, and growing inequality. Rural poverty persists and the growing rural-urban divide in China translates into a reality in which millions of Chinese children, whether living in rural villages or as recent migrants in urban centers, are challenged to secure basic needs. Against this backdrop, advantaged youth may appear to be "little emperors" indeed, whether from one-child or sibling families.

Notes

1. Wealth was measured with an index of durable goods by summing family reports of the total number of goods owned, and assigning households to quartiles based on this sum, as in Adams and Hannum (2005).
2. See Web Table 5.1 on the book web site.
3. See Web Table 5.2 on the book web site.
4. See Web Table 5.1 on the book web site under extra-school activities.
5. Given that these are child reports, we can also speculate that children may understand or report differently on parent behaviors when observed in different sibling contexts. For example, parents may be giving direction to one child or multiple children, which may affect the interpretation by any individual child.
6. See Web Table 5.2 on the book web site for mother-reported interactions with her oldest child age 6–18 on TV viewing.
7. See Web Table 5.3 on the book web site.
8. See Web Table 5.4 on the book web site.
9. See Web Table 5.4 on the book web site.

References

Adams, Jennifer, and Hannum, Emily. (2005). Children's Social Welfare in China, 1989–1997: Access to Health Insurance and Education. *The China Quarterly* 181: 100–121.

Angrist, J., Lavy, V., and Schlosser, A. (2010). Multiple Experiments for the Causal Link between Quantity and Quality of Children. Unpublished manuscript.

Becker, Gary S., and Lewis, H. Gregg. (1973). On the Interaction between the Quantity and Quality of Children. *The Journal of Political Economy* 81, no. 2 (Part 2: New Economic Approaches to Fertility): S279–S288.

Blake, J. (1981). Family Size and the Quality of Children. *Demography* 18: 421–442.

———. (1989). Number of Siblings and Educational Attainment. *Science* 245: 32–35.

———. (1991).Number of Siblings and Personality. *Family Planning Perspectives* 23, no. 6: 272–274.

Chee, Bernadine W. L. (2000). Eating Snacks, Biting Pressure: Only Children in Beijing. In *Feeding China's Little Emperors: Food, Children, and Social Change,* 48–70. Stanford CA: Stanford University Press.

Chen, X. Y. (2006). Family Conditions, Parental Acceptance, and Social Competence and Aggression in Chinese Children. *Social Development* 3, no. 3: 269–290.

Chen, X., Rubin, K. H., and Li, B. (1994). Only Children and Sibling Children in Urban China: A Re-examination. *International Journal of Behavioral Development* 17, no. 3: 413–421.

Cheng, Yingqi. (2010). One Child Norm Breeding Brats, Warn Experts. *China Daily,* February 23. http://www.chinadaily.com.cn/usa/2010-02/23/content_11016156.htm.

Coale, A. J., and Banister, J. (1994). Five Decades of Missing Females in China. *Demography* 31, no. 3: 459–479.

Conley, Dalton, and Glauber, Rebecca. (2006). Parental Educational Investment and Children's Academic Risk: Estimates of the Impact of Sibship Size and Birth Order from Exogenous Variation in Fertility. *The Journal of Human Resources* 41: 722–737.

Dai, Weimin, Feng, Shulan, Yu, Lanqiong, Zhang, Shengping, Zhang, Xingbo, Peng, Qizhi, Zhu, Wei, and Liu, Zhengrong. (2005). The Comparison of the Status of Mental Health of the Singleton and Non-Singleton College Students." *Chinese Mental Health Journal* 19, no. 4: 256–258.

Downey, D. B. (1995). When Bigger Is Not Better: Family Size, Parental Resources, and Children's Educational Performance. *American Sociological Review* 60, no. 5: 746–761.

Du, Xinda. (2007). Divorce Rate Is Rocketing Up among the Post-80s in Beijing: One Third of the Couples Divorced within Five Years of Marriage. *Beijing Evening News,* April 7. http://news.xinhuanet.com/local/2007-04/07/content_5944795.htm. Accessed September 27, 2010.

Falbo, T., and Poston, D. (1993). The Academic, Personality, and Physical Outcomes of Only Children in China. *Child Development* 64, no. 1: 18–35.

Falbo, T., Poston, D., Ji, G., Jing, Q., Wang, S., Gu W., Yin, H., and Liu, Y. (1989). Physical Achievement and Personality Characteristics of Chinese Children. *Journal of Biosocial Science* 21: 438–495.

Fong, Vanessa L. (2002). China's One-Child Policy and the Empowerment of Urban Daughters. *American Anthropologist* 104, no. 4: 1098–1109.

———. (2004). *Only Hope: Coming of Age under China's One-Child Policy.* Stanford, CA: Stanford University Press.

Greenhalgh, Susan. (1993). The Peasantization of the One Child Policy in Shaanxi. In Deborah Davis and Stevan Harrell (eds.), *Chinese Families in the Post Mao Era,* 219–250. Berkeley: University of California Press.

Guo, Guang, and VanWey, Leah. (1999). Sibship Size and Intellectual Development: Is the Relationship Causal? *American Sociological Review* 64: 169–187.

Hesketh, T., Zhen, Y., Lu, L., Dong, Z. X., Jun, Y. X., and Xing, Z. W. (2010). Stress and Psychosomatic Symptoms in Chinese School Children: Cross-Sectional Survey. *Archives of Disease in Childhood* 95, no. 2: 136–140.

Hofferth, Sandra L., and Sandberg, John F. (2001). How American Children Spend Their Time. *Journal of Marriage and Family* 63, no. 2: 295–308.

Jiao, Shulan, Ji, Guiping, and Jing, Qicheng (C. C. Ching). (1986). Comparative Study of Behavioral Qualities of Only Children and Sibling Children. *Child Development* 57, no. 2: 357–361.

Johansson, S., and Nygren, O. (1991). The Missing Girls of China: A New Demographic Account. *Population and Development Review* 17, no. 1: 35–51.

Johnson, K. (1993). Chinese Orphanages: Saving China's Abandoned Girls. *The Australian Journal of Chinese Affairs* 30: 61–87.

Li, H., Zhang, J., and Zhu, Y. (2008). The Quantity-Quality Trade-Off of Children in a Developing Country: Identification Using Chinese Twins. *Demography* 45: 223–243.

Liu, Ruth X., Lin, Wei, and Chen, Zeng-yin. (2010). School Performance, Peer Association, Psychological and Behavioral Adjustments: A Comparison between Chinese Adolescents with and without Siblings. *Journal of Adolescence* 33, no. 3: 411–417.

Lu, Yao, and Treiman, Donald. (2008). The Effect of Sibship Size on Educational Attainment in China: Period Variations. *American Sociological Review* 73: 813–834.

Mare, R. D. (1995). Changes in Educational Attainment and School Enrollment. In R. Farley (ed.), *State of the Union: America in the 1990s. Vol. 1. Economic Trends,* 155–213. New York: Russell Sage.

Mellor, S. (1990). How Do Only Children Differ from Other Children? *Journal of Genetic Psychology* 151, no. 2: 221–230.

Meredith, William H., Abbott, Douglas A., and Ming, Zheng Fu. (1992). Self-Concept and Sociometric Outcomes: A Comparison of Only Children and Sibling Children from Urban and Rural Areas in the People's Republic of China. *The Journal of Psychology* 126, no. 4: 411–419.

People's Daily Online. (2010). China's Second Generation of Only-Child Have More Severe Personality Problems, *People's Daily Online,* February 23. http://english.peopledaily.com.cn/90001/90782/90872/6900095.html.

Popkin, B. M., Du, S., Zhai, F., and Zhang, B. (2010). Cohort Profile: The China Health and Nutrition Survey—Monitoring and Understanding Socio-Economic and Health Change in China 1989–2011. *International Journal of Epidemiology* 39, no 6: 1435–1440.

Poston, D., and Falbo, T. (1990). Academic Performance and Personality Traits of Chinese Children: "Onlies" versus Others. *The American Journal of Sociology* 96, no. 2: 433–451.

Poston, D. L. and Yu, Mei-Yu. (1985). Quality of Life, Intellectual Development and Behavioural Characteristics of Single Children in China: Evidence from a 1980 Survey in Changsha, Hunan Province. *Journal of Biosocial Science* 17: 127–136.

Qian, N. (2009). Quantity-Quality and the One Child Policy: The Positive Effect of Family Size on School Enrollment in China. NBER Working Paper.

Retherford, Robert, Choe, Minja Kim, Chen, Jiajian, Xiru, Li, and Hongyan, Cui. (2005). How Far Has Fertility in China Really Declined? *Population and Development Review* 31, no. 1: 57–84.

Scharping, Thomas. (2003). *Birth Control in China, 1949–2000: Population Policy and Demographic Development.* London: RoutledgeCurzon.

Shen, Jianping, and Yuan, Bao-Jane. (1999). Moral Values of Only and Sibling Children in Mainland China. *The Journal of Psychology* 133: 115–124.

Short, Susan E., and Fengying, Zhai. (1998). Looking Locally at China's One Child Policy. *Studies in Family Planning* 29, no. 4: 373–387.

Short, Susan, Zhai, Fengying, Xu, Siyuan, and Yang, Mingliang. (2001). China's One-Child Policy and the Care of Children: An Analysis of Qualitative and Quantitative Data. *Social Forces* 79, no. 3: 913–943.

Tien, H. Y. (1991). *China's Strategic Demographic Initiative.* New York: Praeger.

Tseng, W. S., Kuotai, T., Hsu, J., Chiu, J. H., Yu, L., and Kameoka,V. (1988). Family Planning and Child Mental Health in China: The Nanjing Survey. *American Journal of Psychiatry* 145: 1396–1403.

Wang, Y., and Fong, V. (2009). Little Emperors and the 4:2:1 Generation: China's Single Child Policy. *Journal of the American Academy of Child and Adolescent Psychiatry* 48, no. 12: 1137–1139.

World Health Organization. (2006). *WHO Child Growth Standards: Length/Height-for-Age, Weight-for-Age, Weight-for-Length, Weight-for-Height and Body Mass Index-for-Age.* Geneva: WHO Press.

Xu, Hongwei, and Minca, Elisabeta. (2008) How Chinese Children Spend Their Time. In Steve H. Murdock and David A. Swanson (eds.), *Applied Demography in the 21st Century,* 299–336. New York: Springer.

Yang, Bin, Ollendick, Thomas H., Dong, Qi, Xia, Yong, and Lin, Lei. (1995.) Only Children and Children with Siblings in the People's Republic of China: Levels of Fear, Anxiety, and Depression. *Child Development* 66, no. 5: 1301–1311.

Yu, Tianyu. (2010). Post 80s Feel the Pressure. *China Daily.* http://www.chinadaily.com.cn/cndy/2010-04/19/content_9745004.htm.

Zajonc. R. B., and Markus, G. B. (1975). Birth Order and Intellectual Development. *Psychological Review* 82: 74–88.

Zhang, Xiaowen. (2001). A Comparison Study of Personality Development and Psychological Health between Single and Non-Single Children College Students. *Journal of Nanjing College for Population Programme Management* 17, no. 2: 36–38.

Chapter 6

Before, During, and After the Baby Carriage

The Division of Family Labor and Wives' Contemporary Marital Satisfaction

W. Bradford Wilcox and Jeffrey Dew

Over the last half-century, demographic, economic, and normative shifts have pushed the trajectory of marriage and family life in the United States in a generally egalitarian direction, with men taking up a larger share of the housework and childcare associated with family life (Bianchi et al. 2006; Robinson and Godbey 1999; Sayer 2005). Nevertheless, the gender revolution of the last half century is incomplete: women still perform the majority of childcare and housework in American families; indeed, in recent years, the percentage of married mothers who are working has stalled out (Bianchi et al. 2006; Hochschild and Machung 1989; Hotchkiss et al. 2008; Stone 2007). In other words, there is much about the division of labor in contemporary family life that remains gendered, especially when couples have children at home.

What is not clear from the scholarly literature is how the relatively egalitarian or traditional character of family life affects the quality of marriages among contemporary women. Some studies indicate that more egalitarian divisions of family labor make married women happier (Amato et al. 2007; Blair and Johnson 1992), whereas other studies suggest that more traditional divisions of family labor make for higher-quality marriages among women (Rogers and Amato 2000; Wilcox and Nock 2006). Surprisingly, research has not considered the possibility that the relationship between the division of family labor and marital happiness may differ as a function of motherhood. Specifically, more egalitarian divisions of family labor may be more likely to foster marital happiness for couples without children in the home whereas a traditionally gendered division of family labor may be more likely to foster marital happiness when children are in the home. Accordingly, this study seeks to extend our understanding of marital quality by exploring the possibility that the relationship between the division of family labor and women's marital happiness varies by the presence of children at home.

We use data from the nationally representative 2000 Survey of Marriage and Family Life (Amato et al. 2007) to see if the relationship between the division of family labor and women's marital quality varies by wives' motherhood status. Wives who do not have children at home may be more attracted to egalitarian models of married life because they can more easily balance the demands of work and family life with their partners. Alternatively, given the contemporary challenges of juggling work, motherhood, and marriage, wives with children at home may be just as happy with more traditional arrangements as they are with more egalitarian arrangements (Amato et al. 2007; Blair-Loy 2003; Hochschild and Machung 1989; Stone 2007). We rely on distributive justice theory to generate hypotheses about the relationship between the division of family labor and women's marital happiness. We also explore the possibility that religion affects women's perceptions of marital equity and marital quality. Finally, this study is particularly valuable because most studies of the divisions of labor and marital quality have relied on data that are more than two decades old.

Predicting how different divisions of family labor relate to marital satisfaction has proven difficult. Some studies find that the division of labor has very little to do with marital satisfaction. For example, a number of studies indicate that the gendered division of labor is not directly related to wives' marital satisfaction, and the indirect relationship has been weak (Voydanoff and Donnelly 1999; Wilkie et al. 1998).

By contrast, some studies have shown that an egalitarian division of family labor is most conducive to marital satisfaction. For example, a few studies indicate that wives are happier in their marriages when their husbands take on a more equal share of housework (Lennon and Rosenfeld 1994; Stevens et al. 2001). Other studies have found that husbands' participation in housework and childcare is linked to higher marital satisfaction for wives (Blair and Johnson 1992; Kalmijn 1999). And one study found that increased egalitarianism within marriage may have also kept aggregate marital satisfaction levels stable over time in spite of other challenges to married life (Amato et al. 2007).

Still other research questions the relationship between an egalitarian division of labor and marital satisfaction, particularly when it comes to income. A number of studies have found that marriages are happier or more stable when the husband earns the majority of the income. Wilcox and Nock (2006), for example, found that women's marital satisfaction was higher in marriages where husbands earned 66 percent or more of the total family income. They also found that husband's housework was not a significant predictor of marital satisfaction. Additionally, couples are more likely to divorce when the husband does not take the lead in providing (Brines and Joyner 1999; Heckert et al. 1998; Nock 2001; Rogers 2004).

Three points may account for these mixed research findings. The first is that studies have often ignored key familial demands, especially motherhood, which may moderate the relationship between the division of family labor and marital quality (for an exception see Pittman and Blanchard 1996). Second, many studies have only considered one aspect of the division of labor, usually paid employment or housework, without considering the ways in which the total division of earning, paid work, and household work affects the quality of married life. Finally, the link between the division of family labor and marital satisfaction may vary over time, with mixed results being attributable to the fact that studies have relied upon samples drawn at different time periods.

The Division of Labor and Perceptions of Marital Unfairness

Scholars have often used distributive justice theory to explain the link between the division of labor and marital satisfaction. Distributive justice theory asserts that perceptions of marital unfairness play a key role in shaping relationship satisfaction and in mediating the relationship between the actual division of labor and marital quality; specifically, perceived marital unfairness, rather than the actual division of labor, is directly associated with marital dissatisfaction (Deutsch 1985; Major 1987). Spouses who feel that aspects of their marriage are unfair to themselves will become dissatisfied and often seek to change or leave their marriage. As marriages have become more egalitarian, and as Americans have embraced egalitarian gender attitudes in larger numbers (Amato et al. 2007; Thornton and Young-DeMarco 2001), the importance of perceived fairness, or equity, within marriage has increased (Gager and Sanchez 2003; Wilcox and Nock 2006).

Although the actual division of household labor matters for perceived unfairness, other factors are just as important in determining whether wives perceive the division of labor as equitable. For example, to perceive their marriages as unfair, women have to feel entitled to a particular division of family labor that they are not receiving and also to feel that nothing justifies not receiving that division of labor (Thompson 1991). Thus, even married women who are in marriages marked by unequal divisions of family labor will not necessarily perceive marital unfairness if they feel that they are not entitled to an equal division of labor or if they think that their family's circumstances justify the lack of an egalitarian division of labor.

Research has empirically validated distributive justice theory regarding the relationship between the division of labor and perceptions of marital unfairness. Studies suggest that the more domestic labor wives performed, the more likely they are to perceive the marital division of labor as unfair (Lennon and Rosenfeld 1994; Stevens et al. 2001; Wilkie et al. 1998). A parallel finding is that the more husbands participated in housework and childcare, the more wives perceive the division of labor to be fair (Blair and Johnson 1992; DeMaris and Longmore 1996). Thus, on average, equality in the division of household labor does tend to predict a sense of marital fairness.

But ideology also colors how wives perceive the division of family labor in their marriage. For instance, studies suggest that wives who have more traditional gender role attitudes are more likely to perceive the division of labor as fair, even when it is not organized in an egalitarian fashion (DeMaris and Longmore 1996; Greenstein 1996; Stevens et al. 2001; Wilkie et al. 1998). Thus, as distributive justice theory would predict, wives with traditional gender role attitudes are less likely to expect or feel entitled to egalitarian divisions of labor. Although wives perceive different divisions of labor to be fair depending on their expectations and personal desires (Greenstein 1996; Grote et al. 2002), in recent years wives' gender role attitudes have become less traditional (Thornton and Young-DeMarco 2001). Thus, on average, contemporary wives are more likely to view egalitarian divisions of labor as the most fair. Accordingly, we offer the following two hypotheses:

> **Hypothesis 1a:** Wives perceive more egalitarian divisions of family labor as fairer than more traditional divisions of labor.
>
> **Hypothesis 2:** Gender role attitudes moderate the relationship between the division of labor and perceptions of unfairness such that women with more traditional attitudes will be less likely to perceive traditional divisions of family labor as unfair.

Motherhood and Perceived Marital Unfairness

Although an egalitarian division of family labor may be seen as most fair, this type of labor can be difficult to realize in the contemporary labor force context. US labor practices are still guided by the assumption that a worker has someone at home engaged in unpaid production (e.g., a wife) (Jacobs and Gerson 2004; Williams 2000). In other words, the paid labor force has yet to fully accommodate the reality that women work and that most women do not leave the paid labor force following the birth of their first child. For example, the most highly remunerated jobs require workers to spend large amounts of time in the workplace, leaving less time for workers to take care of family issues (Jacobs and Gerson 2004; Williams 2000). Another example is the motherhood wage gap. Ever-married mothers earn lower wages than men, childless women, and never-married mothers, even after accounting for interrupted job histories, work hours, and occupational choices (Budig and England 2001). This means that contemporary couples often have an economic incentive to have married fathers participate more in paid labor after the birth of a child, while for married mothers an economic disincentive exists for them to remain in the labor force on a full-time basis.

In addition to economic disincentives, other structural and cultural factors exist that make it more difficult for married couples with children to adapt an egalitarian division of labor. The cost of high-quality childcare is prohibitively expensive for many couples, making it more difficult for parents to contribute equally to family income. Further, social norms frame mothers' participation in the labor force as a question of commitment to their children versus commitment to the labor force (Hays 1996; Williams 2000). Thus, many barriers exist that make it more difficult for married families with children to adapt an egalitarian division of family labor.

In the face of these structural and cultural challenges to an egalitarian model of family life, individuals and families use different "adaptive strategies" to organize their divisions of labor. Adaptive strategies are patterns of behavior that families actively employ in response to family stressors or challenges (Moen and Wethington 1992). For example, in their research on dual-earner couples, Becker and Moen (1999) found that couples' decisions to have one spouse be the main breadwinner invested in a "career" (usually the husband) and one spouse in a "job" to provide more income while caring for children and home (usually the wife) was a strategy designed to help couples meet the dual challenges of work and family life (see also Amato et al. 2007). The second shift arrangement is another example of an adaptive strategy because it combines dual-earner economic strength with a desire to not upset the traditional gender order at home (Hochschild and Machung 1989).

In light of these realities, married mothers with children in the home may be more likely than wives without children in the home to view non-egalitarian divisions of family labor as fair. That is, they may view adaptive non-egalitarian family role strategies as justified by the challenges that they and their spouse face in meeting their work and family obligations (Greenstein 1996; Thompson 1991). The one exception to this openness to non-egalitarian models may be the second shift model of dividing household labor, where wives shoulder the majority of domestic tasks despite earning about as much as or more than their husbands. In this model, women may resent the work-asymmetry that the second shift division of labor presents—particularly the fact that they are doing many more hours of paid and unpaid work than their husband—and feel that such arrangements are unfair (Greenstein 1996). By contrast, a traditional model where husbands earn most of the money while wives undertake the majority of childcare and housework may be acceptable to many contemporary mothers because the total hours that husbands and wives devote to paid and unpaid labor are about equal in such arrangements (Bianchi et al. 2006; Sayer 2005).

Mothers may view another division of labor type, what we call the neo-traditional model, as even more equitable. In the neotraditional model, husbands earn substantially more than their wives, but contribute about or almost as equally to childcare and/or housework as their wives. Mothers may feel that this arrangement is the most ideal because it allows them to benefit from men's higher earning potential while still seeing their husbands live up to contemporary norms of male familial involvement (Amato et al. 2007; Thornton and Young-DeMarco 2001). This arrangement also allows married mothers to focus more on their maternal role without worrying as much about their financial contributions to the family (Wilcox and Nock 2006).

> **Hypothesis 1b:** Wives with children at home will be less likely than wives without children at home to view traditional divisions of family labor as unfair. However, wives with children at home will perceive the second shift arrangement as less fair, given the large and unequal demands this arrangement places on their time.

Motherhood, Divisions of Labor, and Marital Satisfaction

In contemporary marriages, marital equity is an important predictor of marital quality for women (Gager and Sanchez 2003; Wilkie et al. 1998). As the foregoing discussion indicates, perceptions of equity are often more important than the actual division of family labor for women's marital happiness. So although the division of family labor can have a direct effect on women's marital happiness, this division of labor is mainly related to marital satisfaction on an indirect basis. In other words, non-egalitarian divisions of family labor are most likely to be associated with lower levels of marital satisfaction when they generate a sense of unfairness among wives.

For this study, we predict that the link between the division of labor and women's marital happiness depends in part on their maternal status. Wives without children are likely to perceive egalitarian relationships as most fair and, accordingly, to be happiest in such relationships. By contrast, married mothers are less likely to view more traditional arrangements as unfair, insofar as they expect their husbands to focus more on breadwinning and less on housework and childcare once children come along; accordingly, we do not expect more traditional family arrangements to make wives less happy than egalitarian divisions of family labor. By contrast, married mothers who find themselves in second shift marriages where they are taking on the lion's share of breadwinning *and* domestic responsibilities are likely to be less happy in their marriages, insofar as they are likely to perceive their disproportionately large workload as unfair.

Finally, married mothers should be particularly happy in neotraditional arrangements where their husbands take the lead in breadwinning and yet still share housework and childcare with them. Wives with children in the home are likely to be happy when their husbands take the lead in breadwinning because most married mothers would prefer to focus more on domestic affairs than their husbands, either by working part-time (46 percent of married mothers prefer this arrangement) or by staying at home (36 percent prefer this arrangement) (Wilcox and Dew 2008). At the same time, recent shifts in attitudes toward fatherhood have led wives to expect high levels of domestic labor from their husbands, which suggests that they should also be happier when their husbands take on about half of the childcare and housework (Coltrane 1996; Thornton and Young-DeMarco 2001). Furthermore, wives tend to be happier when they spend more time with their husband and children; husbands who do more domestic labor are likely to spend more time with their family members, thereby increasing their wives' marital satisfaction (Dew and Wilcox 2010). Accordingly, wives in neotraditional marriages are likely to be especially happy in their marriages.

> **Hypothesis 3a:** Wives will be most satisfied in their marriage when their division of family labor accommodates their (non-)maternal status.
> **Hypothesis 3b:** The relationship between the division of labor and wives' marital satisfaction is mediated by perceptions of marital unfairness.
> **Hypothesis 3c:** Married mothers are happiest in neotraditional marriages where husbands earn more than 60 percent of the household income and still come close to sharing housework and childcare with their wives.

However, the division of family labor may also relate to marital satisfaction in one other way—by increasing the fit between wives' preferences and the reality of their work-family arrangement. The role of congruity between preferences and work-family realities for women's well-being cannot be overstated (Hakim 2000). For example, in a study of new mothers, wives were happiest when their work preferences and actual work-family arrangement were congruent (Klein et al. 1998). In a review of the literature on the relationship between women's labor force employment and psychological well-being, Spitze (1988, p. 599) asserted, "The key factor, however, appears to be employment preferences. Wives are least depressed when their employment status is consistent with their own and their husbands' preferences and most depressed when they are not employed but would prefer to be." Since the happiest wives are likely to be those whose division of family labor matches their preference (Hakim 2000; Wilcox and Dew 2008), gender role attitudes may moderate the relationship between the division of labor and marital satisfaction. That is, wives with traditional gender role attitudes should be most satisfied in traditional arrangements whereas wives with egalitarian gender role attitudes should be most satisfied with egalitarian divisions of labor.

> **Hypothesis 4:** Family role attitudes moderate the relationship between divisions of family labor and marital satisfaction. Thus, wives will be most satisfied in their marriage when their division of labor reflects their family role attitudes.

Finally, religion should play an important role in structuring wives' perceptions of fairness and happiness in their marriage. Religion endows motherhood and marriage with sacred significance; it also provides social support to women in both of those roles, partly by embedding women in social networks that have large numbers of married mothers who are themselves more likely to offer counsel and encouragement to wives and mothers (Pearce and Axinn 1998; Stolzenberg et al. 1995; Wilcox 2004). Because they are more likely to view these two roles as sacred undertakings, and to receive social support for these roles, religious wives are probably less likely to view the division of housework and child care as unfair. For similar reasons, they are also likely to enjoy higher levels of marital happiness; moreover, perceptions of fairness are likely to mediate the link between religion and women's marital happiness.

> **Hypothesis 5:** Religious wives are less likely to see their marriages as unfair and more likely to be happy in their marriages.

The data for this analysis are taken from the Survey of Marriage and Family Life. The Survey of Marriage and Family life was conducted in 2000. The study gathered a nationally representative probability sample using random-digit dialing and was designed to study marriage closely (Amato et al. 2007). The Survey of Marriage and Family Life had over 2,100 married participants and represented the best data for this particular study for many reasons.

One advantage that strongly influenced the decision to use the Survey of Marriage and Family Life is that it is a recent survey. Studies on gender relations in marriage are still using aging data. For example, two recent studies using older data (the National Survey of Families and Households and the Marital Instability over the Life Course) have found that wives are happier and marriages most stable when their husbands earn the bulk of the income (Wilcox and Nock 2006; Rogers 2004). Unfortunately, the data in the NSFH and the MIOLC are both 20–25 years old. Thus, these findings may not adequately reflect how currently married spouses respond to the way they have divided labor. Since norms and gendered expectations have changed since the NSFH and MIOLC were initiated (Thornton and Young-DeMarco 2001), more recent data better capture the contemporary relationship between gendered divisions of labor and marital satisfaction than these older surveys.

Although even more current data than the Survey of Marriage and Family Life exist (e.g., the 2008 General Social Survey) a second advantage of these data is they are centrally concerned with measuring marital quality. Consequently, the items on marriage in the Survey of Marriage and Family Life are much richer than most other recent nationally representative surveys. For example, the Survey of Marriage and Family Life has a multidimensional scale on marital satisfaction and also includes indicators of perceptions of equity and family role attitudes. Few contemporary national surveys have such rich marital data.

We conducted the analysis using all of the female participants in the Survey of Marriage and Family Life ($N = 1,229$). To test the hypotheses regarding motherhood, we split the sample into three mutually exclusive groups. We split the sample rather than running interaction models because we could not include all of the variables we wanted in the full sample. For example, we could not control for the age of the youngest child in marriages with no children. The three groups were wives who had never had children ($n = 194$), wives with children at home ($n = 753$), and wives who were mothers but whose children were not at home ($n = 282$). The large majority of childless wives were 35 years old or younger, whereas the majority of parents whose children were not at home were 46 years old or older.

The main dependent variable was a mean scale constructed from four items concerning wives' satisfaction with their marriage. These items included wives' satisfaction with the amount of understanding they receive from their husband, the love they feel from their husbands, their sexual relationship, and their husband as someone to do things with. The responses ranged from 1 (Very Happy) to 3 (Not Too Happy). The variables were reverse coded so that higher scores represented higher marital satisfaction. Chronbach's alpha was .84.

To operationalize the couples' division of family labor, we created four categorical variables (see Table 6.1). As opposed to most studies that analyzed either wives' labor force participation or their domestic work, we combined these aspects (Hall and MacDermid 2009). We categorized the division of labor by first considering the percentage of income the wife earned and then considering the proportion of housework and (if applicable) the proportion of childcare they reportedly did. For example, if the wife reported that her husband earned between 60 and 100 percent of the income and that she did more housework and (if applicable) childcare, then she was put into the "traditional" division of labor category. If a wife reported that her husband earned between 60 and 100 percent of the income but that he also did equal amounts of house-work/childcare, or even more housework/childcare than she did, she was put into the "neotraditional" category. If a wife reported that she earned between 40 and 60 percent of the family income and that she and her husband split the housework and childcare equally, then she was put into the "egalitarian" category. Alternatively, if wives earned 40–100 percent of the income and the husband did most of the housework/childcare (e.g., a gender-reversed bread-winning situation), they were also put into the egalitarian category. Finally, if a wife reported that she earned between 40 and 100 percent of the income and also did more housework or childcare, then she was put into the second shift category. The categories were mutually exclusive.

To measure perceived fairness, we used two items that asked wives whether they felt they were doing more of their fair share in housework and childcare. These variables were dichotomized such that any response other than "fair" meant that the division of labor was unfair (1 = Division of Housework/Child-care Unfair). In most of the analyses, perceived unfairness was an independent variable, but it did serve as a dependent variable in the first analysis.

Table 6.1 Attributes of Married Couples (19–55)

	Childless (n = 194)		Children at Home (n = 194)		Children Not at Home (n = 194)	
	Mean	StD	Mean	StD	Mean	StD
Traditional	.23	.42	.48	.50	.32	.47
Egalitarian	.30	.45	.12	.32	.23	.42
Wife second shift	.32	.46	.32	.47	.34	.47
Neotraditional	.14	.35	.08	.27	.12	.32
Housework unfair to self	.20	.40	.29	.45	.24	.43
Childcare unfair to self	—	—	.18	.39	—	—
Number of children in home	—	—	1.89	.87	—	—
Age of youngest child in home	—	—	7.11	5.07	—	—
Participant's age	34.98	9.24	36.99	7.31	47.98	5.94
Number of marriages	1.20	.43	1.20	.48	1.51	.77
Marital duration	7.98	10.24	12.41	7.95	21.43	12.19
Education	15.21	2.53	14.34	2.53	13.73	2.36
Total family income (log transform)	4.70	.49	4.66	.54	4.60	.65
African-American	.03	.17	.06	.24	.09	.28
Other race/ethnic minority	.09	.29	.10	.30	.07	.25

Source: Survey of Marriage and Family Life, 2000.

We measured family role attitudes with a summed scale of three items that assessed wives' views on the roles of men and women. The items questioned whether women's most important life task was to care for her children, whether husbands should earn more than their wives, and whether men should be responsible for breadwinning and women responsible for childcare. We reverse coded the items so that the higher the score, the more traditional participant's family role attitudes were. Chronbach's alpha was .65 for the scale.

We measured religion by taking the mean of two items. The first item asked how frequently participants attended religious worship services. The second asked how important religion was in the participant's daily life. We reverse coded the variables. Chronbach's alpha was .64.

We also included age at the time of the survey, the number of marriages they had had, the marital duration of the current marriage they were in, the number of years of education they had completed, the family's total income, and whether they considered themselves African-American or another minority race/ethnicity (the omitted category was White, Non-Hispanic). In analyses of mothers with children at home, we added two variables pertaining to their children. We operationalized the number of children as the number of children under age 18 on the household roster, and we controlled for the age of youngest child. Because some of the variables had missing values, we used multiple imputation to generate plausible values. Multiple imputation is a statistically better choice than mean imputation or list-wise deleting cases (Rubin 1987).

Our first research question was whether different divisions of family labor predicted marital unfairness in the contemporary sample. We used logistic regression to test whether the division of labor categories predicted wives' feelings that the housework and childcare arrangements were unfair to them. In each wives' subsample, we regressed whether wives felt that the division of housework or childcare was unfair onto the division of labor categories and the control variables. The omitted category was the traditional division of family labor. In the second model we tested whether gender role attitudes moderated the relationship between divisions of labor and marital unfairness by adding three interaction terms.

Finally, we tested whether the division of labor categories predicted wives' marital satisfaction in each wives' category. Specifically, we regressed the marital satisfaction scale variable onto the division of labor categories and the control variables. In the second model, we added the divisions of labor by family role attitude interaction terms. In the third model, we examined whether perceptions of marital unfairness to oneself mediated the relationship between the division of labor and marital satisfaction.

The distinct divisions of family labor we measured for this study—egalitarian, second shift, traditional, and neotraditional—were related in different ways to wives' perceptions of unfairness in housework and childcare. We could not assess fairness for childless women because a complete separation of the data occurred; none of the childless women in a neotraditional arrangement rated their marriages as unfair (a noteworthy finding in itself). Thus, the logistic model could not be fit. However, women with children at home were more likely to view the division of housework as unfair in a second shift arrangement relative to a traditional arrangement. They were less likely to view the division of housework and childcare as unfair in egalitarian and neotraditional arrangements.[1] Mothers who did not have children residing in the home (i.e., empty-nesters) were less likely to feel that the housework was divided unfairly when they were in egalitarian or neotraditional arrangements. These findings support Hypothesis 1a but not Hypothesis 1b; clearly, the presence of children does not moderate the odds that wives consider a traditional arrangement to be unfair. (Nevertheless, the second shift only increases the odds that wives view the division of housework as unfair when they have children.) Moreover, contrary to Hypothesis 2, none of the division of labor category by family role attitude interactions was significant.[2] And, consistent with Hypothesis 5, religiosity reduced feelings of unfairness for mothers with children at home and for mothers whose children were not at home.[3]

The next set of analyses were OLS regressions that measured the relationship between the division of family labor and marital satisfaction and whether marital unfairness mediated this relationship. None of the division of labor categories significantly predicted childless wives' marital satisfaction.[4] However, some of the divisions of labor by family role interactions were significant. These interactions indicate that childless wives with more traditional family role attitudes had lower levels of marital satisfaction when they were in egalitarian or second shift arrangements relative to childless wives with more traditional family role attitudes in traditional arrangements (see Figure 6.1). These findings support Hypothesis 4, which predicted that family role attitudes would moderate the relationship between the division of labor and marital satisfaction. Contrary to Hypothesis 3b, a perception of unfairness in housework was not a mediator because there was no relationship to mediate. Nevertheless, perceptions of unfairness are clearly linked to lower levels of marital quality on the part of childless wives.

The relationship between the division of family labor and marital satisfaction was somewhat different for wives with children at home. As anticipated in Hypothesis 3c, wives with children at home in neotraditional arrangements

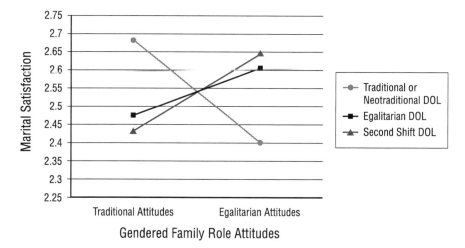

Figure 6.1 Marital Satisfaction among Childless Women
Source: Survey of Marriage and Family Life, 2000.

were happier than wives in traditional arrangements.[5] The magnitude of the relationship was .21 or nearly half a standard deviation of marital satisfaction. By contrast, marital satisfaction among wives with children at home who were in egalitarian or second shift arrangements was no different from wives in a traditional division of labor. Like the childless wives, gender role attitudes moderated these relationships, but only for neotraditional arrangements. Wives with children at home who had traditional gender role attitudes but were not in a traditional arrangement were less satisfied in their marriage; on the other hand, mothers with more egalitarian attitudes were happiest in a neotraditional arrangement (see Figure 6.2). Moreover, unfairness in housework and childcare completely mediated the main effect for the neotraditional arrangement. That is, when unfairness in housework and childcare were added to the model, the relationship between division of labor categories and wives' marital satisfaction went to zero. Follow-up Sobel tests of mediation suggested that both housework unfairness and childcare unfairness could be considered mediators of the relationship between the neotraditional arrangement and marital satisfaction (both at $p < .05$). This suggests that wives with children in the home are happier with neotraditional arrangements because they minimize the possibility that they view their marriage as unfair.

Our empirical analyses of wives with children at home also show that religiosity is a significant predictor of women's marital happiness.[6] Moreover, the

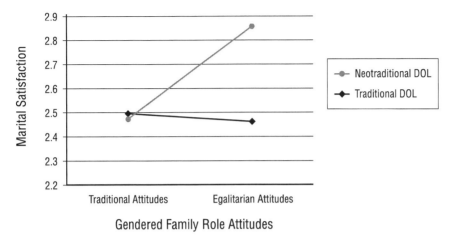

Figure 6.2 Marital Satisfaction among Women with Children at Home
Source: Survey of Marriage and Family Life, 2000.

analyses indicate that more than one-third of the effect of religion is mediated by the measures of housework and childcare fairness. This suggests that one reason religious mothers are happier in their marriages is that they are less likely to view their marriages as unequal, regardless of the actual divisions of family labor in their home.

Mothers whose children were not at home had happier marriages when the division of family labor in their marriage was organized along egalitarian lines.[7] This finding is consistent with Hypothesis 3a. Again, the magnitude of the association was equal to about half a standard deviation of wives' marital satisfaction. Unlike childless wives and wives with children at home, none of the divisions of labor by family role attitude interactions was significant. Further, although perceptions of housework unfairness were negatively associated with marital satisfaction, the egalitarian coefficient did not decline very much. A follow-up Sobel test of mediation showed that housework unfairness was not a mediating variable. Consistent with Hypothesis 5, our analyses also indicate that religion is positively related to the marital happiness of wives who do not have children at home and that perceptions of fairness mediate the link between religion and marital quality for this group.

A mixed body of research has emerged regarding the link between the egalitarian or traditional division of family labor and women's marital happiness. Some research suggests that women are happier in their marriages when their marriages are organized along more egalitarian lines (e.g., Stevens et al. 2001), whereas other research suggests that women are happier in more traditional marriages (e.g., Wilcox and Nock 2006). Using data from the 2000 Survey of Marriage and Family Life, we find evidence that the link between the family division of labor and women's marital happiness turns in part on their maternal status.

Wives who have children in the home were happiest in neotraditional marriages where their husbands take the lead in breadwinning (earning more than 60 percent of the household income) and yet also share the domestic work associated with housework and childcare. This arrangement could be particularly attractive to mothers because their husbands' material contributions may allow them to cut back on paid work and devote more attention to their children. This is noteworthy because most married mothers wish to work part-time (46 percent) or stay at home full-time (36 percent) (Wilcox and Dew 2008). Having a husband who takes the lead in providing may give them the opportunity to make good on this preference. At the same time, in part because of new norms about equality and paternal participation (Coltrane 1996), women clearly think that neotraditional arrangements are fairer than more traditional arrangements, and this helps to account for why the neotraditional division of family labor is popular among married mothers. Finally, it is interesting to note that the neotraditional arrangement is especially appealing to progressive-minded mothers with more egalitarian family role attitudes (see Figure 6.2).

But even though married mothers are more likely to think that egalitarian marriages are fairer than traditional marriages, they are not happier in such marriages. This may be because they are more likely to believe that the challenges they and their husbands face in meeting work and family responsibilities force them to deviate from an egalitarian model of marriage. Some women who are in traditional marriages may also accept an inegalitarian division of family labor because their husbands' work allows them to focus more on their children. Regardless, egalitarian divisions of labor are not associated with happier marriages for wives who have children at home.

By contrast, our analyses also indicate that wives whose children are no longer in the home are happier in more egalitarian marriages. This is partly because they view such marriages as more equitable. But equity is not the whole story. It may also be that more egalitarian marriages provide empty nesters with more time together, more common work and domestic experiences, and are more congruent with broader cultural shifts towards family role egalitarianism.

Surprisingly, we did not find that childless wives as a whole were happier in egalitarian marriages. On the other hand, childless wives who hold egalitarian attitudes are happier in their marriages when they enjoy a more egalitarian division of family labor (see Figure 6.1). This same pattern was not evidenced for egalitarian-minded wives with children at home. So, overall, this study does provide some evidence in support of the notion that an egalitarian division of family labor is more attractive to wives who are not engaged on a day-to-day basis with their maternal roles; by contrast, married mothers are happiest in neotraditional marriages that enable them to focus more on their maternal responsibilities and still enjoy high levels of domestic support from their husbands. In general, then, this study indicates that the link between the division of family labor and women's marital happiness is contingent on their active maternal status.

This study also indicates that religion plays a role in shaping women's happiness and their perceptions of equity in their marriage. Religious wives are generally happier in their marriages, and they are less likely to perceive them as unfair. This may be because religious wives sanctify their marriages in ways that encourage them to view their marriages through rose-colored lenses; that is, because they are more likely to view their marriages as sanctioned by God, religious wives may be inclined to focus on positive aspects of their marriage and to overlook negative aspects of their marriage (Wilcox 2004). It may also be because religious women enjoy access to family-centered social networks of other women who provide them with social support for their family roles and responsibilities (Stolzenberg et al. 1995). Regardless, this study shows that religion plays a role in shaping women's perceptions of the quality and equity of their marriages.

Our study also confirms that equity is an important and abiding value for women in contemporary marriages (e.g., Wilkie et al. 1998). Women who rate the division of housework or childcare as unfair in their marriage are significantly less satisfied in their marriages than women who consider the division of domestic labor to be fair. In fact, perceptions of equity are some of the most consistent and important predictors of marital happiness in this study.

But it is important to note that perceptions of equity are more important than the reality of equity for most wives. In fact, as Table 6.1 indicates, less than 30 percent of wives are in egalitarian marriages but more than 70 percent of wives do not consider their marriages to be unfair when it comes to the division of domestic work. Thus, for most wives, being in a non-egalitarian marriage does not automatically make them view their marriage as unfair. Rather, this study suggests that religion, family role ideology, and the division of family labor all play some role in determining wives' perceptions of marital equity.

Conclusion

We find that there is no straightforward connection between the division of family labor and marital satisfaction among contemporary wives. For wives who do not have children in the home, an egalitarian arrangement is associated with markedly higher levels of marital quality. Likewise, for childless wives with egalitarian family attitudes, an egalitarian division of family labor is also associated with higher levels of marital satisfaction. But for wives who do have children in the home, a neotraditional arrangement is associated with a markedly higher level of marital quality, and egalitarian arrangements are not more successful than traditional arrangements for married mothers. Thus, this study suggests that the presence or absence of children in the day-to-day lives of married women has a lot to do with the kind of division of family labor that is most likely to leave wives happily married.

Notes

1. See Web Table 6.1, Model 1, on the book web site.
2. See Web Table 6.1, Model 2, on the book web site.
3. See Web Table 6.1, Model 2, on the book web site.
4. See Web Table 6.2, Model 1, on the book web site.
5. See Web Table 6.2 for details on the empirical predictors of marital satisfaction among wives with children at home.
6. See Web Table 6.2.
7. See Web Table 6.2 for details on the empirical predictors of marital satisfaction among wives whose children no longer live at home.

References

Amato, P. R., Booth, A., Johnson, D. R., and Rogers, S. J. (2007). *Alone Together: How Marriage in America Is Changing.* Cambridge, MA: Harvard University Press.
Becker, P. E., and Moen, P. (1999). Scaling back: Dual-earner couples' work-family strategies. *Journal of Marriage and the Family* 61: 995–1007.
Bianchi, S. M., Robinson, J. P., and Milkie, M. A. (2006). *Changing Rhythms of American Family Life.* New York: Russell Sage Foundation.
Blair, S. L., and Johnson, M. P. (1992). Wives' perceptions of the fairness of the division of household labor: The intersection of housework and ideology. *Journal of Marriage and the Family* 54: 570–581.

Blair-Loy, M. (2003). Globalization, work hours, and the care deficit among stockbrokers. *Gender and Society* 17: 230–249.

Brines, J., and Joyner, K. (1999). The ties that bind: Principles of cohesion in cohabitation and marriage. *American Sociological Review* 64: 333–355.

Budig, M. J., and England, P. (2001). The wage penalty for motherhood. *American Sociological Review* 66: 204–225.

Coltrane, S. (1996). *Family Man: Fatherhood, Housework, and Gender Equity.* New York: Oxford University Press.

DeMaris, A., and Longmore, M. A. (1996). Ideology, power, and equity: Testing competing explanations for the perception of fairness in household labor. *Social Forces* 74: 1043–1071.

Deutsch, M. (1985). *Distributive Justice: A Social-Psychological Approach.* New Haven, CT: Yale University Press.

Dew, J., and Wilcox, W. B. (2010). Competing devotions? Family time, spousal time, and marital satisfaction. Working Paper. Charlottesville: Department of Sociology, University of Virginia.

Gager, C. T., and Sanchez, L. (2003). Two as one? Couples' perceptions of time spent together, marital quality, and the risk of divorce. *Journal of Family Issues* 24: 21–50.

Greenstein, T. N. (1996). Gender ideology and perceptions of the fairness of the division of household labor: Effects on marital quality. *Social Forces* 74: 1029–1042.

Grote, N. K., Naylor, K. E., and Clark, M. S. (2002). Perceiving the division of family work to be unfair: Do social comparisons, enjoyment, and competence matter? *Journal of Family Psychology* 16: 510–522.

Hakim, C. (2000). *Work-Lifestyle Choices in the 21st Century: Preference Theory.* New York: Oxford University Press.

Hall, S. S., and MacDermid, S. M. (2009). A typology of dual earner marriages based on work and family arrangements. *Journal of Family and Economic Issues* 30: 215–225.

Hays, S. (1996). *The Cultural Contradictions of Motherhood.* New Haven, CT: Yale University Press.

Heckert, D. A., Nowak, T. C., and Snyder, K. A. (1998). The impact of husbands' and wives' relative earnings on marital disruption. *Journal of Marriage and the Family* 60: 690–703.

Hochschild, A. R., and Machung, A. (1989). *The Second Shift.* New York: Avon.

Hotchkiss, J. L., Pitts, M. M., and Walker, M. B. (2008). Working with children? The probability of mothers exiting the workforce at time of birth. Federal Reserve Bank of Atlanta Working Paper 2008-8.

Jacobs, J. A., and Gerson, K. (2004). *The Time Divide: Work, Family, and Gender Inequality.* Cambridge, MA: Harvard University Press.

Kalmijn, M. (1999). Father involvement in childrearing and the perceived stability of marriage. *Journal of Marriage and the Family* 61: 409–421.

Klein, M. J., Hyde, S., and Essex, M. J. (1998). Maternity leave, role quality, work involvement, and mental health one year after delivery. *Psychology of Women Quarterly* 22, no. 2: 239–266.

Lennon, M. C., and Rosenfeld, S. (1994). Relative fairness and the division of housework: The importance of options. *The American Journal of Sociology* 100: 506–531.

Major, B. (1987). Gender, justice, and the psychology of entitlement. In P. S. C. Hendrick (ed.), *Sex and Gender,* 124–148. Newbury Park, CA: Sage.

Moen, P., and Wethington, E. (1992). The concept of family adaptive strategies. *Annual Review of Sociology* 18: 233–251.

Nock, S. (2001). The marriages of equally dependent spouses. *Journal of Family Issues* 22: 756–777.

Pearce, L., and Axinn, W. (1998). The impact of family religious life on the quality of mother-child relations. *American Sociological Review* 63: 810–828.

Pittman, J. F., and Blanchard, D. (1996). The effects of work history and timing of marriage on the division of household labor: A life-course perspective. *Journal of Marriage and the Family* 58: 78–90.

Robinson, J. P., and Godbey, G. (1999). *Time for Life.* University Park: Pennsylvania State University.

Rogers, S. J. (2004). Dollars, dependency, and divorce: Four perspectives on the role of wives' income. *Journal of Marriage and Family* 66: 59–74.

Rogers, S. J., and Amato, P. R. (2000). Have changes in gender relations affected marital quality? *Social Forces* 79: 731–753.

Rubin, D. B. (1987). *Multiple Imputation for Non-Response in Surveys.* New York: Wiley.

Sayer, L. C. (2005). Gender, time, and inequality: Trends in women's and men's paid work, unpaid work and free time. *Social Forces* 84: 285–303.

Spitze, G. (1988). Women's employment and family relations: A review. *Journal of Marriage and the Family* 50, no. 3: 595–618.

Stevens, D., Kiger, G., and Riley, P. J. (2001). Working hard and hardly working: Domestic labor and marital satisfaction among dual-earner couples. *Journal of Marriage and Family* 63: 514–526.

Stolzenberg, R. M., Blair-Loy, M., and Waite, L. J. (1995). Religious participation in early adulthood: Age and family life cycle effects on church membership. *American Sociological Review* 60: 84–103.

Stone, P. (2007). *Opting Out? Why Women Really Quit Careers and Head Home.* Berkeley: University of California Press.

Thompson, L. (1991). Family work: Women's sense of fairness. *Journal of Family Issues* 12: 181–196.

Thornton, A., and Young-DeMarco, L. (2001). Four decades of trends in attitudes toward family issues in the United States: The 1960's through the 1990's. *Journal of Marriage and Family* 63: 1009–1037.

Voydanoff, P., and Donnelly, B. W. (1999). The intersection of time in activities and perceived unfairness in relation to psychological distress and marital quality. *Journal of Marriage and the Family* 61: 739–751.

Wilcox, W. B. (2004). *Soft Patriarchs, New Men: How Christianity Shapes Fathers and Husbands*. Chicago: University of Chicago Press.

———, and Dew, J. (2008). No one best way: Gender, work-family strategies, and marital happiness. Working Paper. Charlottesville: Department of Sociology, University of Virginia.

———, and Nock, S. L. (2006). What's love got to do with it? Equality, equity, commitment and women's marital quality. *Social Forces* 84: 1321–1345.

Wilkie, J. R., Ferree, M. M., and Ratcliff, K. S. (1998). Gender and fairness: Marital satisfaction in two-earner couples. *Journal of Marriage and the Family* 60: 577–594.

Williams, J. W. (2000). *Unbending Gender: Why Family and Work Conflict and What to Do about It*. New York: Oxford University Press.

Chapter 7

Sacralization by Stealth?

The Religious Consequences of Low Fertility in Europe

Eric Kaufmann

Europe stands at the confluence of two great outriders of modernity: secularization and the demographic transition. Indeed, it is commonly viewed as the exemplar of both. The first demographic transition—from a static population based on high birth and death rates to a new equilibrium based on low birth and death rates—took place gradually in western Europe between 1750 and 1950. During this period, depending on the country, the population of western Europe expanded three to eight times (Skirbekk 2009). However, since then, native populations in Europe have plateaued and begun to fall. Period total fertility rates (TFRs) in many western countries dipped below two children per woman in the late 1960s or 1970s. Most demographers foresaw a rebound, as per Easterlin's cyclical theory, but as we now know, the anticipated "correction" never arrived (Easterlin 1976). In fact, total fertility rates seem stuck at low levels in most of the developed world. The slight recent uptick in TFR in some of the most developed countries of Europe is no real cause for optimism since it largely reflects a tempo effect of older women realizing some of their desired fertility as well as the peculiar historical features of France and Scandinavia (Myrskylä et al. 2009). In any event, completed Europe-wide TFR looks unlikely to approach replacement levels. The persistently downward trends took most demographers by surprise.

Did religion play a part in this decline? Theorists of the second demographic transition (SDT) posit that the first demographic transition occurred in the context of a bourgeois family structure. Families were small but patriarchal, while expressive individualism was muted. Declining fertility was driven by material considerations like falling infant mortality and the move to the cities. These reduced the benefits and raised the costs of children. It thus made more sense to invest heavily in a smaller number of offspring (Becker 1991). The second demographic transition—which is accompanied by the trend to below-replacement fertility—is, by contrast, stimulated by value changes rather than material shifts.

In the first instance, attitude shifts involve a transition from traditional and communal values to expressive-individualist orientations (Lesthaeghe 2007). A major expansion of a centralized television media and higher education helped disseminate liberal values from an avant-garde cultural elite to wider strata of the population (Kaufmann 2004). Public attitudes changed during a period of vastly increased survey activity, and value changes are thereby solidly grounded in data (Mayer 1992). One large-scale American study looked at high school seniors and their parents in 1965 and 1973. Observing the value positions of youth and parents across five cultural issues, the authors concluded that opinions had changed radically, in a more liberal direction, especially among youth. The reasons for the change had less to do with events like Vietnam than with the changing education—and educational aspiration—levels of the younger generation. Within similarly educated groups from both generations, changes were minor (Jennings et al. 1981). In Europe as well, Inglehart (1990) powerfully shows how value orientations across most western societies changed, with post-1960s cohorts more liberal than their parents.

Contemporary observers were stunned by the rapidity of the change: "The life-style once practiced by a small *cenacle*," remarked Daniel Bell, a leading New York intellectual of the 1940s and 1950s, "is now copied by many … [and]

this change of scale gave the culture of the 1960s its special surge, coupled with the fact that a bohemian life-style once limited to a tiny elite is now acted out on the giant screen of the mass media" (Bell 1996). Consumer hedonism must be viewed as a product of both an older capitalist ethos and a newer expressive orientation. This explains how the new middle classes managed to combine an "antinomian" countercultural individualism with the materialistic values of postindustrial capitalism. The bourgeois-bohemian, or "bobo," is the end result. In fact, some argue that the anti-puritan hedonism of the counterculture was necessary to stimulate modern consumerism. Bohemia fulfils the function of a "social and cultural laboratory for modern society," remarks Campbell, "as crucial in connection with consumption as science and technology is for production" (Bell 1973).

The social upheaval of the 1960s, unsurprisingly, had an enormous impact on fertility. For example, while more than half of those over 65 in developed countries in Europe, North America, and Asia in 1981 claimed that a woman needs children to be fulfilled, just 35 percent of those ages 15–24 agreed (Inglehart 1990). These attitudes soon translated into concrete behavior. In twelve nations of the European Community between 1960 and 1985, we find a steady rise in divorce and children born out of wedlock occurring at the same time as a decline in total fertility rates. These three trends are all connected to a rise in expressive individualism. In Inglehart's words, expressive individualists "place more emphasis on self-fulfilment through careers, rather than through ensuring the survival of the species." What Inglehart terms—somewhat misleadingly— "postmaterialism" shifts the focus of life "out of the family toward broader social and leisure activities" in pursuit of individuality (Inglehart 1990). The value changes of the 1960s have proven exceptionally enduring: cultural shifts have been consolidated by subsequent generations, as have sub-replacement levels of fertility. Though the attitude changes of the 1960s began to flatten out by the 1990s, they had reached a new, liberal plateau far removed from the situation at mid-century (Thornton and Young-DeMarco 2001).

Religiosity and Fertility

One element of what Inglehart terms "traditional" values is religion. In almost every Western country, religiosity fell sharply among the baby boom generation, which entered adulthood in the 1960s and continued to decline thereafter (Inglehart 1990). The United States is not an exception to this rule—baby boomers are less religious than their parents and their kids even more so—though the impact of the 1960s was less pronounced in America than in Europe (Putnam 2009; Hout and Fischer 2002).

Correlation between more secular attitudes and smaller families does not, however, confirm a causal link. At the country level, using the 1999–2000 World Values Survey (WVS), the association between religiosity and fertility disappears when we add an indicator for female educational enrollment (Kaufmann 2008). However, *within* countries, we find an extremely robust association between an individual woman's level of religiosity and her fertility, which holds up in both developed and developing countries under multivariate analysis. Religiosity is arguably as important as education or income in predicting how many children a woman will bear (see Table 7.1).

Some aver that the relatively high (i.e., near replacement) fertility of extremely secular France and Scandinavia refutes the contention that declining religiosity leads to population decline. The socially progressive nature of these societies enables higher levels of fertility than in more patriarchal southern Europe or East Asia. Proponents add that fertility in countries with the highest levels of human development has risen over the past 5–10 years (Baizan 2006). There is some truth in this analysis. It makes sense to adopt public policies that smooth the path for women to combine careers with childrearing. However, those who argue that "feminism is the new pronatalism" are stretching the argument (Goldberg 2009). First of all, for each example of a progressive country with relatively high fertility one finds another with low fertility (e.g., Austria or Canada, notably Quebec). Equally, one discovers countries with high fertility that are more traditional, like Ireland and the United States. As in the world as a whole, there is not (yet) a statistically significant relationship at the macro-level between religiosity and fertility when GDP per capita and education controls are applied.

However, at the micro-level, there *is* a robust association between religiosity and fertility that survives multivariate scrutiny. And it runs in the opposite direction from that posited by progressive optimists. Thus, feminist-friendly social policies cannot explain why those of religious bent, in almost all Western societies, bear significantly more children than the non-religious. This is the case even when we account for their education, income, age, and other characteristics. In feminist France, for instance, practicing Catholic white women have a half-child fertility advantage over non-religious women and this has been increasing over time. The religious are also advantaged over seculars in Scandinavia (Berman et al. 2005).

Several recent studies examine the connection between religiosity—whether defined as attendance, belief, or affiliation—and fertility. Traditionally, education was considered the main determinant of a woman's fertility. Yet in

Table 7.1 Individual Fertility of Women in 45 Countries, 1999–2000

	GDP per capita >$20,000	GDP per capita <$5,000
Unmarried	−.253*** (.012)	−.281*** (.009)
Age	.021*** (.001)	.065*** (.001)
Individual religiosity	.203*** (.047)	.258** (.042)
Individual education	−.024*** (.004)	−.045*** (.003)
Personal income	−.092*** (.010)	−.026** (.008)
Country secondary school enrollment percent	.001 (.002)	.009*** (.001)
Country GDP per capita	−.170* (.074)	−.828*** (.145)
Country population 65+	−.825*** (.091)	−1.411*** (.051)
Constant	3.677*** (.279)	−.443 (.251)
R^2	.192	.451
N	4186	6402

$*p < .05; **p < .01; ***p < .001.$

Note: Country Total Fertility Rate was dropped from the analysis due to problems with multi-colinearity. Country variables have been standardized. The 45 countries include France, United Kingdom, Spain, Netherlands, Denmark, Belgium, Albania, Ireland, Algeria, Sweden, Iceland, Argentina, Bangladesh, Bosnia and Herzegovina, Canada, Chile, China, India, Indonesia, Iran, Israel, Japan, Jordan, Korea, Mexico, Moldova, Morocco, Nigeria, Pakistan, Peru, Philippines, Puerto Rico, Singapore, Vietnam, South Africa, Zimbabwe, Turkey, Uganda, Macedonia, Egypt, Tanzania, United States of America, Venezuela, Serbia, Montenegro.

Source: Regression coefficients calculated from 1999–2000 World Values Survey.

many European studies, a woman's level of religiosity is as or more important than her education in determining the number of children she will bear. In Spain, women who are practicing Catholics have significantly more children than non-practicing Catholics—even holding income, marital status, education, and other factors constant. This wasn't the case as recently as 1985, when many still practiced for social reasons, occluding the pro-natalist impact of committed belief (Adsera 2004).

In the United States, theological conservatism, attendance, and congregational participation all play a part in raising fertility—independent of controls for the usual demographic indicators. Utah Mormons and the most conservative Protestant denominations (e.g., independent Baptists, Foursquare Gospel, or the Anderson Church of God) enjoy at least a one-child TFR advantage over other Americans (Hackett 2008). Curiously, better-educated, wealthy Mormons tend to have larger families than poorer Mormons (Heaton 1986). Secular Americans in the General Social Survey have the lowest fertility, 1.66, of any ethnoreligious group apart from Jews and Buddhists. American women who are pro-life on abortion bear two-thirds of a child more than pro-choice women, and this advantage has been increasing since the GSS began in 1972. The same is true for other measures of traditionalism-modernism such as belief in the literal truth of the bible or support for gay rights. The fact that differentials have been widening provides support for the SDT interpretation that values come to play an ever more important role in determining fertility in modern societies (Skirbekk et al. 2010).

Across most Western countries, secular fertility is consistently lower than that of the religious (see Table 7.2). Muslims have higher fertility than practicing Christians. They, in turn, tend to outbirth nominal Christians who in turn bear larger families than the nonreligious. European Muslim fertility is typically higher than that of European whites—often by a multiple of two or three—because most European Muslims are recent immigrants from high fertility countries. Euro-Muslim TFR likewise remains elevated because they are more religious than European Christians. However, like the Protestant-Catholic fertility gap in the United States and Europe, the Christian-Muslim difference is rapidly closing (Westoff and Frejka 2007).

Table 7.2 Total Fertility Rates by Religion, Europe and the USA, 2001–2003

	Spain	Austria	Switzerland	USA
Catholic	—	1.32	1.41	2.3
Active Catholic	1.77	—	—	—
Nominal Catholic	1.41	—	—	—
Protestant	1.45*	1.21	1.35	2.21
No religion	1.00	0.86	1.11	1.66
Muslim	1.57*	2.34	2.44	2.84
Average	1.37	1.33	1.50	2.08

* Denotes few observations.

Source: Vegard Skirbekk and Anne Goujon, IIASA, World Population Program, 2007–2009.

What is not converging, however, is the more enduring, SDT-driven cleft between religious and secular fertility. As general fertility declines, the proportional fertility premium enjoyed by the religious—especially the fundamentally religious—grows. For instance, the Mormon advantage over other Americans has hovered around one child for many decades, but a TFR of 3 versus 2 is a 50 percent advantage, whereas 5 versus 4 is only 25 percent higher. Or consider the Laestadian Lutherans of Finland, who number 80,000–100,000 and have long opposed birth control. They experienced some fertility decline over the course of the twentieth century, but as of 1985–1987, the Laestadian TFR remained high, at 5.47. The Finnish average declined more abruptly, reaching 1.45 by this date. Thus the Laestadian advantage over other Finns climbed from under 2:1 in the 1940s to nearly 3:1 in the 1960s to almost 4:1 by the late 1980s.

A slower growing but much larger religious group is the Orthodox Calvinists of Holland, who form 7 percent of the population. Among women born during 1945–1949, Calvinist TFR was 3.0, compared to 2.3 for other Protestants, 1.9 for Catholics, and 1.7 for seculars. In a secularizing Holland, this gives Calvinists a near 40 percent fertility premium over many other (Haandrikman and Sobotka 2003). We can discern the same pattern within European Jewry: as secular and moderate Jewish fertility has declined, the advantage of the ultra-Orthodox has greatly expanded. In Britain, for instance, the ultra-Orthodox average 6.9 children whereas other Jews have a TFR of around 1.65 (Wise 2008).

Earlier, we noted a disjuncture between macro and micro trends, with religious fertility only affecting the micro-level of individuals. However, when fundamentalist groups grow large enough, their fertility begins to exert compositional effects at macro-levels of geography. Thus, in Utah, Mormons increased through fertility from 60 percent of the population in 1920 to 75 percent in 1998, despite large-scale non-Mormon immigration (Phillips 1999). Nationwide, conservative Protestants expanded from one-third to two-thirds of white Protestants during the twentieth century. Three-quarters of this growth was due to higher fertility. Evangelical growth created the constituency that was eventually mobilized as the New Christian Right by the Reagan administration in 1980 (Bruce 1998). Individual relationships are reproduced at a state level: Lesthaeghe and Neidert, for example, convincingly show a correlation of .78 between an American state's white TFR and its vote for George W. Bush in 2004 (Lesthaeghe and Neidert 2006). The relatively high fertility of the United States among developed countries—even in the absence of subsidized daycare and child benefits—may be related to its unusually high (for developed countries) levels of religiosity, especially conservative religiosity.

In Europe, we see a reflection of this in the endurance of Calvinism in Holland. Dutch Orthodox Calvinists are large enough (7 percent of the Dutch population) that their high fertility has affected the religious composition of the Netherlands. Once outnumbered 6 to 1 by the established Dutch Reformed Church, Calvinists now equal them when it comes to weekly worshippers. Demography is not the only reason for the reversal, but it is a central chapter in the story (Berghammer 2009). As with American fundamentalist Protestants, the micro-level association between religiosity and fertility begins to affect macro trends when religious groups pass a certain population threshold.

This is most evident in the Jewish population. In Britain, ultra-Orthodox Jews account for just 12 percent of the Jewish population but 75 percent of Jewish births. They are expected to comprise the majority of both American and British Jews by 2050. 2008 was also the first year since World War II that Jewish birth rates in Britain exceeded death rates. Between 2005 and 2008, the Jewish population of Britain increased for the first time in living memory (Wise 2008). In the United States, the majority of modern and ultra-Orthodox Jews tend to vote Republican and are rapidly increasing their share of American Jewry at the expense of their heavily Democrat-leaning, liberal Jewish co-ethnics. The growing Orthodox-ization of American Jewry may explain why American Jews were the only ethnoreligious group to swing against Obama in the 2008 election (Smidt et al. 2010). It is worth noting that the ultra-Orthodox have simultaneously increased their share of Israeli Jewry. In 1960, they comprised little more than 5 percent of primary schoolchildren. They now comprise a third of Jewish first-graders (Cincotta and Kaufmann 2009).

We have seen that the individual-level relationship between religiosity and fertility can eventually recast the religious composition of groups and territories. Fundamentalists benefit most, seculars the least, from these dynamics. But with the exception of America's "values voters" and Israel's ultra-Orthodox, we have been focusing on groups whose share of the national population is small. What can we say about the European majority—or plurality—that remain religious? Here it is vital to parse out three major groups: seculars, Christians, and Muslims. We also must distinguish between societies that have experienced long-term religious decline, such as France, the Czech Republic, and Scandinavia, and those where declines in personal piety are more recent, namely, much of Catholic Europe.

Seculars

Secularization theorists explain religious decline as the inevitable outcome of the modernization process. The differentiation of society, first between work

and home, then between various occupational specialties, spins ever more func-
tions out of the orbit of religious control. Social services, law, and education are
provided by the state, leisure and conviviality by the market, and so forth. These
spheres legitimate themselves in their own secular terms: education is for its
own sake rather than to further God's purposes, health care to promote better
health in this world, and so on. This tends to reduce religion to merely one com-
partment in individuals' lives, and a shrinking one at that. Culturally, religious
toleration and pluralism spawn an awareness of multiple truths and lead to
interfaith marriages, reducing belief in a religion's exclusive truth (Bruce 2002).

Intellectually, ethics and art become detached from their religious roots,
beginning with natural law in the sixteenth and seventeenth centuries and
coming to fruition with the Enlightenment and Romantic movements of
the eighteenth and nineteenth centuries (Taylor 2007). Large-scale growth
in secular schools, universities, and the media helped diffuse secular ideas
about the irrationality of religion to a wider segment of the population (Gray
2007). Meanwhile, some suggest that improved levels of health, income, and
education produce the human security and trust in secular institutions that
renders religious explanations less compelling (Norris and Inglehart 2004).
Even the "religious markets" theorists that challenge secularization theory accept that religious decline can occur—especially in societies with established,
monopolistic religions (e.g., Catholicism, Lutheranism). These are held to
have become lazy and ineffective in ministering to people's spiritual needs, as
compared with their American counterparts who must address the needs of
their mobile parishioners in order to compete in a vibrant religious marketplace
(Stark and Iannaccone 1994).

What becomes clear when examining cohort trends in Europe is that there
are two groups of countries. The first has high—but declining—religiosity and
largely consists of Catholic countries like Ireland and Spain whose religiosity
has fallen more recently. The second group has low religiosity, but religiosity
levels have been quite stable among successive cohorts born after 1945–1960.
In other words, while Scandinavian or French grandparents (those born pre-
1960) are more religious than their parents (born 1950s–1970s), the children
and young adults (born 1970s onward) are no less religious than their parents
(Voas 2009). In France and Scandinavia, for instance, only about 5 percent of
the population attend church weekly, but there has been no decline beneath
this level among generations born after 1945. This may reflect a trend wherein
those who derive greater marginal utility from religion remain resistant to the
secular norms at play in the wider society.

Perhaps 5 percent of those in the most secular countries attend church
weekly, but 45 percent consider themselves to be "a religious person" and

60–70 percent say they believe in God. My own projections using data from the European Values Surveys (EVS) for six of the most secular countries of western Europe suggest this may well prove to be a stable long-run equilibrium for Europe. Given (a) the 10–20 percent fertility advantage—after standard controls—of European women who say they "are a religious person" over those that reply that they are "not religious" or an atheist; and (b) the female-skewed sex ratio in the childbearing age ranges in favor of the religious, we expect the secular proportion of the population to begin to age relative to the religious.

After 2050, the religious share of these countries' population would begin to grow, leading to desecularization (see "expected" line in Figure 7.1). Even in the absence of a religious fertility premium, the trough of secularization among post-1945 generations will produce a stable 40 percent "religious" population—with perhaps 5 percent weekly attendance—as seen in the "no fertility gap" curve in Figure 7.1.

The above suggests that while seculars will continue to increase their share of the population via cohort replacement throughout Europe—a process that will end sooner in Protestant than in Catholic Europe—an increasingly resistant remnant of religious Christians is emerging. The heightened self-consciousness

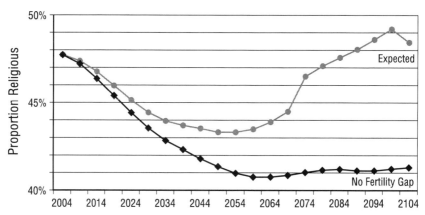

Figure 7.1 Projected Religious Population, France, Britain, and Four Scandinavian Countries, 2004–2104

Note: "Expected" refers to a scenario where the existing religious fertility advantage over seculars persists throughout the projection period. "No Fertility Gap" scenario plots the religious-secular population balance if there were no religious fertility premium over seculars.

Source: Hout 2006.

and intensity of Europe's remaining devout population can be seen in the rise of charismatic Christianity within Catholicism, Lutheranism, and other mainstream denominations. Indeed, charismatics, together with evangelicals and Pentecostals, are estimated to form over 8 percent of the European population and are increasing at the same rate as Muslims. The rise of charismatic Christianity is associated with the surge of interest in performing pilgrimages to sacred sites like Lourdes in France or Santiago de Compostela in Spain (Johnson and Grim 2009).

Muslims and Other Faiths

Much of the previous discussion uses European values surveys that undersample Europe's growing population of non-European descent. Yet to a large extent, Europe's ethnic future will be a non-European one. David Coleman estimates that at current levels of non-European immigration—even under the assumption that ethnic fertility gaps will converge over time—perhaps a quarter of the population of Britain will be non-white in 2050 and over a third will be of non-British ancestry.[1] Though Britain's minority population leans toward the high side for Europe, many western European countries are expected to fall in the 10–15 percent visible minority range by 2050 (Coleman 2006). Thus Britain's experience may be taken as indicative of the kind of changes that will emerge in western Europe. Such shifts will be revolutionary, amounting to what Coleman dubs a "third demographic transition." Indeed, by 2100, those of unmixed white background in Britain are projected to form a minority of less than 40 percent of the population (Coleman and Scherbov 2005).

Immigration could be reduced by popular ethnonationalist pressure, as has occurred in both Denmark and Holland since 2002. However, across Europe, levels have remained steady for some time, and there are a number of reasons why we might expect non-European inflows to continue or even exceed current levels. First, the rapid aging of European societies will generate growing demand for working-age immigrants in the period up to 2050 as the proportion of the total population over 60 increases from just over 20 percent to close to 40 percent; second, ethnic networks tend to generate and channel co-ethnic migration, whether legal (often through family reunification) or illegal; and third, intra-European source regions, such as southern and eastern Europe, are unlikely to produce as many emigrants as their populations age and economically develop (Parsons and Smeeding 2006). Differentials in age structures and fertility rates between European and non-European groups will also power ethnic change for decades even in the absence of immigration.

Ethnic change brings religious change. Most non-European immigrants to Europe are religious—be they Christian, Muslim, Hindu, or other—and far more devout than the host population. This introduces a second, indirect, religio-demographic effect beyond the direct pro-natalism of Christian, Muslim, and Jewish fundamentalists mentioned earlier. In France, for instance, the number of evangelical Protestants has jumped from 50,000 to 400,000 inside fifty years, mainly because of African immigration. In Britain, a tenth of all Christians attending Sunday services are now of African or West Indian origin, rising to 44 percent in London. If we add other non-whites, the London figure rises to 58 percent, which doesn't include the more than one million eastern European immigrant Londoners, who make up a significant share of the white attendance total. Thanks largely to immigration and high immigrant fertility, Christian attendance in relatively secular London barely budged between 1989 and 2005 while it plummeted 40 percent in the rest of the country (Johnson and Grim 2009; Parsons and Smeeding 2006).

Of course it is always possible that the immigrants and their descendants will lose their religion over generations. Will immigrants and their progeny follow the natives into irreligion? Secularization theory provides one answer. Where religion can find a secular function, it may persist in spite of secularizing forces. One of the foremost secular tasks to which religion is suited is the marking of ethnic boundaries. Catholic Poles assert their faith against Orthodox-cum-atheist Russians; Muslim Arabs brandish Islam against Jews in Palestine; even Catholic Bretons and Basques wield their faith against the secularism of Paris and Madrid. In all these cases, ethnic identity politics insulates religion from secularization (Bruce 2002).

The fact that newcomers to Europe are both ethnically and religiously different from the white host population means that religion finds a secular purpose as a marker of ethnicity. This is clearest for non-white Muslims, Sikhs, and Hindus, who identify against the white secular majority. It is more problematic for white Muslims like Bosniaks or non-white Christians such as West Indians, who share some features in common with the majority. Thus their religiosity only benefits obliquely from the identity politics effect. In Britain, successive ethnic minority surveys show that Pakistani and Bengali Muslims have near-perfect religious retention between the immigrant and British-born generations. In Figure 7.2, the solid and cross-hatched bars for "BP Muslims" are nearly identical: 35–40 percent of both foreign and UK-born Bangladeshi and Pakistani Muslims attend worship regularly and, while the second generation has somewhat lower self-reported practice (80 versus 88 percent), the levels remain extremely high. By contrast, British Afro-Caribbean Christians secularize considerably between the foreign-born and native-born groups; attendance drops from around 50 to nearer 30 percent between the two.[2]

In 2001, 71.4 percent of British-born Muslims said their Muslim identity was important to them, considerably *more* than the 64.7 percent of foreign-born Muslims who answered likewise. Between the immigrant and second generation, the proportion of British Pakistanis and Bangladeshis reporting themselves to have no religion barely budges, from 0.32 to a mere 0.68 percent (Mirza et al. 2007). A recent Dutch study confirms these results: the proportion citing "no religion" among second-generation Turkish (4.8 percent) and Moroccan (3.1 percent) Dutch respondents is far lower than the general population and differs little from Muslims of the first generation (Phalet and Haker 2004). Pooled Muslim samples for western Europe from the European Social Survey (ESS) and European Values Survey (EVS) confirm the findings

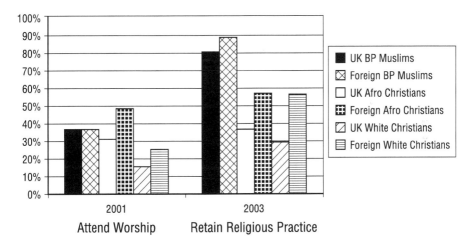

Figure 7.2 Religious Retention by Faith and Birthplace, UK, 2001–2003

Note: "BP" designates Bangladeshi and Pakistani, and "Afro" refers to African and Caribbean. Excludes non-identifiers.Worship attendance and practice is self-reported as "yes" or "no."

Sources: Home Office, 2003, Communities Group and BMRB, Social Research, Home Office Citizenship Survey, UK Data Archive Study No. 4754; Office for National Statistics and Home Office, 2005, Communities Group, Home Office Citizenship Survey, 2003, UK Data Study No. 5367.

from ethnic minority surveys: there is no difference between the religiosity (whether defined as practice or affiliation) of younger and older Muslims (European Social Survey 2004).

These proclivities are reflected in intermarriage behavior. In most European societies, with their secular norms, the tendency in interfaith marriages—or where one partner is secular—is for the children to be raised in the default culture, that is, to become nonreligious (Voas 2009). Across a number of major western European countries, residents of West Indian origin tend to marry out at the rate of 40 percent (rising to over half in the second generation), whereas Muslim intermarriage averages just 8 percent (10.5 percent in the second generation) (Lucassen and Laarman 2009). From British census data, we find exogamy to be much rarer among South Asian Muslims, Hindus, and Sikhs (10 percent or fewer of married couples) than Africans, Caribbeans, or East Asians.[3]

Here ethnic endogamy reinforces religious endogamy. For instance, inter-ethnic marriage between Bangladeshi and Pakistani Muslims is almost un-heard of; it is far more unusual than Bengali or Pakistani unions with whites.[4] Algerian Muslims in France are the one glaring exception to the endogamy rule—most Franco-Algerian men now marry non-Muslims and over half of Franco-Algerians claim not to be religious. This may be because a majority of Franco-Algerians are of Kabyle Berber or Algerian loyalist descent, both of whom bear anti-Islamist grievances (Silverstein 2004).

Looking Ahead: The Future of Secularization in Europe

The future of religion in Europe will be heavily determined by the relative pull of three factors: secularization, religious fertility, and religious immigration. The first force erodes religion while the others contribute to its revival. Secularization must therefore run to stand still. In fact, it may well be the case that *individuals* leave religion at a steady rate while *society* as a whole becomes more religious. To some extent this is what is happening at the global level due to population explosion in the religious global South more than offsetting losses to secularism in the secular North (Norris and Inglehart 2004). However, while Norris and Inglehart locate secularization in the West and religious demography in the global South, our analysis suggests that this geographic disjuncture cannot be sustained. Indeed, religious demography may be more powerful in the West than elsewhere because religiosity is a more powerful source of fertility advantage in wealthier, second-demographic transition contexts and religious immigration is a more potent factor in rich Western societies.

Census questions on religious affiliation are asked in only four European countries.[5] Switzerland and Austria have the longest running data. Using parameters for religious fertility and age structure derived from their censuses, and applying source-country religious composition data to current net immigration inflows, my colleagues Anne Goujon and Vegard Skirbekk at IIASA's World Population Program have developed cohort component projections for Austria and Switzerland. For brevity, we focus on two distinct religious populations: seculars and Muslims. Muslims are expected, on current trends, to treble their share of the population of Switzerland and quadruple their position in Austria between 2001 and 2051. Their growth curves, buoyed by high fertility, both display a concave shape.[6]

Will Muslims take over Europe, as prophets of "Eurabia" predict? Bernard Lewis warns that Muslims will form a majority in western Europe by the twenty-first century at "the latest." George Weigel allows a further half century before Eurabia arrives. Others—including the authors of the 10-million-plus-hit YouTube video "Muslim Demographics"—are similarly convinced. In addition, jihadists like Omar Bakri and enthusiastic Muslim leaders like the late Moammar Qaddafi have both spoken of Islam's demographic conquest of Europe. However, as we shall see, Eurabia is an unlikely prospect. "Plurope" is more plausible, in which Muslims, Christians (white and nonwhite), other non-Christians, and seculars share an increasingly polyglot public sphere (Kaufmann 2010).

How so? Austria and Switzerland have relatively representative Muslim populations in western Europe, though Austrian Muslims have a stronger fertility advantage over others than their Swiss counterparts, along with higher migration rates. We know that Muslim fertility is converging with that of native Austrians and Swiss, so the Muslim population will almost certainly begin to stabilize: if fertility convergence is attained by 2016, Muslims will—despite some immigration—level off at around 10 percent of the Swiss total and 22 percent of the Austrian population by the end of the century. With no further convergence in fertility between Muslims and others, Muslims could comprise 36 percent of Austrians in 2050 and a majority of its schoolchildren.[7] But this would fly in the face of trends in Muslim European TFRs, which have halved in a generation. For some Muslim ethnic groups—such as Iranians or some Turkish populations—Euro-Muslim fertility is already at or below host levels (Westoff and Frejka 2007).

The non-religious are also expected to reshape the religious direction their countries take as elderly Christians die off and young seculars take their place. Seculars will also form a larger chunk of women in the childbearing age ranges—though not as large as their share of men in these age groups. The projections also assume that current high rates of religious defection to non-religion will continue. This may be unrealistic given the tapering of secularism in countries where it has been in train longest. The resistance of Muslims to religious decline also speaks against it.[8] The extremely low fertility among those of no religion ("nones") in both countries and the paucity of secular immigrants will lead to an aging of the secular population and, ultimately, desecularization. If religious decline stops[9] the desecularization point could be reached as early as the 2020s in both countries, with Austrian Muslims overtaking "nones" by 2040.

Desecularization is, however, more likely to occur around 2050. Depending on the secularization assumption deployed, we project thirty-six possible outcomes for the nonreligious population of Austria.[10] It is notable that the proportion of non-religious can only continue to rise if there is some degree of Muslim secularization—an unlikely assumption from current survey trends. Any slackening in rates of religious decline—which, as we saw, also seems to be true of the most secular societies of Europe—will lead to desecularization before mid-century. In major urban, immigrant-receiving areas, we can therefore expect religion to return far sooner. Given the role of metropolitan regions in politics and the mass media, this may translate into increased religious influence in the west European public sphere within the next decade or two.

Already, religious fundamentalism (chiefly Muslim) has sent issues of security, women's rights, multiculturalism, and freedom of expression soaring to the top of the political agenda. The murder of Dutch filmmaker Theo Van Gogh in 2004, the Danish cartoons controversy of 2005, or the ructions that followed the Madrid (2004) and London (2005) bombings are merely the most visible signs of the new dispensation. From honor killings to the headscarf, government programs for training imams to multiculturalism, naturalization ceremonies to citizenship classes, there has been an enormous increase in the profile given to religiously inflected issues in Europe. Broadly speaking, Europe is in the process of rolling back its commitment to multiculturalism and open immigration in response to the challenge of Islam. Secular liberal nationalism rests its case on the irrationality of religion, especially fundamentalist Islam. This has led to Christian and Jewish religious voices joining moderate Islam in this societal conversation, where they have often—as in the case of Pope

John Paul II's outreach to Islam or Catholic UK Prime Minister Tony Blair's support for an anti-religious-hate law—backed Muslim demands for limits to secular liberalism (Caldwell 2009).

Conclusion

Secularization and religious resurgence can occur simultaneously. We should expect a continued flow of people from Christianity into non-religion in Europe in the near future. However, Europe's population will probably begin to become more religious at some point between 2020 and 2070—probably around 2050. Demography provides the missing link in this equation. Religious Europeans—still a majority of the population—have more children than seculars. Religious fundamentalists, a relatively small minority, have far more children than others and benefit from high religious retention. Women are also disproportionately religious, especially in the childbearing age ranges, which redounds to the advantage of the pious.

Immigrants are reshaping Europe's population, and those of unmixed European origin may well be in the minority in western Europe in 2100. Immigrants are more religious than natives and tend—especially if non-Christian—to retain their faith as a marker of ethnic identity. Against these demographic sources of religious growth must be set the continued appeal of secularism. However, the *rate* of religious decline has been falling in the more secular countries because those Christians and Jews most inclined to leave religion have generally already done so. In other words, the micro-level forces of religious decline may be ebbing while the macro-level ones powering the rise of religion are waxing.

Based on current rates of fertility, immigration, and secularization, our cohort component projections find that secularization will peak in western Europe around 2050. This will take place far sooner in European gateway capitals like Paris, London, Amsterdam, Brussels, and Moscow, as well as in high-immigrant provincial centers like Malmö, Marseilles, or Leicester. Already, these are among the most religious parts of their respective countries, islands of religious growth in Europe's secular sea. Given these urban zones' proximity to national sources of media and political power, we may witness religion's reentry into the European public sphere in short order. In this sense, contemporary concerns about security, women's rights, multiculturalism, and freedom of expression may merely prove the thin edge of Europe's new religious wedge.

Notes

1. British ancestry refers to those of English, Scottish, Welsh, or Irish descent.
2. The white categories do not reflect intergenerational dynamics in the same way. Rather, this should be read as showing that foreign-born (largely East European) whites are more religious than British whites.
3. See Web Figure 7.1 on the book web site.
4. Of more than 12,000 couples in the ONS Longitudinal Survey 2001 British sample involving a Pakistani or a Bengali, there were a mere 25 Pakistani-Bengali ones (ONS Longitudinal Survey 2001).
5. These are Austria, Switzerland, Britain, and Slovakia.
6. See Web Figure 7.2 on the book web site.
7. Projections to 2100 courtesy of Anne Goujon, IIASA World Population Program (unpublished).
8. Even if we bracket these questions, notice that secular growth curves in Web Figure 7.2, in contrast to the Muslim ones, are convex.
9. See the "low" scenario presented in Web Figure 7.2 on the book web site.
10. See Web Figure 7.3 on the book web site.

References

Adsera, A. 2004. "Marital Fertility and Religion: Recent Changes in Spain." IZA Discussion Paper 1399. University of Chicago: Population Research Center, p. 23.

Amiraux, Valérie. 2004. "L'Islam en France." In *Encyclopaedia Universalis France*. Paris.

Baizan, Paul. 2006. "Do Childcare Arrangements Matter for Fertility Decisions? The Effects of Men's Involvement in Childcare, and of Formal and Informal Options." European Population Conference, Liverpool.

Becker, Gary S. 1991. *A Treatise on the Family.* Enl. ed. Cambridge, MA: Harvard University Press.

Bell, Daniel. 1973. *The Coming of Post-Industrial Society: A Venture in Social Forecasting.* New York: Basic Books, p. 115.

———. 1996 [1976]. *The Cultural Contradictions of Capitalism.* New York: Harper Collins, p. 54.

Berghammer, C. 2009. "Causality between Religiosity and Childbearing: Evidence from a Dutch Panel Study." Paper presented at IUSSP conference, Marrakesh, Morocco, 2009.

Berghammer, C., D. Philipov, and T. Sobotka. 2006. "Religiosity and Demographic Events: A Comparative Study of European Countries." Paper delivered at European Population Conference, Liverpool, 2006.

Berman, E., L. Iannaccone, and G. Ragusa. 2005. "From Empty Pews to Empty Cradles: Fertility Decline among European Catholics." National Bureau of Economic Research working paper.

Brooks, D. 2001. *Bobos in Paradise: The New Upper Class and How They Got There.* New York: Simon and Schuster.

Bruce, Steve. 1998. *Comparative Protestant Politics.* Oxford: Oxford University Press, p. 148.

———. 2002. *God Is Dead: The Secularisation of the West.* Oxford: Blackwell.

Caldwell, Christopher. 2009. *Reflections on the Revolution in Europe: Immigration, Islam, and the West.* New York: Doubleday, p. 230.

Campbell, Colin. 1987. *The Romantic Ethic and the Spirit of Modern Consumerism.* Oxford: Basil Blackwell, p. 208.

Cincotta, Richard, and Eric Kaufmann. 2009. "The Changing Face of Israel." *Foreign Policy,* June 1.

Coleman, D., and S. Scherbov. 2005. "Immigration and Ethnic Change in Low-Fertility Countries—Towards a New Demographic Transition?" Paper presented at the annual meeting of the Population Association of America, Philadelphia, March 31–April 2.

Coleman, David. 2006. "Immigration and Ethnic Change in Low-Fertility Countries: A Third Demographic Transition." *Population and Development Review* 32 (3, September): 414.

Easterlin, Richard A. 1976. "The Conflict between Aspiration and Resources." *Population and Development Review* 2: 418–425.

Economist. 2006. "A New Jerusalem." *Economist,* September 21.

European Social Survey (ESS). 2004. http://www.europeansocialsurvey.org/.

European Values Survey (EVS). 1999–2000 wave. http://www.worldvaluessurvey.org/.

Frejka, T., and C. F. Westoff. 2008. "Religion, Religiousness and Fertility in the US and in Europe." *European Journal of Population–Revue Europeenne De Demographie* 24 (1): 5–31.

Goldberg, Michelle. 2009. *The Means of Reproduction: Sex, Power, Population and the Future of the World.* New York: Penguin Press, p. 222.

Gray, John. 2007. *Black Mass: Apocalyptic Religion and the Death of Utopia.* London: Penguin, p. 289.

Haandrikman, K., and T. Sobotka. 2003. "The Dutch Bible Belt: A Demographic Perspective." Working paper, University of Groningen, Population Research Centre.

Hackett, Conrad. 2008. "Religion and Fertility in the United States." PhD Dissertation. University of Texas at Austin, pp. 37–42.

Heaton, T. B. 1986. "How Does Religion Influence Fertility: The Case of the Mormons." *Journal for the Scientific Study of Religion* 25 (2): 253–256.

Hout, M. 2006. "The Demographic Imperative in Social Change: Political Implications." Presented at Political Demography: Ethnic, National and Religious Dimensions, London School of Economics, September.

Hout, M., and C. Fischer. 2002. "Why More Americans Have No Religious Preference." *American Sociological Review* 67 (2): 165–190.

Hout, M., A. Greeley, and M. Wilde. 2001. "The Demographic Imperative in Religious Change in the United States." *American Journal of Sociology* 107 (2): 468–500.

Inglehart, Ronald. 1990. *Culture Shift in Advanced Industrial Society.* Princeton, NJ: Princeton University Press.

Jenkins, Philip. 2007. *God's Continent: Christianity, Islam, and Europe's Religious Crisis.* Oxford: Oxford University Press, pp. 61–62, 75.

Jennings, M. Kent, and Richard G. Niemi. 1981. *Generations and Politics: A Panel Study of Young Adults and Their Parents.* Princeton, NJ: Princeton University Press, pp. 100, 160, 261, 267–269.

Johnson, T., and B. Grim. 2009. *World Religion Database.* Leiden: Brill.

Kaufmann, Eric. 2004. *The Rise and Fall of Anglo-America: The Decline of Dominant Ethnicity in the United States.* Cambridge, MA: Harvard University Press, pp. 189, 195–196.

———. 2008. "Human Development and the Demography of Secularisation in Global Perspective." *Interdisciplinary Journal of Research on Religion* 4, Article 1.

———. 2010. *Shall the Religious Inherit the Earth?* London: Profile Books, ch. 6.

Klausen, Jytte. 2005. *The Islamic Challenge: Politics and Religion in Western Europe.* Oxford: Oxford University Press.

Lesthaeghe, R. 2007. "Second Demographic Transition." In *Encyclopedia of Sociology,* ed. G. Ritzer. Oxford: Blackwell.

Lesthaeghe, R., and L. Neidert. 2006. "The 'Second Demographic Transition' in the United States: Exception or Textbook Example?" *Population and Development Review* 32 (4): 669–698.

Lucassen, Leo, and Charlotte Laarman. 2009. "Immigration, Intermarriage and the Changing Face of Europe in the Post War Period." *The History of the Family* 14 (1): 52–68.

Martin, David. [1978] 1993. *A General Theory of Secularization.* Aldershot: Gregg Revivals, p. 47.

Mayer, William G. 1992. *The Changing American Mind: How and Why American Public Opinion Changed between 1960 and 1988.* Ann Arbor: University of Michigan Press, p. 18.

Mirza, Munir, Abi Senthilkumaran, and Zein Ja'far. 2007. *Living Apart Together: British Muslims and the Paradox of Multiculturalism.* London: Policy Exchange.

Myrskylä, M., H. P. Kohler, and F. C. Billari. 2009. "Advances in Development Reverse Fertility Declines." *Nature* 460 (7256):741–743.

Norris, Pippa, and Ronald Inglehart. 2004. *Sacred and Secular: Religion and Politics Worldwide.* Cambridge: Cambridge University Press.

Parsons, Craig, and Timothy M. Smeeding. 2006. "What's Unique about Immigration in Europe." In *Immigration and the Transformation of Europe,* ed. C. Parsons and T. M. Smeeding. Cambridge: Cambridge University Press, pp. 1–29.

Phalet, K., and Frea Haker. 2004. "Moslim in Nederland. Diversiteit en verandering in religieuze betrokkenheid: Turken en Marokkanen in Nederland 1998–2002." In *SCP-werkdocument 106b*: Sociaal en Cultureel Planbureau, Utrecht, and Ercomer-ICS, Universiteit Utrecht, pp. 17–22.

Phillips, Rick. 1999. "The 'Secularization' of Utah and Religious Competition." *Journal for the Scientific Study of Religion* 38 (1): 75–77.

Putnam, Robert D. 2000. *Bowling Alone: The Collapse and Revival of American Community.* New York: Simon and Schuster, p. 352.

———. 2009. Interview with author, Harvard University, May.

Regnier-Loilier, Arnaud, and France Prioux. 2008. "Does Religious Practice Influence Fertility Behaviour in France?" Paper presented at the European Population Conference (EPC), Barcelona, July 9–12.

Silverstein, Paul A. 2004. *Algeria in France: Transpolitics, Race, and Nation.* New Anthropologies of Europe. Bloomington: Indiana University Press, pp. 124–127.

Skirbekk, V. 2009. "Human Fertility and Survival across Space and Time." World Population Program, IIASA, Working Paper.

Skirbekk, V, A. Goujon, and Eric Kaufmann. 2010. "Secularism, Fundamentalism or Catholicism? The Religious Composition of the United States to 2043." *Journal for the Scientific Study of Religion* 49, no. 2: 293–310.

Smidt, Corwin, Kevin den Dulk, Bryan Froehle, James Penning, Stephen Monsma, and Douglas Koopman. 2010. *The Disappearing God Gap? Religion in the 2008 Presidential Election.* Oxford: Oxford University Press.

Stark, Rodney, and Laurence R. Iannaccone. 1994. "A Supply-Side Reinterpretation of the 'Secularization' of Europe." *Journal for the Scientific Study of Religion* 33 (3): 230–252.

Taylor, Charles. 2007. *A Secular Age.* Cambridge, MA: Belknap Press of Harvard University Press.

Thornton, Arland, and Linda Young-DeMarco. 2001. "Four Decades of Trends in Attitudes toward Family Issues in the United States: The 1960s through the 1990s." *Journal of Marriage and the Family* 63 (4): 1009–1037.

UK Census. 2001. Table 4.11, "Religion by Ethnic Group and Country of Birth."

Voas, D. 2003. "Intermarriage and the Demography of Secularisation." *British Journal of Sociology* 54 (1): 83–108.

———. 2009. "The Rise and Fall of Fuzzy Fidelity in Europe." *European Sociological Review* 25 (2): 155–168.

Westoff, C. F., and T. Frejka. 2007. "Religiousness and Fertility among European Muslims." *Population and Development Review* 33 (4): 785–809.

Wise, Yaacov. 2007. "Majority of Jews Will Be Ultra-Orthodox by 2050." University of Manchester press release, July 23.

———. 2008. "Britain's Jewish Population on the Rise: Britain's Jewish Population Is on the Increase for the First Time since the Second World War, According to New Research." *Telegraph Online,* May 20.

Chapter 8

Feminism as the New Natalism

Twenty-First-Century Prescriptions for Addressing Low Fertility

Leonard Schoppa

Fertility rates have been falling in most of the developed world since the 1950s, falling below the replacement rate of 2.1 in many countries in the 1970s before reaching "lowest-low fertility rates" of 1.2–1.4 in Japan, Korea, Germany, Austria, Italy, Spain, Greece, and many of the former socialist eastern European nations in the first decade of the 2000s.[1] For much of this period, this "second demographic transition" has been celebrated as a rational result of the birth control technologies and wealth that have enabled families in the industrialized nations to reduce the size of their families in order to invest in the education and nurturing of a smaller number of children. We celebrated the fact that, in the industrialized world at least, mankind has been able to avoid the threat of over-population forecast by demographers since Malthus made his predictions of disaster 200 years ago.

By the 1990s, however, policy-makers and social commentators in several of the countries with the lowest fertility rates had begun worrying that the fall in rates had gone too far. After the total fertility rate (TFR) in Japan fell to a record low of 1.57 in 1989, one government commission forecast that Japan would become extinct as a nation if the rate remained that low for several centuries. "Just as in the last days of the Roman empire," it intoned, "the decrease in the number of children is a sign of the decline of civilization" (Suzuki 1995).

While these reactions were extreme, the concerns were based on real economic and demographic calculations. According to the formulas used by demographers, a sustained TFR of 1.3 will reduce the size of a nation's population by 75 percent over the course of a century (McDonald 2002). A fall-off in births of this pace threatens to up-end the finances of pension and health insurance programs that rely on tax-paying workers to cover the cost of providing benefits to retirees. These programs were designed to be self-sustaining under stable population growth, with worker-to-retiree ratios on the order of 4:1. Policy-makers in charge of these programs warned that low fertility rates would produce worker-to-retiree ratios below 2:1 that would put a crushing tax burden on the younger cohorts that would be called upon to cover their elders' pension and health obligations.

Since the 1990s, therefore, policy-makers in nations with the lowest fertility rates have been studying the forces that have driven their rates to record lows. Noting that fertility rates were 1.70 or higher in many OECD countries,[2] officials and analysts in those with the lowest rates have begun devoting significant energy to exploring ways in which they might push rates up to a level where the nation would not have to deal with such a rapid decline in the working age population. In this chapter, I examine this policy debate, focusing in particular on the emergence of a feminist policy prescription that has called on the governments of nations with traditional male-breadwinner-oriented labor market policies and gender norms to adopt work-family reconciliation policies such as expanded childcare services, childcare leave policies that encourage fathers to take time off from work after the birth of each child, and reforms in labor-market rules to make it easier for mothers and fathers to move flexibly between "fast-track" jobs with long working hours and part-time or flex-time work more compatible with the care obligations of parents with young children. Ironically, I argue, feminists who initially celebrated the decline in birth rates as a sign that women were taking advantage of new freedoms to choose roles other than mother have recently become the "new natalists," selling work-family reconciliation policies as a tonic to cure the problem of too-low fertility rates.

The chapter is organized as follows. In the first section, I examine the attitudes of feminists toward the population debate when low fertility rates first began to be described as a problem. I then look at how they gradually came to embrace a policy line, growing out of studies conducted under the purview of the OECD that revealed that higher fertility rates in the industrialized world were correlated with high rates of work and pay for women. In this section, I lay out this policy prescription and examine the evidence that has been put forth by feminists and others to support taking these steps in order to boost birth rates. Finally, in the third section, I look at the track record of those who have advocated this policy prescription, emphasizing the limited degree to which advocates have been able to leverage fertility concerns to move policy sharply in the direction they favor. I focus in this section primarily on the record of reform in Japan, Germany, and Italy.

Is Low Fertility a "Problem"?

When fertility rates first fell below 1.60 and conservatives began forecasting the end of civilization, Japanese feminists' first reaction was to disagree with the characterization of falling rates as a "problem." Chizuko Ueno, a sociologist specializing in gender issues, took the lead, titling an article "The Declining Birthrate: Whose Problem?" The view that a nation's strength depended on the size of its population, she argued, was an "antiquated idea of the nineteenth century" (Ueno 1998). If there were not enough workers to cover the costs of retirement programs, this problem could easily be solved by bringing more immigrants into the country. She noted that the decline in fertility in Japan closely tracked the decline in marriage rates, but she argued that this development should be celebrated. It was the earlier pattern, when 97 percent of men and 98 percent of women in cohorts coming of age in the 1960s and 1970s married at least once during their lives, that was abnormal. It was "normal for any society to have a 'remain single' population at the 10 percent level," she argued, and welcomed the falling marriage and fertility rates as a sign that "as social pressure for marriage is now being relaxed, people consider marriage as an option in life" (Ueno 1998).

Yuriko Ashino, a leader of the Family Planning Federation of Japan, was similarly adamant, asking "what is wrong with the low birthrate?" (Suzuki 1995). Population control deserved praise rather than criticism, she argued, vowing that "you won't find today's women having babies for the sake of their country or because someone told them to" (Suzuki 1995). Her reference to "today's women" recalled, by way of contrast, *yesterday's* women who had been victims of Japanese wartime policies that restricted access to birth control and exhorted women to "go forth and multiply" (*umeyo, fuyaseyo*) in order to produce the manpower needed to fight the war and increase wartime industrial production. Many parents struggled after the war to feed their large families, generating a powerful allergy to any suggestion that the government might once again be trying to boost the fertility rate. Ueno, Ashino, and other feminists worried that if the government succeeded in characterizing the fall in fertility rates as a problem, it might then use this pretext as a basis for rolling back abortion rights or access to family planning services.

Early reactions to hand-wringing about falling fertility rates in Germany and Italy were greeted similarly in these nations, which had also seen wartime governments attempt to boost fertility rates in the "national interest" (Gauthier 1996). Italian feminist Mariarosa Dalla Costa, for example, echoed several of the points made by Japanese feminists in writing that those who worry about Italy's low fertility rate should remember that "women's refusal to function as machines for reproducing labor-power, demanding instead to reproduce themselves and others as social individuals, has represented a major moment of women's resistance and struggle" (Dalla Costa 1996).

From "Not a Problem" to Opportunity

Even as women's movement leaders and activists were arguing against any quick move to label steep fertility declines a problem, however, they also began using the trend as a hook for promoting the Scandinavian model of work-family reconciliation. Keiko Higuchi, a commentator known for being outspoken on women's issues in Japan, was one of the first to point to Sweden's high fertility rates in Japan's debate about the causes of the fertility decline (Suzuki 1995). At the time she voiced this argument, in 1995, some conservatives in Japan were blaming the drop in births on women's rising labor market participation and higher levels of education. Sweden's high rates of fertility gave lie to this claim, Higuchi argued, for that nation had seen fertility rates rebound and reach levels close to 2.0 even though 80 percent of women in their thirties were in the workforce, in comparison to just 50 percent of women in the same age bracket in Japan. More education and more work did not directly lead to low fertility.

As Japanese academics and officials began exploring the forces that were pushing fertility rates to record lows there, they soon began to focus more closely on the puzzle posed by the comparison of Sweden and Japan. Why was it that higher educational levels and working rates among young women were associated with a falling fertility rate in Japan while high rates of working coexisted with higher fertility rates in Sweden, France, and the United States? It came down to "opportunity costs," according to labor economist Machiko Osawa, who published a mass market book promoting this explanation in 1998 (Osawa 1998).

Japanese career jobs—the ones that came with job security and seniority wages—demanded long hours and uninterrupted commitment to the employer. Government support for childcare leave and services, and husbands' support at home, was not sufficient to allow most mothers to live up to these employer demands; so most new mothers quit their jobs upon the birth of a child. If a new mother left a career job in this way, she was usually unable to find a job with similar pay or benefits and was instead consigned to poorly paid part-time work. As a result, motherhood imposed a stiffer price on Japanese women than on women in many other industrialized nations. That was why the fertility rate had fallen so low.

In no time, this argument became the mainstream view among policy-makers and scholars, promoted not only by women's movement figures such as Higuchi and academics with similar sympathies like Osawa but also by mainstream economists and career officials inside Japan's Ministry of Health and Labor. A particularly vocal advocate of the opportunity cost argument was Naohiro Yashiro, whose 1999 book *Economics for a Declining Fertility/Aging Society,* advanced a similar line of argument (Yashiro 1999). Yashiro was known as an advocate of liberal, market-oriented reforms (and not a feminist), so when he advanced an argument in favor of gender equality on economic grounds, it gave the view added credibility. Of course, as an advocate of market-oriented reforms, Yashiro did not prioritize increased government spending or services. Instead, he pointed to ways in which tax and benefit rules could be changed to reduce women's opportunity costs. He pointed out that tax and pension rules offering special deductions to "dependent" spouses (with limited income of their own) created incentives for wives to cut back on their working hours, artificially limiting their earnings and adding to the opportunity costs they paid for being mothers. For similar reasons, he called for reforms to Japan's employment rules that gave (mostly male) career workers job protections in exchange for complete loyalty and long hours—a system that forced men to rely on wives to do everything at home and made it difficult for mothers to stay in these jobs. The fertility decline, he argued, was a result of a market failure created by policies like these.

Like Higuchi, Yashiro pointed out that fertility rates were higher in places where women's career work did not force many of them to give up motherhood. But rather than using a single case, like Sweden, to make his point, Yashiro included in his book a figure showing that this pattern reflected the experience of industrialized nations in general. The two-dimensional figure correlated each nation's gender equality (he used the "gender development index") and its fertility rate, showing that fertility rates were highest in places like Norway, France, Canada, and the United States where the GDI was highest and were lowest in places like Japan and Italy where the GDI was low. Regression lines of this type subsequently appeared in a variety of government reports, reinforcing this message. The one in the *Gender Equality White Paper,* published by the Office of the Prime Minister (2000), showed higher fertility linked to higher employment rates for women ages 25–35. I have reproduced a similar figure, updated to reflect more recent data, in Figure 8.1.

At around the same time, officials within the Ministry of Health and Welfare were struggling to draw up "declining fertility countermeasures" (*shōshika*

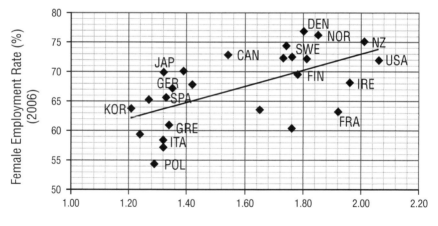

$R^2 = 0.3583$

Figure 8.1 Fertility Rates and Employment Rates by Country

Source: OECD Family Database, online at http://www.oecd.org/document/4/0,3746, en_2649_34819_37836996_1_1_1_1,00.html#structure, accessed February 6, 2012. For TFR, see Web Table 8.1. Annual TFR data can be found on the above web site under SF2.1 Fertility Rates. Women's employment rate data can be found under LMF 1.2 Maternal Employment.

taisaku). This task had been given to them after the nation's official demographic projections issued in 1997 showed that fertility rates were trending even lower than had been projected five years before. After that earlier projection, the same bureaucrats had drawn up "The Angel Plan," which called for an expansion in childcare services. But by the late 1990s, officials under team leader Michiko Mukuno had come to realize that reducing opportunity costs for mothers would require more than marginally longer childcare hours (Schoppa 2006). They needed to reform labor market rules so that new mothers would have an easier time taking a leave of absence and returning (with flexible hours) to their workplace. They needed husbands to help out more at home. They needed a more gender-equal society.

Toward this end, the Ministry of Health and Welfare published a white paper in 1999 that focused on the declining fertility problem and linked it to the unequal distribution of childcare and housework in the family. Japanese fathers of children under six spent just 17 minutes a day, on average, on childcare and only 37 minutes on housework. Women spent over 10 hours a day on these tasks (Ministry of Health and Welfare 1999).[3] Even when the mother worked full-time, she spent many more hours on caregiving than the father. Listing specific tasks, the white paper reported that the work was rarely split evenly or done primarily by the father. Fathers accounted for just 27 percent of the time spent changing diapers; 7.4 percent of the time cooking; 18.3 percent of the time picking up children from the childcare center; and 19.2 percent of the time taken off from work when a child was sick (Ministry of Health and Welfare 1999). The report made no attempt to suggest a legislative solution to this problem, but by linking the unequal distribution of childcare and housework burdens to the declining fertility problem, the government was implicitly taking the side of the feminists. And this was at a time when Japan was still ruled by a predominantly male and very conservative Liberal Democratic Party.

The European nations dealing with the lowest-low fertility rates were going through a similar embrace of "feminism as the new natalism" during these same years. Writing for an OECD publication about declining fertility concerns in her native Italy and other "lowest low fertility" nations, Saraceno noted already in 1997 that the relationship between the level of women's participation in the labor market and fertility rates had flipped. In the 1970s, the nations with the highest fertility rates were those (like Ireland) with the lowest rates of women in the workforce. Yet the most recent data showed that "the fertility rate is now lowest in countries where women's participation in the labor force is lowest" (Saraceno 1997).[4] Like Higuchi in Japan, she mentioned Sweden as an example of how "some countries which have a high level of labor participation by women ... also have the highest levels of fertility." Saraceno jumped straight to the policy implications of these data: "This must be due not only to cultural differences, but also to the different ways in which national policies deal with family obligations and have responded to the growth of female employment" (Saraceno 1997).

OECD Publications on Family Policy and Fertility

The flipping of the relationship between women's work and fertility would go on to be one of the most-reproduced findings in European publications on family policy and fertility over the next several years. In its high-profile report on new social policy challenges in 1999 (*A Caring World: The New Social Policy Agenda*), the OECD featured a pair of correlation figures showing how the relationship between labor force participation for women and completed fertility for mothers went from clearly negative for mothers born in 1930 to strongly positive for mothers born in 1960 (OECD 1999).[5] While the OECD stopped short of drawing a clear policy lesson from these data (noting that "such simple comparisons do not prove that increasing female labor force participation will inevitably increase fertility rates"), it did recognize that the data at least should increase confidence that nations should be able to increase women's labor force participation without worrying that this would cause fertility rates to drop further.

In 2001, the OECD *Employment Outlook* included a more extended analysis of the connection between women's employment and fertility. The analysis began by noting that in virtually all OECD countries, the correlation between women's work and fertility *over time* has been negative. Earlier cohorts of women worked less and had more babies than recent cohorts, suggesting that women's work was driving the trend toward lower fertility rates. Juxtaposing this finding with the cross-national correlation that showed a *positive* correlation (the *Caring World* figures), the report went on to investigate how to reconcile these two patterns. The authors of the report ultimately reconciled them in this way: many countries (like Japan, Italy, and Spain) had indeed seen women have fewer children as they entered the workforce in slightly higher numbers. But the cross-national pattern was driven by the ability of a few countries (the authors mentioned "the United States and the Nordic countries") to create environments in which there was less of a trade-off between work and family, so that women were able to both work and have children at higher rates (OECD 2001).

The personnel involved with these OECD reports, especially Willem Adema, went on to lead the OECD's well-known *Babies and Bosses* studies of work-family reconciliation policies (Mahon 2008). This set of four reports, published between 2002 and 2005, focused closely on how policies in thirteen countries eased (or did not ease) the ability of parents to reconcile work with their childrearing responsibilities at home. A synthesis published in 2007 included data on a more comprehensive set of countries and featured the project's most important findings. As Rianne Mahon, who has written about the *Babies and Bosses* project, notes, the policy lessons drawn by the OECD staff overseeing the series of country studies evolved over the course of time (Mahon 2008). The project had grown out of earlier OECD efforts to advise member countries on how to bring more women into the workforce in order to reduce women's poverty (especially of single mothers) and avoid a looming labor shortage as populations aged. As the quotes from the *Caring World* report above suggest, the OECD's earlier work touched on fertility rates only in order to assure members that more women could be brought into the workforce without pushing fertility rates lower.

As the project began investigating the relationship between women's work and fertility and looking closely at problems in specific countries, however, the project team began to present work-family reconciliation as a way of *actually increasing fertility rates*. Thus the *Babies and Bosses* synthesis report concludes that "systems which provide a continuum of support to families—support for parents at home when the child is very young, leading on to a childcare place, pre-school, school and out-of-school-hours care activities—perform best in helping parents reconcile work and family life. Such an approach stimulates birth rates as parents can realistically plan their work and family commitments" (OECD 2007).

Equally striking is the menu of policies the synthesis report recommends. As Mahon has noted in her study of the project, the OECD team initially focused mostly on the need to offer new mothers childcare leave and childcare services to ease their transition to motherhood without ending their attachment to the workforce. However, as the team investigated problems in "lowest low fertility" countries such as Japan, they concluded that more far-reaching changes of the kinds advocated for many years by feminists were needed before the opportunity costs paid by mothers could be reduced to the point that more would choose motherhood. In places where tax and benefit systems favored the male-breadwinner model, with the wife staying at home to care for the children, the report recommends changing these rules "to give both parents in couple-families equally strong incentives to work" (OECD 2007).

Equally striking were the report's recommendations on how to design childcare leave policy in order to maximize women's labor market participation and fertility. The report concludes that paid leave policies, which in some countries encouraged women to stay home with their children for three years, needed to be of "moderate length," which it defined as a period of four to six months: "If leave periods are shorter, mothers are often not ready to go back to work, while the use of longer leave periods by mothers can permanently damage their labor market position" (OECD 2007). Behind this recommendation was the correlation the authors of the study had observed between generous leave policies in places like Germany and Austria and low women's work and fertility rates in these places. But adjusting leave lengths, the report found, was not enough. Leave policies needed to be changed to draw more fathers into taking leave and thereby developing a more equitable sharing of childrearing work from the earliest stages of an infant's life. It was not enough to make fathers eligible for leave. Neither was it enough to give fathers a week or two of leave when a child was first born. The report had the most praise for Iceland, which has gone the furthest in creating "paid leave entitlements that are non-transferable between the parents" so that parents who wish to maximize their leave benefits have an incentive to split the leave evenly.

The report's remaining recommendations called on OECD member nations to make high-quality childcare, preschool, and after-school care available so that mothers and fathers would more easily be able to balance work and family commitments after the mothers' and fathers' periods of leave were over, and to supplement these programs with incentives for businesses to offer family-friendly policies (flex-time, part-time, sick leave). Interestingly, the report praised the Nordic countries for providing high-quality care to a large segment of children but deemed the Nordic model "not directly exportable to other OECD countries." Instead, it recommended the Australian and Dutch approach of providing parents with vouchers that could be redeemed for a variety of care services that might be more closely tailored to their needs (OECD 2007). Finally, the report argues that good policies in the area of childcare leave and services are not enough to help women reconcile work with their family obligations when "the workplace is not family-friendly." If holding onto a job requires long hours, offers little flexibility to parents of young children, and features a seniority-based wage system that penalizes workers who take time off to care for their children, workers will be unable to "balance work and caring activities" (OECD 2007).

While I have emphasized the surprising degree to which OECD and government analysts have embraced elements of the feminist agenda as a solution to the low fertility problems in some countries, I should emphasize that the agenda just described does *not* insist that policies force all fathers and mothers to divide housework and paid work exactly evenly at all times and live completely "gender-free" lives. The policies advocated are instead designed to offer couples *choices* so that they can raise children without paying opportunity costs. Many of the prescribed policies deliver benefits to couples where a mother with "adaptive" preferences (see Hakim in this volume) can take most of the leave benefits or exit and reenter the workforce while children are young. But the prescription calls for policies to make it easier for mothers to retain their attachment to the workforce so that those who wish to work continuously, or again later, are able to do so.

Before concluding this section on the policies that define "feminism as the new natalism," I need to touch on one more far-reaching policy that has been recommended explicitly or implicitly by some feminists as a way of increasing birth rates—but was not featured in *Babies and Bosses.* A variety of demographers have observed that fertility rates are highest in countries that have a more flexible view of marriage: where cohabitation is high, single parenthood is high and divorce rates are high. The United States and Sweden, for example, score high on all of these dimensions, while Japan, Italy, Spain, and many of the other nations with the lowest-low fertility rates have the lowest rates in the OECD on these measures. Ueno Chizuko was one of the first observers in Japan to note this pattern, observing in her 1998 article that the low fertility rate there was no doubt driven in part by the fact that "the age when Japanese couples begin living together may well be the oldest in the industrialized world." Although she admitted that the Japanese government would never consider this solution, she suggested that "encouragement of out-of-wedlock children is an option to increase the birthrate" (Ueno 1998).

By 2000, a demographer employed by the Japanese government, Miho Iwasawa, was arguing in a mass market monthly that virtually all of the differences in birth rates between Japan and the high-fertility industrialized countries were accounted for by children born and raised outside of traditional marriage. The number of children born inside marriage had declined everywhere, but in some places, such as Scandinavia and the United States, this decline was offset by a rise in births outside marriage. If Japan truly wanted to increase birth rates, she argued, it needed to create a society that welcomed these alternative family arrangements (Iwasawa 2000).

European investigations into the forces driving the fertility decline there have similarly focused on the connection between traditional family norms (and laws) and low fertility. As Sleebos wrote in an OECD working paper, "OECD countries where divorce and out-of-wedlock birth are more frequent have, at the end of the 1990s, lower fertility rates than other countries." She pointed to Sweden and the United States as examples of places where high out-of-wedlock birth rates were associated with higher fertility rates and Italy and Spain as places where the opposite pattern prevailed. These patterns, she wrote, "suggest that marriage laws that are more neutral with respect to the form of relationship may be an important condition for sustaining fertility" (Sleebos 2003).

It should be noted, however, that most of these analysts have been careful to qualify their recommendations. While arguing that higher fertility is connected to liberal attitudes toward family structure and that fertility *would probably increase* if nations with more conservative attitudes toward family structure adopted more flexible attitudes toward cohabitation, divorce, and out-of-wedlock births, most have been mum on the question of whether this increase would deliver benefits that exceed the possible costs associated with the breakdown of the traditional two-married-parent household. A wide variety of studies have found that children of divorce and children raised by single parents suffer emotionally, educationally, and economically (Amato 2005).[6] Policy-makers in nations like Japan, Spain, and Italy have therefore been much less attracted to the policy prescription implied by these observations than they have to the work-life-balance agenda that is the focus of this chapter.

Efforts to Implement the Feminism-as-New-Natalism Agenda

The previous section documents the surprising degree to which policy-makers and other opinion leaders—even in nations with entrenched male-breadwinner traditions—have embraced the view that increasing women's participation in the labor force promises to be an important means of boosting fertility rates. Despite this paradigm shift, policy-makers in the lowest-low fertility nations have had persistent difficulties in moving policy in this direction. In this final section, I focus on progress, or the lack thereof, in supportive policy initiatives in Japan, Germany, and Italy. As Table 8.1 shows, some twenty years after concerns about falling fertility rates reached the top of the agenda, and almost a decade after the OECD and top policy-makers identified "reducing opportunity costs for mothers" as an important strategy for reversing this trend, the three low fertility countries continue to be characterized by: (1) a tendency of new mothers to leave the workforce, (2) large gender gaps in pay, and (3) low rates of young children in formal care and preschool. Fertility rates, too, have not budged much from lows early in the decade. In 2008, rates were up to 1.37 in Japan, 1.38 in Germany, and 1.41 in Italy.

Table 8.1 Work-Family Reconciliation Data for High and Low Fertility Countries

Country Fertility 2000–08	Mothers of <2 in Work Force	Mothers of 3–5 Work Force	Gender Pay Gap 2006	Children 0–2 in Formal Care	Children 3–5 in Care or School	Births Outside of Marriage	Cohabitation among Those Ages >20
Italy 1.32	47.3	50.6	**	28.6	99.4	20.7	2
Germany 1.35	36.1	54.8	23	28.3	87.6	30	5.3
Japan 1.32	28.5	47.5	33	28.3	87.6	2.1	2.1
Sweden 1.74	71.9	81.3	15	45.3	85.6	54.7	**
France 1.92	53.7	63.8	12	42.9	100	50.4	14.4
USA 2.06	54.2	62.8	19	31.4	58.4	38.5	5.5

Source: Fertility data from Web Table 1: Work rate data for 2006 from OECD, *Babies and Bosses Synthesis*, 2007, p. 16; the gender pay gap is for median earnings of full-time employees; the formal care for children rates are for 2006 (2005 for US); births outside of marriage data are for 2007 (2006 for Japan); cohabitation data are for 2000; all but work rate data are from the OECD Family Database, online at http://www .oecd .org/els/social/family/database, accessed February 11, 2010.

** = No data available.

Each nation, however, has seen policy-makers adopt *some* policy changes in line with the policy recommendations made by the OECD *Babies and Bosses* project. Prior to 1990, Japan offered no childcare leave benefits beyond the eight weeks of maternity leave guaranteed to all new mothers, and childcare services for newborns were in short supply. In 1989, just 4.4 percent of newborns ages zero to 1 and just 13.2 percent of children 1–2 were in childcare, and waiting lists in suburban areas of large cities were so long that many new mothers were forced to give up work because of their inability to find a childcare spot (Zenkoku Hoiku 1990). Over the course of the 1990s, the government addressed both of these deficits to some degree. It created and expanded a childcare leave program so that new parents today are entitled to ten months of leave beyond maternity leave, at 60 percent of their pay (but note that this leave is only available to one parent, the one who is primarily responsible for childcare, and only when both parents work full-time). Meanwhile, it increased funding for childcare services in order to create more spaces for children 0–2, increasing the proportion of this age group in care to 28.3 percent in 2006. It also introduced changes in labor law, asking employers to "endeavor to take necessary measures" on behalf of workers with children under age six, such as flex-time. In addition, one of the tax breaks available to dependent spouses was removed, reducing the incentive for part-time working mothers to limit their work so as to remain under the $10,000 threshold (Schoppa 2006).[7]

Despite these changes, however, the proportion of mothers of young children in the Japanese labor force remains at just 28.5 percent. Since 90 percent of single childless women work, this means that over 60 percent of women continue to leave employment after marriage or motherhood, foreclosing the opportunity to climb career ladders in a Japanese labor market that continues to give seniority wages and other preferences to "lifetime employees" who do not interrupt their careers. This means mothers continue to pay a steep opportunity cost for the decision to marry and have children (which continue to go together in most cases).

Analysts attribute the lack of progress to a number of ways in which Japanese policies, labor market practices, and gender role norms about the division of work at home continue to fall short of the gender-equal society that is supposed to reduce opportunity costs and deliver higher fertility rates. Leave benefits, at just 40 percent of pay, discourage the primary earner—usually the husband—from taking leave, so that just 0.55 percent of new fathers took leave at the start of the 2000s. When Junichiro Koizumi took over as prime minister in 2001, he vowed to encourage more fathers to take leave. Under his "Plus One" plan, employers were encouraged to allow new fathers to take up to five "daddy days" (available regardless of their wife's employment status) and to set targets for their workers aimed at boosting the proportion of fathers taking at least five days of leave to 10 percent. Some employers did so, but as of 2008, just 1.56 percent of fathers were taking leave (Japanese Ministry of Health, Labour, and Welfare 2010). Finally, realizing that these nudges were not proving sufficient to challenge expectations on the part of employers, parents, and society that mothers will be the ones taking virtually all of the childcare leave, the new Democratic Party of Japan (DPJ) government that took over in September 2009 pushed through a policy resembling Sweden's two-month "daddy quota." Since June 2010, under the "Mom and Dad Childcare Leave Plus" program, couples have been entitled to a total of 14 months of leave, rather than just 12, if a second spouse took at least two months of leave. It remains to be seen whether this policy will succeed in boosting fathers' leave rate above 1.56 percent.

Reforms have been similarly tentative in many other areas affecting the ability of mothers in career track jobs to meet employer expectations. Until 2010, when a DPJ-initiated reform made it mandatory, employers had an obligation only to "endeavor" to offer shortened working hours for new parents. Even after the reforms, firms that refuse to be flexible or penalize mothers who claim these benefits face few sanctions. As a result, just 58 percent of women who continue working and are eligible for leave take the full leave to which they are entitled. The latest surveys on the division of housework between spouses continue to show that mothers do the bulk of the work, even when they work full-time.

A final sign of how hesitant the Japanese have been to challenge traditional gender role patterns was the decision of the new ("progressive") DPJ government to spend virtually all its budget aimed at improving the welfare of families on *child allowances*. The expenditure, coming to about 1 percent of GDP when it is fully funded and giving every child under 13 an allowance of $276 a month, is significant.[8] But this money may actually encourage more mothers to quit their jobs, by giving them the income support to do so, rather than sustaining their attachment to the workforce. If social norms were not involved, this policy—which is neutral in terms of how it affects male breadwinner and dual-income families—might be the ideal policy for boosting fertility rates. It subsidizes families where women prefer to take time off from work (Catherine Hakim's "adaptive" women), but it offers the same subsidy to families where both spouses work. It therefore supports childrearing (and encourages fertility) among all types of women. In a society where norms strongly push women, regardless of preferences, to quit their jobs after the birth of children, and the labor market makes reentry into similar work very difficult, however, this neutral subsidy likely will perpetuate the gender-segregated labor market.

To the extent that this perpetuates a structure that imposes opportunity costs on women, the DPJ's latest package of reforms continues to fall short of the *Babies and Bosses* prescription and means that Japan still has not done enough to be a test case for the argument that gender equality will significantly boost fertility rates.

The stories of policy change in Germany and Italy are similar. Influenced by the paradigm shift captured in the *Babies and Bosses* series and under pressure from the European Union to change policies in the areas of childcare leave and childcare services to improve work-family reconciliation, both nations have adopted some reforms, but they fall far short of the feminist natalism prescription. In 1996, the European Union issued a directive requiring all member states to provide at least a minimal level of parental leave, and in 2002, it followed up with a recommendation that members improve support for childcare services to the point where at least 33 percent of children under three were in formal care by 2010 (Neyer 2003).[9] While both Italy and Germany have adopted some reforms in response to these EU initiatives and national dialogues about how to improve work-family reconciliation, neither comes close (yet) to the *Babies and Bosses* ideal.

In Germany, a set of policies encouraging mothers to leave the workforce and stay home with children under three has been blamed, for some time, for perpetuating gender inequality and lowering fertility rates. Starting in 1986, the German government began providing a generous childcare leave allowance to new mothers that (in 2000) gave them a flat payment of €307 a month for twenty-four months, with an option to take another year of leave (Morgan and Zippel 2003). As Henninger et al. (2008) explain, "in combination with gendered norms, tax penalties for dual-earner couples, gender discrimination on the labor market, and a lack of childcare institutions, the benefit created incentives for mothers to stay at home and care for their children and made it difficult for them to return to the labor market afterwards." In response to criticism that this leave system pushed mothers to separate from the labor market for so long that their careers were often sidelined, the German government began considering changes designed to increase "both the labor-force participation of women and the birth rate" (Henninger et al. 2008). After studying a variety of reform proposals, the grand coalition government finally pushed through changes in 2007 that made the German parental care leave system resemble much more closely the Swedish model. The leave benefit is now available for only 14 months, and it is pegged to income at a rate of 67 percent so that it comes closer to replacing the income lost by higher-earning women and men taking time off from their careers to care for their newborns.[10] In addition, the new system requires that a second parent take two months of care leave if the couple wishes to claim the full 14 months, thereby mimicking the Nordic effort to draw fathers into splitting childcare leave with mothers.

While German reforms come close to bringing their parental leave system into line with the *Babies and Bosses* recommendations, the government has been unable to expand childcare services at a sufficient pace to meet the demand from full-time working parents. Because childcare services are the responsibility of the Länder (German regional governments) and because local governments and care services for small children are very expensive, the central government had difficulty pushing them to expand. A 2007 compromise provides for the central government to help fund expansion in exchange for the Länder's commitment to provide enough childcare spots to serve 33 percent of all children under three, but the target date for implementation was put off to 2013. At mid-decade (2004), only 10 percent of children in the western Länder were being served by childcare facilities, so it remains to be seen if this target will be reached (Henninger et al. 2008).

Finally, an examination of policy change in Italy suggests that it has seen the least change. The area where Italian reforms have been most significant is in the area of parental leave. In 1999, largely in response to the EU directive in this area, Italy created a program offering ten months of parental leave, at 30 percent of pay, in addition to the five months of maternity leave available previously. Furthermore, to encourage fathers to split this leave with mothers, it offered an extra month of leave to fathers who took at least three months of leave. Nevertheless, sizable gaps remain in Italy's work-family reconciliation policies—especially the lack of affordable childcare services for children under three and rigidities in the labor market that make it difficult for mothers (or fathers) to adjust work hours to meet family needs. Spaces for children under three in formal care centers are extremely scarce in Italy, with just 7.4 percent in this type of care (just 2 percent in the far south) at the start of the 2000s (Del Boca et al. 2004). In addition, the available care services for children under age three have been expensive: about €460 a month (Del Boca 2002). The other problem making work-family reconciliation difficult in Italy is the rigidities in the labor market that have made part-time work difficult to find and made taking time off from work unattractive because the high unemployment rate and job protections make firms reluctant to hire workers (Del Boca 2002). While these problems have been on the agenda, the Italian government has done little to address them.

Conclusion

This brief survey of efforts to implement the new natalist agenda in response to steep fertility declines in Japan, Germany, and Italy shows that none has been able to implement the full set of recommended reforms. As a result, these nations have seen limited increases in women's workforce participation and only slight increases, in the last several years, in fertility rates. This uneven record raises a number of questions about the reform agenda. First, the claim that these reforms will deliver higher fertility rates is based on the cross-national correlation between high fertility and high rates of women in the workforce in places like Sweden, France, and the United States. But we don't know exactly which of the work-family reconciliation policies in place in these nations are necessary and sufficient to bring about the promised fertility increase. Will partial reforms of the types adopted in Japan, Italy, and Germany begin to boost rates, or does it take the full set?

Second, the uneven record of reform in Japan, Germany, and Italy raises questions about whether they have the political will to implement policies that attempt to radically change gender roles, merely to boost birth rates. Feminists have played a role in criticizing current male-breadwinner-oriented policies, but they do not have the political clout in these countries to push through reforms on their own. Technocrats, informed by the OECD studies and other analyses, have joined them, but it remains to be seen whether this coalition can implement a top-down, bureaucracy-led gender role revolution in the name of long-term population growth.[11]

Finally, we know that high fertility nations such as Sweden, France, and the United States have other characteristics in common besides work-family reconciliation policies. In particular, all of them have higher rates of out-of-wedlock births and a more flexible view as to whether children need to be born only in the context of a traditional marriage. What if it turns out that higher fertility rates in these countries are largely a product of these liberal attitudes toward marriage and childbirth? Even if Japan, Italy, and Germany come to adopt the full set of pro-natalist reforms, they might still find that fertility rates stay low if they, at the same time, maintain conservative attitudes toward family.

Notes

1. See Web Table 8.1 on the book web site.
2. See Web Table 8.1 on the book web site.

3. The white paper (Ministry of Health and Welfare 1999) did not present any correlation analysis or other quantitative evidence linking declining fertility to housework patterns; but it implied the connection by devoting almost twenty pages to the topic in a volume focused on the declining fertility problem. The father's housework minutes reported here can be found on p. 83.

4. Chesnais (1996, p. 737) makes a similar point.

5. OECD (1999, p. 17). The OECD has continued to feature this pair of charts showing the "flipped" correlation between women's work rates and fertility in more recent publications, including Sleebos (2003) and OECD (1997).

6. For a review of these effects in the United States, see Amato (2005).

7. See also Peng (2002, pp. 425–426).

8. The DPJ funded half of the benefit in its first year in office but delayed funding the second half in 2010 after concerns about fiscal deficits and the party's poor performance in upper house elections caused the party to back-pedal on this commitment. Officially, the second half has only been delayed, but as of this writing it remains to be seen when, if ever, the full sum will be allocated.

9. On the EU role in shaping policy in this area, see also Mahon (2002).

10. The income replacement formula applies to income up to ¥2,700 a month, yielding a benefit of up to ¥1,800 (much higher than the flat ¥307 available previously) for one year (instead of two). But note that the benefit under the new arrangement can actually be lower for parents who did not have income prior to birth, who are given just ¥300 (Henninger et al. 2008).

11. I argue in my book *Race for the Exits* that in Japan, at least, the "exit" of women from the work-family reconciliation challenge by opting out of motherhood or work has forced the nation to rely on this (largely ineffective) top-down approach. This is a poor substitute for a gender role revolution led by mothers struggling to balance work and family and driven by their difficulties to demand change from their employers, husbands, and government.

References

Amato, Paul R. 2005. The Impact of Family Formation Change on the Cognitive, Social, and Emotional Well-Being of the Next Generation. *Future of Children* 15, no. 2 (Fall): 75–96.

Chesnais, Jean-Claude. 1996. Fertility, Family, and Social Policy in Contemporary Western Europe. *Population and Development Review* 22, no. 4 (December): 737.

Dalla Costa, Mariarosa. 1996. Capitalism and Reproduction. *Capitalism, Nature, Socialism* 7 (4): 111–121.

Del Boca, Daniela. 2002. The Effect of Child Care and Part Time Opportunities on Participation and Fertility Decisions in Italy. IZA Discussion Paper No. 427, p. 5.

Del Boca, Daniela, Marilena Lacatelli, and Daniela Vuri. 2004. Child Care Choices by Italian Households. IZA Discussion Paper No. 983, p. 5.

Gauthier, Anne Helene. 1996. *The State and the Family: A Comparative Analysis of Family Policies in Industrialized Countries.* Oxford: Clarendon Press, pp. 139–140.

Henninger, Annette, Christine Wimbauer, and Rosine Dombrowski. 2008. Demography as a Push Toward Gender Equality? Current Reforms of Germany Family Policy. *Social Politics* 15 (3): 287–314.

Iwasawa, Miho. 2000. Kekkon shinai henjintachi: Hikongata kappuru wo mitomeru shakai e. *Chuō Kōron* 115: 13.

Japanese Ministry of Health, Labour, and Welfare. 2010. Introduction to Revised Child Care and Family Care Law. http://www.mhlw.go.jp/english/policy/affairs/dl/05.pdf, p. 23. Accessed November 18, 2010.

MacDonald, Peter. 2002. Low Fertility: Unifying the Theory and the Demography. Paper prepared for Session 73, Future of Fertility in Low Fertility Countries, 2002 Meeting of the Population Association of America, Atlanta, May 9–11, 2002.

Mahon, Rianne. 2002. Child Care: Toward What Kind of "Social Europe"? *Social Politics* (Fall): 344–379.

———. 2008. Babies and Bosses: Gendering the OECD's Social Policy Discourse. In Rianne Mahon and Stephen McBride (eds.), *The OECD and Transnational Governance,* 260–275. Vancouver: UBC Press.

Ministry of Health and Welfare (Japan). 1999. Reflections on Declining Fertility: Creating a Society Where Having and Raising Children Is a "Dream." White Paper.

Morgan, Kimberly J., and Kathrin Zippel. 2003. Paid to Care: The Origins and Effects of Care Leave Policies in Western Europe. *Social Politics* 10: 49–85.

Neyer, Gerda. 2003. Family Policies and Low Fertility in Western Europe. Max Planck Institute for Demographic Research Working Paper 2003–021, p. 4.

OECD. 1999. *A Caring World: The New Social Policy Agenda.* Paris: OECD, p. 17.

———. 2001. *2001 Employment Outlook.* Paris: OECD, p. 153.

———. 2007. *Babies and Bosses: Reconciling Work and Family Life: A Synthesis of Findings for OECD Countries.* Paris: OECD, p. 18.

Office of the Prime Minister. 2000. Danjo kyoudou sankaku hakusho (Gender Equality White Paper). Tokyo: Sourifu.

Osawa, Machiko. 1998. *Atarashii kazoku no tame no keizai gaku.* Tokyo: Chuo Shinsho.

Pcng, Ito. 2002. Social Care in Crisis: Gender, Demography, and Welfare State Restructuring in Japan. *Social Politics* (Fall): 411–443.

Saraceno, Chiara. 1997. Family Change, Family Policies and the Restructuring of Welfare. In OECD (ed.) *Family, Market and Community: Equity and Efficiency in Social Policy,* 85. Paris: OECD.

Schoppa, Leonard. 2006. *Race for the Exits: The Unraveling of Japan's System of Social Protection.* Ithaca, NY: Cornell University Press.

Sleebos, Joelle. 2003. Low Fertility Rates in OECD Countries: Facts and Policy Responses. OECD Social, Employment, and Migration Working Papers, 15, p. 20.

Suzuki, Kazue. 1995. Women Rebuff the Call for More Babies. *Japan Quarterly* 42, no. 1 (January–March): 14.

Ueno, Chizuko. 1998. The Declining Birthrate: Whose Problem? *Review of Population and Social Policy* 7: 106.

Yashiro, Naohiro. 1999. *Shōshi kōreika no keizaigaku.* Tokyo: Tōyō Keizai Shinpōsha.

Zenkoku Hoiku, and Dantai Renrakukai. 1990. *Hoiku hakusho.* Tokyo: Sōdo Bunka, p. 252.

Chapter 9

What Do Women Really Want?

Designing Family Policies for All Women

Catherine Hakim

In the last three decades of the twentieth century, the focus of social policy in the European Union, and perhaps in all OECD countries, has been the elimination of the entrenched sexism and racism that pervaded all labor markets and replacing them with a new ethos of equal opportunities for all in meritocratic economies. Arguably, this battle has now been won, and debates on social policy have moved on to other issues: immigration and the social problems it creates, declining fertility across affluent modern societies, and aging societies. But whatever the current concern, full-time homemakers and mothers tend to be left out of the picture by policy-makers and academics alike. Homebodies are not an exciting group; they do not provide dramatic news stories on battles won, mountains climbed, dangers overcome, successful managerial strategies. Children are dealt with exclusively by childcare policies for working mothers, with the family role ignored.

One notable feature of current research in demography and the sociology of the family is the absence of any central guiding theory on the relative importance of childbearing in women's (and men's) lives. Family policy debates are constrained by the fear of promoting "traditional" or "conservative" pro-natalist policies, in case this is linked to eugenics and Nazi Germany policies, which cast a long shadow in Europe. Hence Sweden invariably insists that it has never had pro-natalist policies, only "gender equality" policies that help women to have larger families early in life.

This chapter presents preference theory and research results showing that preference theory offers a realistic framework for analyzing women's lifestyle choices and values in modern societies. It shows that fertility tends to be highest among family-centered women and lowest among the careerist women who are currently the focus of public policy, and that full-time employment is highest among careerist women and lowest among family-centered women. Preference theory helps to identify policies that can reliably be expected to raise fertility in modern societies, most notably the homecare allowance first developed in Scandinavian countries but still relatively unknown elsewhere, despite its huge popularity wherever it is introduced. We examine Swedish policies and show why their achievements are illusory rather than real, with costs that are far higher than most polities can realistically consider.

Preference Theory

Preference theory provides a new theoretical basis for analyses of women's choices between paid work and family work in modern societies and for the development of social policy and family policy as they affect women in the twenty-first century. It is especially helpful for identifying the policy levers that will be effective with particular groups of women.

Preference theory is a historically informed, empirically based, multidisciplinary and predictive theory about women's choices between market work and family work in rich modern societies (Hakim 2000, 2003a, 2003b). It argues that a series of social and economic changes (Text Box 9.1) produce a new polarization between three groups of women making distinctive life choices (Table 9.1). Work-centered or careerist women give priority to their jobs, often remain childless even if married, and endorse the competitive, achievement-oriented values of the marketplace. Home-centered or family-centered women prefer not to work after marriage and childbearing, often have many children, and espouse caring and sharing family values. Adaptive women seek a balance between employment and family work over the life cycle as a whole; they tend to be torn between the two competing value systems of the marketplace and family life. Female heterogeneity emerges clearly only from the 1970s onwards, after the contraceptive and equal opportunities revolutions are fully implemented in a society, and is reflected in three sharply differentiated lifestyle choices[1] that are identified by longitudinal studies as well as in cross-sectional data.

Preference theory has already been operationalized and tested in national surveys in four contrasting European countries: Britain and Spain (Hakim 2003a, 2003c), the Czech Republic (Rabusic and Manea 2009), and Belgium (Corijn and Hakim 2009). In all countries, three lifestyle preference groups were identified, as expected, with very similar national distributions, close to those posited by Hakim and shown in Table 9.1. Lifestyle preference groups were also identified among men, on a more rough and ready basis in Britain and Spain (Table 9.2). The key finding was that, in modern societies where all five social and economic changes are completed, such as Britain, Belgium, and the US, lifestyle preferences can predict women's employment and fertility more strongly than the "social structural" variables usually underlined as most important, notably educational qualifications (Table 9.3).

In Belgium, lifestyle preferences strongly predict fertility among women, but do not differentiate between careerist and adaptive men, perhaps because their wives' preferences overrode the husbands' views. Lifestyle preferences also strongly predict Belgian women's decisions to have paid jobs, or not, but again have no impact on men's employment patterns. Whatever their preferences, men are obliged to stay in full-time employment, and most wives prefer things this way (Corijn and Hakim 2009).

In the Czech Republic, the typology differentiates women's sex-role attitudes and lifestyle values. However, there is only a weak correlation with fertility levels, largely because the Czech Republic has only recently made the transition from a socialist regime to a liberal democracy, and the norm of the two-child family is still observed by everyone, with little diversity in fertility patterns, in contrast with Britain and Belgium (Rabusic and Manea 2009).

A rather chaotic and disorganized research report by Hattery (2001) also identified the three lifestyle preference groups among mothers of new babies in the US. The mothers were all well educated and financially secure. What differentiated them were their ideologies: family-centered "conformists," work-centered "nonconformists," and the middle group of "innovators" trying

Box 9.1 The Four Central Tenets of Preference Theory

1. Five separate historical changes in society and in the labor market that started in the late twentieth century are producing a qualitatively different and new scenario of options and opportunities for women. The five changes do not necessarily occur in all modern societies and do not always occur together. Their effects are cumulative. The five causes of a new scenario are

- the contraceptive revolution, which, from about 1965 onward, gave sexually active women reliable control over their own fertility for the first time in history;
- the equal opportunities revolution, which ensured that for the first time in history women had equal access to all positions, occupations, and careers in the labor market; in some countries, legislation prohibiting sex discrimination went further, mandating equal access to housing, financial services, public services, and public posts;
- the expansion of white-collar occupations, which are far more attractive to women than most blue-collar occupations;
- the creation of jobs for secondary earners, people who do not want to give priority to paid work at the expense of other life interests; and
- the increasing importance of attitudes, values, and personal preferences in the lifestyle choices of affluent modern societies.

2. Women are heterogeneous in their preferences and priorities regarding family and employment. In the new scenario they are therefore heterogeneous also in their employment patterns and work histories. These preferences are set out, as ideal types, in Table 9.1. The size of the three groups varies in rich modern societies because public policies usually favor one or another group.

3. The heterogeneity of women's preferences and priorities creates conflicting interests between groups of women: sometimes between home-centered women and work-centered women, sometimes between the middle group of adaptive women and women who have one firm priority (whether for family work or employment). The conflicting interests of women have given a great advantage to men, whose interests are comparatively homogeneous; this is one cause of patriarchy and its disproportionate success.

4. Women's heterogeneity is the main cause of women's variable responses to social engineering policies in the new scenario of modern societies. This variability of response has been less evident in the past, but it has still impeded attempts to predict women's fertility and employment patterns. Policy research and future predictions of women's choices will be more successful in future if they adopt the preference theory perspective and first establish the distribution of preferences between family work and employment in each society.

Adapted from Hakim (2000).

Table 9.1 Classification of Women's Work-Lifestyle Preferences in the Twenty-First Century

Home-Centered 20% of women (varies 10–30%)	Adaptive 60% of women (varies 40–80%)	Work-Centered 20% of women (varies 10–30%)
Family life and children are the main priorities.	This group is most diverse and includes women who want to combine work and family, plus drifters and unplanned careers.	Childless women are concentrated here. The main priority in life is employment or equivalent activities in the public arena such as politics, sports, art, etc.
Prefer not to work.	Want to work, but not totally committed to work career.	Committed to work or equivalent activities.
Qualifications obtained as cultural capital.	Qualifications obtained with the intention of working.	Large investment in qualifications, training, employment, and other activities.
Number of children is affected by government social policy, family wealth, etc. Not responsive to employment policy.	Very responsive to government social policy, employment policy and propaganda, economic cycles such as recession or growth; responsive to income tax and social welfare benefits, educational policies, school timetables, childcare services, public attitudes toward working women, legislation promoting female employment, trade union attitudes toward working women, availability of part-time work and similar work flexibility, economic growth and prosperity, and institutional factors generally.	Responsive to economic opportunity, political opportunity, artistic opportunity. Not responsive to social and family policies.
Family values: caring, sharing, non-competitive, orientation, communal, focus on cohesion.	Combination values: conflicting set of values.	Marketplace values: competitive rivalry, achievement, individualism, excellence.

Adapted from: Hakim (2000).

181

Table 9.2 National Distributions of Lifestyle Preferences among Women and Men

	Family Centered	Adaptive	Work Centered
Britain			
All women ages 16+	17	69	14
Women in full-time work	14	62	24
Women in part-time work	8	84	8
All men ages 16+	?	<48	52
Men in full-time work	?	<50	50
Men in part-time work	?	<66	34
Spain			
All women ages 18+	17	70	13
Women in full-time work	4	63	33
Women in part-time work	7	79	14
All men ages 18+	?	<60	40
Men in full-time work	?	<56	44
Belgium-Flanders			
All women	10	75	15
Women with partners	12	75	13
All men	2	23	75
Men with partners	1	22	77
Germany			
Women	14	65	21
Men	?	33	67
Czech Republic			
All women ages 20–40	17	70	13
Women in employment	14	69	17
Wives ages 20–40	14	75	11
Switzerland			
Mothers with at least one child at home	57	30	13
Sweden			
Women in 1955 birth cohort: actual lifestyle choices by age 43 (1998)	4	64	32
Japan			
Ideal lifecourse of unmarried women			
1987	37	55	8
2002	21	69	10
2005	20	70	10

Source: Data for Britain and Spain, 1999, extracted from Tables 3.14 and 3.15 in Hakim (2003a: 85, 87). Data for Belgium-Flanders extracted from Corijn and Hakim (2009) based on a 2002/2003 survey. Data for Germany extracted from Bertram et al. (2005). Data for Czech Republic from Rabusic and Manea (2009) based on a November 2005 survey. Data for Sweden extracted from Huang et al. (2007) reporting analysis of a longitudinal data set. Data for Switzerland from Stahli et al. (2009) based on a 1998/1999 survey of couples. Data for Japan from National Institute of Population and Social Security regular surveys of Views of the Unmarried about Marriage and Family in Japan provided by professor Akihide Inaba, Tokyo Metropolitan University.

Table 9.3 The Relative Importance of Lifestyle Preferences and Education

(A) Full-time employment rates

Lifestyle Preferences	% Working Full Time		Distribution	
	Highly Qualified	Other Women	Highly Qualified	Other Women
Home centered	28.00*	34.00	11.00	14.00
Adaptive	48.00	26.00	71.00	78.00
Work centered	93.00	65.00	18.00	8.00
All wives 20–54	54.00	30.00	100.00	100.00
Base = 100%	119.00	589.00	119.00	589.00

(B) Fertility

Lifestyle Preferences	Average Number of Children at Home <16 Years of Age			Percent with No Children at Home		
	Highly Qualified	Other Women	All Women	Highly Qualified	Other Women	All Women
Home centered	2.00*	1.18	1.29	8.00*	42.00	37.00
Adaptive	1.00	1.09	1.08	39.00	42.00	42.00
Work centered	.71	.62	.65	68.00	64.00	65.00
All wives 20–54	1.08	1.08	1.08	41.00	44.00	44.00
Base = 100%	119.00	708.00	708.00	119.00	589.00	589.00

*Indicates base numbers too small for result to be reliable.

Notes: Married women ages 20–54 who have completed their full-time education. In the absence of information on educational qualifications, the highly qualified are defined as those completing their full-time education at age 21 and later, because in Britain first degrees are normally completed by age 21. People completing full-time education at age 20 or earlier are assumed to have qualifications below tertiary education level.

Source: Hakim (2003b).

to combine motherhood and family work with paid jobs. The last group was most susceptible to influences on them, as predicted by preference theory. Hattery explains her differentiated results by the motherhood ideology without being able to explain why some women accept and others reject this ideology in the US.

Broadly similar results for the US are reported by Dau-Schmidt et al. (2007) from a study of graduates of Michigan Law School. Although the men and women were equally well qualified, they made very different career and family choices, so that their employment patterns and earnings diverged increasingly with time in the workforce. The study identified three distinct groups, with different value systems, personalities, and career trajectories:

> People with no children (28 percent of women and 19 percent of men)
> People with children, but who did little childcare themselves (32 percent of women and 78 percent of men [whose wives did the childcare])
> People with children doing childcare themselves (3 percent of men and 40 percent of women)

The last group had the highest career satisfaction and were happiest with their work-life balance.

A study based on the 2000 Survey of Marriage and Family Life found that only one-fifth of married mothers ideally prefers to remain in full-time employment. About half prefer to work part-time only, and a full one-third prefer not to do paid work while they raise children. Interestingly, husbands' perceptions of wives' preferences are tilted even more strongly towards full-time motherhood (Wilcox 2012, in this volume). This study also shows that enthusiasm for segregated family roles, with one spouse in full-time work and one responsible for home and family, plateaued in the US from the 1980s onwards, at about 40 percent of all couples, a very high level compared with European countries (Hakim 2003a). The social costs of symmetrical family roles became more obvious over time, and the crusading spirit of the 1970s faded away.

A recent study in Britain analyzed how attitudes to family roles and values changed and developed over the twenty-two years between 1986 and 2008 (Dench 2010). It confirms the polarization of attitudes and values between childless women (many of whom are focused on their careers) and mothers, especially mothers of young children who supported the "traditional" (in fact, modern) division of labor in the family. More important, it reveals a remarkable intergenerational change of perspective on motherhood. Young women under 30–35 years of age increasingly reject the idea of lifelong employment in favor of full-time motherhood and a homemaker career, either temporarily or permanently, in sharp contrast to their mothers' generation (women ages 50 and older) who underline employment careers as liberating. The idea that gender equality requires a lifelong commitment to wage labor and an independent income is rejected by around half of young women, who dislike the "double shift" this creates.

Surveys carried out in Germany, Switzerland, Sweden, and Japan have yielded classifications of lifestyle preferences, or actual life choices, that fit the preference theory typology (Table 9.2). However, we would not necessarily expect preferences to predict behavior unless the five socioeconomic changes set out in Text Box 9.1 are achieved in a country, which is not the case in the majority of European countries, let alone globally.

Preference theory deals only with social processes in modern societies, after the contraceptive and equal opportunities revolutions, and is forward-looking rather than retrospective in orientation. It is predictive, combines historical and psychosocial explanations, and incorporates micro-level qualitative research on how women choose between employment and family work as well as longitudinal study findings. It provides a framework for understanding how social policies, family policy, and employment policies work, in terms of their success and failure within particular groups of women (Hakim 2000, pp. 223–253).

Even in the new scenario of modern societies, we do not expect convergence in women's employment and fertility rates. Even the most liberal society and laissez faire polity still has social and economic institutions, laws, customs, national policies, and cultures that shape and structure behavior. Choices are not made in a vacuum. Social and economic factors still matter and will produce national variations in employment patterns and lifestyle choices, as illustrated by the contrasts between countries in Table 9.2. In addition, the choices people make are molded by an unpredictable constellation of events: economic recessions and booms, wars, changes of government, as well as events in private lives, individual ability, accidents or ill health, and marital unhappiness or happiness. There is also an element of path-dependence in all careers. So there will still be variation among women with the same lifestyle preference due to contextual factors and individual life events. However, the three groups differ in their responses to all these experiences.

For example, Japan has seen rapid changes in attitudes and values concerning gender roles and family roles in response to social and economic change that has transformed a predominantly agricultural economy (in which most women worked in the family farm or business) into a modern industrial economy in a very short period, with greater separation of personal and professional lives (Suzuki 2007). On the one hand, the full-time homemaker wife is a recent innovation in Japan and an indicator of prosperity. At the same time, the careerist wife and the child-free lifestyle are also modern innovations, prompted in part by economic recession and equal opportunities policies. Societal norms for women place Japan close to South Korea,[2] but almost all women accept that paid work will feature in their lives, given lower fertility levels. Data on personal ideals and expected life patterns suggest that, overall, Japanese women are able to live the life of their choice, although policies to facilitate work-life balance would reduce the conflict between changing values and rigid employment structures, notably low labor mobility and the lack of genuinely part-time jobs.[3,4] Even here, family-centered women are unable to achieve their goals.

The contraceptive revolution marks a qualitative change in women's perspective on childbearing. We can thus expect an immediate decline in fertility wherever modern contraception is introduced, even in developing countries, where nearly all (93 percent) of contraception involves modern methods.[5] After the contraceptive revolution, it is women's values and lifestyle preferences that become the driving factor in fertility decisions, with the social and economic context facilitating or impeding the realization of women's preferences. On the evidence for at least two countries (Spain and the US), women's lifestyle preferences are not closely linked to, or shaped by, political and religious values (Hakim 2003a, pp. 189–208). The correlation is weak in the US.[6] Similarly, the three lifestyle preference groups cut across education levels, social class, and income levels, so none of these variables can be used as a proxy indicator for lifestyle preferences (Hakim 2000, 2003a, p. 206).

Why do women display diversity in their lifestyle preferences, certainly more diversity than occurs among men? Social psychologists have so far been unable to explain this variation, which occurs among women raised in the same family and in the same country, so it cannot be explained simply by family socialization or the type of welfare state (Hakim 2000, pp. 185–189). Cultural factors are important, as demonstrated by sharp differences in work orientation, sex-role ideology, and ideal models of the family between ethnic and cultural groups in Britain. These ideologies shape women's employment patterns and careers (if any) very strongly, so that black British women have the highest employment rates, while women with origins in the Indian subcontinent have the lowest employment rates, especially Muslims (Hakim 2003a, pp. 143–147). However, none of these distinctive cultural groups is able to create homogeneous attitudes and values, not even the white community. On the contrary, in all ethnic minority groups, just like the white majority, we find work-centered, family-centered, and adaptive women. Proportions in each group vary, but all three groups are present in every community.

It appears that there is no single dominant factor that determines women's lifestyle preferences. There will always be a complex mix of several factors—including some accidental influences (Hakim 2000, p. 185). Another perspective is that heterogeneity and diversity are normal.[7] Humans are exceptionally diverse. We should be suspicious of countries where there is little or no diversity, as it implies either no freedom of choice or a strong cultural pressure regarding a single correct lifestyle, as in Sweden.[8] The whole point of modern liberal societies is that they allow people to choose how to live, and invisibly small incidents and personal predilections may tip the balance in one direction or another. For most women, childbirth and childrearing offer real alternatives to being a wage worker in the marketplace. Path dependence then magnifies small diverging choices into distinctive lifestyles and careers. Looking at it this way, it is men's uniform dedication to careers and achievement in the public sphere that needs to be explained.

We should now focus on women's values, life goals, and priorities as well as the social and economic context. We need data on women's *personal* preferences as regards employment and fertility, as well as data on their partner's preferences. This is not the same as collecting data on societal norms regarding fertility, gender roles, and women's employment. These societal norms differ between countries, but display relatively little variation within countries (Philipov 2005), whereas personal preferences vary a great deal. For example, most people regard the two-child family as the ideal family size, even when they themselves prefer to have no children at all or a large family of four or more. Most people will agree that smoking is harmful, yet many still choose to smoke themselves. People can be aware of societal norms and confirm them but still reject them in their own lives; it is only personal preferences that predict respondents' behavior (Hakim 2003b, 2004b).

The preference theory perspective suggests that social and family policy should be neutral among the three groups of women, instead of focusing on one group to the exclusion of all others, as tends to be the practice currently across Europe. In the past, the bias toward careerist or family-centered women was determined by whichever party was in power. Currently the European Commission focuses on working women almost exclusively because its legal policy remit does not extend much beyond the labor market and the free movement of labor within the European Union. This has encouraged a bias toward policies for working women across Europe, to the exclusion of those who choose to become full-time mothers. Given this bias, there is an opportunity to add policies to support family-centered women as well as working women. For example, a homecare allowance for full-time mothers would balance working women's right to paid maternity/parental leave for up to three years after the birth—in Sweden and Finland, for example.

The Swedish Illusion

Among feminist academics in Europe and North America, the Swedish model is regularly held up as the ideal social and family policy.[9] Sweden has vigorously promoted itself as a social utopia, with family-friendly policies that deliver gender equality as well as high female employment rates and high fertility. The European Commission endorses this policy perspective, claiming that gender equality solves all social problems and quite a few business problems as well.

There are two problems with this diagnosis and policy prescription. First, Sweden (like all the Scandinavian countries) is a tiny country with a strongly homogeneous society in terms of religion, race, ethnicity, language, culture, and politics—a homogeneity that has produced an extremely conformist and authoritarian society (Brown 2010, pp. 19–20). With a population of only 9 million and a workforce of 4.5 million, Sweden is by far the largest Nordic country,[10] yet it contributes only 2 percent of the European Union population and workforce. Social experiments that may work in tiny, socially homogeneous and well-integrated communities may not work as well, or even at all, in large societies that are socially, ethnically, and culturally heterogeneous, such as the United States, with a population of over 300 million, or even the EU as a whole with a diverse population of 500 million. The distinctive characteristics of Scandinavian societies are routinely ignored by policy analysts.

More important, recent research has shown that Sweden never did deliver gender equality, that high female employment rates are illusory, and that other European societies deliver high fertility and/or high employment rates without the massive social engineering and social pressure to conform that restricts individual liberty and choice of lifestyle in Sweden (Hakim 2000, pp. 236–243, 2004a, 2011).

Swedish social scientists are slowly drawing back the veil of propaganda to reveal the unadorned reality. Swedish employment rates are inflated by including all the women who are at home caring full-time for their young children because they have the right to return to their jobs eventually (Jonung and Persson 1993). Among women of working age, the official labor force participation rate of 85 percent (in 1988) is revealed to be completely misleading. In reality, only 64 percent of Swedish women are genuinely at work; the other 21 percent of "working" women are at home full-time caring for their children (and this rises to 31 percent of women with children under seven years of age). A similar pattern of misleadingly high employment rates is found across the Nordic countries. Studies that focus on average actual hours of paid work and (unpaid) household work hours show that Sweden and the United States are identical on these two measures, along with France (Jonung and Persson 1993).

The sexual segregation of occupations and industries is higher in Sweden (and the Scandinavian countries generally) than in any other advanced industrial society. Indeed occupational segregation is high enough to put Sweden on a level with poor developing countries and Muslim countries of the Middle East (Hakim 2004a, pp. 170–175). The pay gap in Sweden has not been eliminated, contrary to official reports. At around 15 percent, the pay gap is no lower than elsewhere in Europe (Hakim 2004a, pp. 171–173). Swedish wives with jobs are just as financially dependent on their husbands as wives elsewhere in Europe, the only difference being that the fiscal system forces all wives into paid jobs, so that dual-earner couples are more common (Hakim 2004a, p. 73). Finally, it is now generally recognized that generous family-friendly policies have not delivered higher achievements for working women in Sweden. On the contrary, they have created a glass ceiling that did not previously exist and have led to systematic (even if covert) discrimination against women in the labor force (Albrecht et al. 2003; Hakim 2004a, 2006, 2008, 2011). Study after study has shown that women are more likely to achieve the highest grade professional and managerial positions in the liberal economies of the United States and Britain than under the socialist policies of Sweden (Hakim 2006, 2008; Thörnqvist 2006; Henrekson and Stenkula 2009). It is hard to see why the Swedish illusion continues to persuade so many feminist scholars. Perhaps the grass always looks greener on the other side of the fence. Perhaps women always want to believe that an easy solution to the conflict between career and family is lying out there, somewhere.

One disadvantage of the Swedish illusion is that it prevents social scientists from focusing on other policy tools that could make a genuine difference. For example, virtually all European countries have school timetables that in one way or another are not family-friendly. Yet it is within the power of governments to change school policy and timetables. In Germany, for example, schools send all children home at mid-day, to eat lunch at home and do schoolwork at home in the afternoon under parental supervision. Mothers are effectively trapped at home long after their children reach school age—thus negating the potentially positive effects of generous parental leave schemes on German fertility rates.

In the US, the fact that employer health benefits are normally offered only to full-time workers has pushed many women into full-time jobs who might otherwise prefer to work part-time. In Europe, universal access to free health care has allowed women to choose freely between part-time and full-time jobs, so that part-time work is twice as common as in the US.

No single policy has an effect independently of related social policies, which may work together (as in Sweden) or cancel each other out (as in Germany). Integrated social and family policy is necessary in order to garner large benefits. Policies must also work "with the grain" rather than against the grain—by taking account of lifestyle preferences. It is this factor that probably explains the exceptional success of the homecare allowance.

The Homecare Allowance

The homecare allowance is a very successful but little-known policy applied in some European countries. It was never designed to raise fertility levels or to prevent them falling yet further. Yet it appears to have had this effect. It is normally introduced to give greater fairness between mothers using and not using state-subsidized childcare services. It is often seen as eliminating a bias against immigrant women with conservative values who prefer to raise their children themselves, at home.

Introduced in 1985 in Finland and extended in 1990, the homecare allowance was a tremendous success in a country where public childcare services were never lacking and where most women have full-time jobs. The success of the scheme in Finland led to a very similar scheme (called Cash for Care) being introduced in August 1998 in Norway, then expanded in January 1999, again very successfully. French family policy has also moved in the same direction with the APE (Allocation Parentale d'Education), with similar high take-up rates. In Britain, the Policy Exchange think tank recommended the introduction of a version of the French scheme. The success of the homecare allowance shows that, for the majority of women, being paid to look after your own children is preferable to accessing childcare in a public nursery, a benefit in kind that is not subject to parental control and is less flexible (Ilmakunnas 1997; Hakim 2000, pp. 232–235, 2010; Ronsen 2001; Ellingsæter 2003; Schone 2004; Ellingsæter and Gulbrandsen 2007; Hakim et al. 2008; Aassve and Lappegard 2009; Lappegard 2010; Sipila et al. 2010). However, the entire focus of European Commission policy is on getting all small children into collective (institutional) childcare so that mothers can return immediately to employment to meet the fixed targets set down in a Lisbon agreement (Penn 2009; Plantenga and Remery 2009).

The homecare allowance pays a salary to any parent (typically the mother) who does not use public nurseries and makes their own childcare arrangements. The money becomes a salary for stay-at-home mothers who do the job themselves. Alternatively, it can be used flexibly to pay for informal childcare (by grandparents, trusted neighbors, or friends) or to subsidize private childcare costs. In Finland, the salary is equivalent to around 40 percent of average female wages, and it increases with the number of children. It is popular with local municipalities because it is around half the cost of providing a place in a public nursery. In Finland, only 26 percent of babies ages two and younger are in state nurseries, compared to 70 percent in Denmark where there is no homecare allowance. The allowance is now offered to carers of all children under seven years, and by age five one-quarter of Finnish children have never attended day care (Sipila et al. 2010, pp. 51–52, 146). In Norway, the salary is around 450 Euros per month, roughly equivalent to the state subsidy per child in public daycare centers. The schemes differ among Finland, Norway, and France, and have changed and developed over time. The allowance is usually paid up to the youngest child's third birthday, is not dependent on the parent's employment record (so is truly universal), and can be linked to job-protected parental leave. The popularity of the policy is reflected in take-up rates of 80 to almost 100 percent. Around 10 percent of users are fathers (Sipila et al. 2010).

In Finland and France, popularity of the schemes led to a small decline in employment among mothers of young children. Norway has seen no material change in female employment levels, but users of the policy accelerate childbearing significantly. In Norway and Finland, the policy is raising the proportion of mothers who have a third child, thus raising fertility rates overall, even above the level in high-fertility Sweden (Hoem 2005). It seems fairly clear that the long-term effect of these programs is to raise fertility among the family-centred group, which has the highest take-up rates and the highest potential fertility. In the short term, it allows couples to achieve their desired fertility, in part by accelerating childbearing into an earlier and shorter period.[11]

Sweden classified the homecare allowance for full-time parenting as a right-wing policy associated with conservative political parties, and it was rejected by the mainstream social democratic party and feminists (Hoem 2005). However, a version of the policy was introduced in Sweden in July 2008. By 2010, only one-third of municipalities had introduced it, so the majority of Swedes do not have access to it. It pays full-time parents (typically the mother) 3,000 Kronas monthly from the child's first birthday to age three if they do not use the public childcare services. It cannot be held with any other benefit, so it is mainly used for first children, whereas in other countries it is most heavily used for second and subsequent children. Initial results suggest 60 percent take-up rates among foreign-born communities but lower usage among native Swedes. Official statistics on the impact of the program were not expected to be available until late 2010, but were still not published by 2012. The Swedish coalition government remains focused on employment as the first priority for all adults, including parents.

Germany introduced a new parental allowance in January 2007 that also has the effect of stabilizing or raising fertility rates in West and East Germany and raising mothers' return to employment (European Commission 2009). Like the homecare allowance, it is paid to parents of newborns to enable them to stay at home caring for the child for a full year, whether or not they were employed before the birth and without excluding high earners. The allowance pays between 300 and 1,800 Euros a month, and between 67 and 100 percent replacement of earnings for twelve or fourteen months. It does not prohibit part-time work.

A recent Belgian study (Corijn and Hakim 2009) identified the homecare allowance as the only policy that would help Belgians to achieve their desired family size. Apart from straightforward financial support for additional children, no other family policy (of the many proposed in the survey) attracted substantial public support, including all the family-friendly employment policies currently championed by the European Commission that are modeled on Swedish policies. These results are all the more surprising because Belgium is a country with high female employment rates, high levels of full-time female employment, and one of the lowest pay gaps between men and women in Europe—in short, a country that displays equal or greater gender equality than Sweden. Yet even here, the homecare allowance was welcomed as a necessary policy to support parents.

Searching for Policy Levers to Raise Fertility

Demographers and social policy specialists have always been reluctant to claim that family policy can reverse a declining fertility trend. As McDonald (2005) points out, this was partly because demographers have never been certain of any of their forecasts; they were never sure they understood the underlying processes and relied on the "tempo effects" thesis to assume fertility decline was only a temporary dip, rather than a long-term slide. Indeed, Sobotka's

(2004) detailed analysis of the postponement thesis concludes that current low fertility rates are temporary and will rise again in Europe over the next decade or so. In addition, pro-natalist policies are regarded as expensive and politically sensitive due to their historical link with fascism and eugenics (McIntosh 1983). Many European countries rely on controlled immigration to make good any deficits in labor supply—notably Britain, Germany, France, Italy, and Spain. Small homogeneous countries, such as Sweden, opted for pro-natalist policies early on, from fear of being swamped by alien cultures if immigration was actively encouraged; but it always presented them as gender equality policies (McIntosh 1983; Hoem 2005; Thörnqvist 2006, p. 318). The positive view of immigration as the easy solution was buttressed by the fact that the US, along with Australia, Canada, and other countries in the Americas, were built entirely on active immigration policies.

However, many believe that fertility has reached such low levels, and is so widespread a problem in Europe, that immigration alone cannot solve the problem (Grant et al. 2004, p. 135). Some argue that the claimed benefits of higher immigration are not proven (Coleman and Rowthorn 2004).[12] There are signs that the tide has turned, with a new perspective on family policy, pro-natalism, and cross-national migration emerging in the twenty-first century.

Paradoxically, the change of perspective is most obvious within economics. Throughout the twentieth century, economics focused almost exclusively on market work and largely ignored women's employment until the equal opportunities revolution made sex and race discrimination standard topics in labor economics. But there is now a new determination in OECD countries to measure household work and other unpaid work within national statistics and national accounts, despite the technical difficulties. European statistical offices are committed to publishing satellite accounts on the household economy, prompting innovative research based on the new time budget survey data that have to be collected (Hakim 2004a, pp. 27, 56–57). Reproductive and other household work becomes more visible and gains importance from public valuations stating that it adds anywhere from 50 percent to 100 percent to GDP.

The change in perspective is illustrated in a comprehensive economic literature review on women's work in OECD countries (Boeri et al. 2005). Instead of the customary focus on market work alone, this review gives equal attention to women's reproductive work and to the (negative) impact of rising female employment on fertility, on children's development and welfare, and on household income distribution. It points out the need for structural changes in the labor market to resolve the conflict between full-time employment and childrearing work, notably opening up part-time work options on a large scale. Similarly, a recent economic research synthesis on the family notes that the emphasis on child quality rather than on quantity shifts attention to the mother's time investment in childrearing (Ermisch 2003). Today, economists no longer ignore reproductive and other unpaid work and are willing to discuss its contribution to the economy.

Policy-makers are also looking at the costs of pro-natalist family policy in a new light. In the first decade of the twenty-first century, the European Commission began to be openly concerned about declining fertility and the economic consequences of an aging population, an aging workforce, and little or no population growth. Europe no longer has a "demographic motor," has lost its "demographic engine," it worried. Comparisons are drawn with the US, "where fertility is now 40 percent higher than Europe." However the invariable response from the Commission is to reiterate gender equality policies, demanding rising female employment, family-friendly employment arrangements, and more public childcare (European Commission 2003, 2005a, 2005b), solutions that actually aggravate the problem of declining fertility (Dey 2006) instead of solving it.

The European Commission commissioned a Rand study of the causes and economic consequences of declining fertility and the policy options for solving it (Grant et al. 2004). This report recognizes that adequate fertility rates are a crucial contribution to economic growth and avoiding a decline in human capital (Grant et al. 2004, p. 135). The review admits the difficulty of demonstrating conclusively that particular policies have visible effects on fertility rates and concludes that it is impossible to show the impact of any individual policy, because the wider pro-natalist culture can be crucial to the effectiveness of programs (Grant et al. 2004, pp. 96, 131). However, the study concludes that policies aimed at increasing or sustaining fertility rates can have an impact, sometimes a strong impact. France's long-term pro-natalist family policies have maintained relatively high fertility rates.[13] In Spain, fertility rates collapsed under democracy, after Franco's pro-natalist policies were withdrawn. Fertility rates collapsed in East Germany after reunification, and in Poland after the transition to capitalism, when economic uncertainty made forward planning more risky. The study also recognizes that policies to raise female employment can exacerbate the problem of low fertility and population aging in the longer term (Grant et al. 2004, p. 140). The report concluded that no single policy can be recommended as universally effective and that policies can only be effective if substantial funding is invested in family policy. Weak policy effects are typically due to the low (and declining) economic value of family allowances and tax benefits, for example. Population policy can be expensive, but then so are other social policies that are now taken for granted, such as income support for the unemployed, the disabled, the sick, and the retired.

Research now distinguishes between benefits in kind and programs that put money in people's pockets. The former are unattractive to parents while the latter obtain strong support. This is shown by Gauthier and Hatzius's (1997; see also Gauthier 1996a, 1996b, 2007) conclusions from a study of twenty-two modern countries over the twenty-year period from 1970 to 1990. Family-friendly (or, more realistically, work-friendly) programs such as maternity leave have no impact on fertility. In contrast, family allowances do raise fertility, but the cash benefits need to be substantial rather than nominal in order to show a worthwhile impact. Another cross-national comparative study reiterated the difficulty of measuring child costs, but nevertheless concluded that institutionally driven child costs affect fertility patterns in modern societies (Diprete et al. 2003).

The Rand report for the European Commission is unusual in recognizing that there are many ways of achieving the same goal, and that there is no universal solution to the problem of fertility decline. Preference theory explains why it is that many different policies can all have an impact and why it is so difficult to identify the impact of any single policy. Each policy favors one or more subgroup of women, and its effect depends in part on the relative size of the three groups and how well policies are targeted. Most are poorly targeted, because they focus on the typical or average woman and family, which do not in fact exist. Thus, the wide availability of part-time jobs, including jobs with very short hours and flex-time, in the Netherlands and Britain can be just as effective as strong fiscal support for families in the US and France (Castles 2003; Bernardi 2005).[14]

The Rand report underlines one key reason why population policies rarely attract government support: such policies only bear fruit in the medium or long term, while politicians who need to be reelected every four to five years generally focus on short-term policies. One politician who is not afraid of taking the broader, long-term perspective is Frank Field, a Labour Member of Parliament in Britain. He has proposed a motherhood endowment of £24,000 (36,000 Euros) for each child born, as an illustration of a serious investment in pro-natalist policies (Field 2004). In Singapore and Quebec, baby bonus programs have raised fertility (Bernardi 2005). One objection to such policies is the idea that they encourage the "wrong sort of people" to have more children. Work-life balance policies are more attractive because they seem to encourage fertility among the "right sort of people"—meaning those in employment. So eugenics informs current policy perspectives, however invisibly. Given that so-called family-friendly policies are in reality work-friendly policies, it is not surprising that they have little or no impact on fertility. Around half of careerist women remain childless (Hakim 2003c), so they are fairly impervious to such policies.

Most theories explaining changing patterns of fertility are macro-level theories that address broad changes in societies, not micro-level theories that address individual-level decision-making.[15] Preference theory works at both levels and also helps to identify appropriate policy options. The IPPAS survey in Belgium (Flanders) shows that preference theory helps to differentiate the beneficiaries of policies (Corijn and Hakim 2009). More important, it helps to identify policies with the greatest potential for success and effectiveness. As Gauthier (2007) points out, the mixed results obtained for the impact of social policies on fertility can be explained by the increasing heterogeneity and polarization of families, which vary across countries. Preference theory helps us to address this heterogeneity.

Social policy specialists are now challenging the EU's focus on gender equality in the labor market to demand that the work ethic is balanced by a new emphasis on the care ethic (Dey 2006). There is a recognition that care work cannot ever be completely transferred to the market, so domestic care work needs to be re-valued and rewarded (Lewis and Giullari 2005). Preference theory provides a theoretical framework encompassing family work and market work and shows that social policy is currently biased toward women who specialize in market work and ignores women who specialize in family work (Hakim 2000, p. 253). A change of direction in social policy thus requires some movement away from values that prioritize competitive rivalry and achievement in the marketplace over the caring and sharing values of family life.

Conclusion

Preference theory is a new theory that helps to make sense of current debates, explain current and future patterns of employment and fertility among women, and develop social policies that address the interests of all women and all families. It offers empirically based statements about the relative priority women accord to market work and careers versus family work and private life (corresponding to three distinct models of the family) and recognizes that women are heterogeneous in their lifestyle preferences, to a greater extent than are men. Preference theory also specifies the historical context in which these core values become important predictors of behavior. It notes that five historical changes collectively produce a qualitatively new scenario for women in rich modern societies in the twenty-first century, giving them options that were not previously available to them. The theory provides a basis for analyzing the biases embedded in most current social policies, which are focused on working women and careerists to the exclusion of full-time parents and part-time workers.

Declining fertility is prompting a revaluation of motherhood and reproductive work and a change in emphasis in public policy. The bias toward support for working mothers needs to be balanced by new measures to support home-centered women as well. Many family-friendly employment policies are of wide appeal to all workers and could potentially be made even less discriminatory. However, the emphasis on publicly subsidized childcare, which benefits only work-centered women and some adaptive women, should be replaced by a diversity of policies supporting all groups of women to an equal degree, even if in different ways. Some policies are flexible enough to offer benefits for all women, such as the hugely popular homecare allowance in Finland and Norway as well as cafeteria-style employer benefits.

Apart from raising family allowances to help compensate for the costs of children, we have identified a new policy—the homecare allowance—that promises to be equally or more effective in encouraging women to achieve their ideal family size and potentially raise fertility. The homecare allowance involves paying one parent (typically the mother) a salary for their work as full-time carer and is offered to families who do not use state-subsidized childcare, thus ensuring parity between users and non-users among parents. The money can be regarded as a wage for childcare at home, as a partial replacement for earnings foregone, or it can be used as a subsidy for purchased childcare services that enable the parent to return to work, full-time or part-time. It has proved a popular alternative to state nurseries because it allows parents to choose their own timetables and childcare—including the option of paying close neighbors or relatives for their help. The homecare allowance has proven popular in Finland, Norway, and France because of this flexibility.

However, feminists regard it as controversial because it rewards full-time motherhood and family work. For example, Heitlinger (1991) rejects all subsidies for full-time mothers as sexist and only endorses family policies that keep mothers in the labor market throughout their lives.[16] Since the program is available to whichever parent stays at home, it is not sexist. It is attractive to family-centered men as well as women, and some fathers choose to use it. The main problem with feminist objections is that they fail to recognize and accept the heterogeneity of women's (and men's) lifestyle preferences and insist on one-size-fits-all policies. Policies are differentially attractive to family-centered, work-centered, and adaptive men and women. So it makes sense to have programs that benefit family-centered parents as well as the (frequently childless) careerist minority and adaptive people. As Gauthier et al. (2004) point out, people who choose to become parents today are an increasingly self-selected group with a particular interest in children, a conclusion reiterated by Jones and Brayfield (1997). Time budget studies show that parents' investment of time in childrearing activities is increasing long-term. However, non-employed mothers are a particularly self-selected minority, and their time investment in their children's development has risen more sharply over the past three decades than that of fathers and employed mothers (Gauthier et al. 2004). Female heterogeneity is producing a polarization of women's lifestyles. The current policy emphasis on working women thus needs to be counterbalanced by family policies that support home-centered women as well. The interests of women and children are not always compatible, and across Europe feminist women are least likely to value children (Jones and Brayfield 1997, p. 1260). Population policy cannot be subordinated to gender equality policy, and they do not always mesh neatly.

Notes

1. For some purposes, the three groups can be regarded as a continuum. However, they espouse sharply different and conflicting values.
2. See Web Table 9.1 on the book web site.
3. See Web Table 9.2 on the book web site.
4. However, some studies indicate a large conflict, for men as well as women. A 2003 survey asked parents about their relative priorities between paid work and family work (childcare and domestic work). The mothers' ideal priorities were paid work primarily 14 percent, family primarily 27 percent, and a balance between paid work and family work 59 percent. However, the reality of mothers' lives was reported as paid work primarily 6 percent, family primarily 81 percent, and a balance between paid work and family work 13 percent. For fathers, the ideal priorities were paid work primarily 31 percent, family primarily 17 percent, and a balance between paid work and family work 52 percent. And the reality of fathers' lives was reported as paid work primarily 65 percent, family primarily 8 percent, and a balance between paid work and family work 26 percent. This survey shows mothers' and fathers' ideals to be very similar, with small minorities preferring sex-role differentiation. The reality of parents' lives displays sharp sex-role differentiation, which is clearly not welcomed by the majority of Japanese. Results of UFJ Institute 2003 Research Report on Childrearing Support Measures reported in Yajima (2007).
5. Goldin and Katz (2002) identify the introduction of the pill as a key turning point in women's life choices in the US. Tsui (2001, p. 191) quotes a United Nations study summarizing

contraceptive patterns in fifty-seven developing countries: 58 percent of married women of reproductive age used some form of contraception, and this was almost invariably modern methods, mainly sterilization, the oral pill, and IUDs (United Nations 1996, Table 15). Some fast-moving Asian countries, such as Singapore, have already switched family policy to a pronatalist position.

6. The statistically significant correlation coefficient between religiosity and lifestyle preferences is only 0.14 in the US National Survey of Marriage and Family Life. See the chapter by Wilcox and Dew in this volume for a full analysis of these survey data.

7. Diversity is necessary for evolutionary adaptations to change, so may be genetically determined in combination with social influences.

8. Sweden must be the only modern society with a well-educated population where it is feasible for citizens to say that it is comforting and reassuring to live in a society where "the government knows what is best for us all." It is inconceivable for such confidence in strong government to be expressed in large and diverse societies such as the US, Britain, Germany, or France. As Swedish commentators have pointed out, Sweden is an extremely conformist and authoritarian society (Brown 2010, pp. 19–20), in which a single party, the Social Democrats, have been in power for sixty-five of the last seventy-eight years.

9. For example, Gornick and Meyers (2003) write enviously about the generous welfare state benefits offered in Europe. They describe European social and family policies in glowing terms, without any reference at all to the high tax rates required to pay for subsidized and free childcare and long parental leaves. (Personal tax rates in Sweden start at 30 percent and rise to a top rate of 59 percent. In Denmark, tax rates start at 28 percent and rise to a top rate of 63 percent. In contrast, the top tax rate in the US is 35 percent.) European policies are often described as if they come free of charge, simply for the asking, without explaining why Americans are foolish enough not to have already voted them into existence.

10. Denmark has a total population of 5.5 million, Finland has 5.3 million. Norway and Iceland (not members of the European Union) have 4.9 million and 0.4 million, respectively.

11. One factor limiting the impact on fertility levels in Finland and Norway may be the strong two-child family norm, with few couples having a third child. Similarly, the Czech survey found no important fertility differences among the three groups of women, possibly because there is little divergence from the strong two-child norm (Rabusic and Manea 2009).

12. Coleman and Rowthorn (2004) argue that the costs can outweigh the benefits and also that the nature of the causal link between the US's growing economy and positive immigration policy is not proven: it is more likely that the dynamic economy attracts immigrants than that immigration itself is the primary cause of economic growth.

13. France also seems to be the first country to modify and update policies to take account of social change, as illustrated by the prime minister's announcement, at a conference on family life in 2005, that the government proposed to pay up to £700 (1,000 Euros) per month, double the current maximum and close to the 1,200 Euros minimum wage, to women who have a third child, in an attempt to encourage highly paid and professional women to have larger families (Randall 2005).

14. Gauthier (2007, p. 331) also points out that the much advertised reversal of the negative correlation between national female employment rates and national fertility rates has been shown to be due to country effects. Overall, high rates of female employment imply lower fertility.

15. These theories are reviewed in the 2001 *Population and Development Review* Supplement on *Global Fertility Transition* (Bulatao 2001).

16. Some feminists reject any division of labor in the family as sexist and disadvantageous to women. However, economists have pointed out that even a minor (female) advantage in childrearing, or a minor (male) advantage in earnings, would lead to a rational division of labor in the family (Ermisch 2003).

References

Aassve, A., and T. Lappegard. 2009. "Childcare cash benefits and fertility timing in Norway." *European Journal of Population* 25: 67–88.

Alberdi, I., and C. Hakim 2007. "Ideas y valores que influyen en los comportamientos familiars." In *Encuesta de Fecundidad, Familia y Valores 2006,* ed. Margarita Delgado, Opiniones y Actitudes No. 59, pp. 143–215. Madrid: Centro de Investigaciones Sociológicas.

Albrecht, J., A. Björklund, and S. Vroman. 2003. "Is there a glass ceiling in Sweden?" *Journal of Labor Economics* 21: 145–177.

Bernardi, F. 2005. "Public policies and low fertility: rationales for public intervention and a diagnosis for the Spanish case." *Journal of European Social Policy* 15: 123–138.

Bertram, Hans, W. Rösler, and N. Ehlert. 2005. *Nachhaltige Familienpolitik* (Sustainable Family Policy). Berlin: Bundesministerium für Familie, Senioren, Frauen und Jugend (Ministry for the Family, Pensioners, Women and Children).

Boeri, Tito, Daniela Del Boca, and Christopher Pissarides, eds. 2005. *Women at Work: An Economic Perspective,* a report for the Fondazione Rodolfo Debenedetti. Oxford: Oxford University Press.

Brown, A. 2010. "The Sweden Democrats party." *Guardian,* September 18, pp. 17–20.

Bulatao, R. A., ed. 2001. *Global Fertility Transition, Population and Development Review* 27 (Suppl.): 1–332.

Castles, F. 2003. "The world turned upside down: below replacement fertility, changing preferences and family-friendly public policy in 21 OECD countries." *Journal of European Social Policy* 3: 209–227.

Coleman, David, and Robert Rowthorn. 2004. "The economic effects of immigration into the United Kingdom." *Population and Development Review* 30: 579–624.

Corijn, M., and C. Hakim. 2009. "Applying Hakim's preference theory in population policy research." Unpublished paper.

D'Addio, A., and M. D'Ercole. 2005. *Trends and Determinants of Fertility Rates: The Role of Policies.* OECD Social Employment and Migration Working Paper No. 27. Paris: OECD Publishing.

Dau-Schmidt, K. G., M. Galanter, K. Mukhopadhaya, and K. E. Hull. 2007. *Gender and the Legal Profession: The Michigan Alumni Dataset 1967–2000.* Indiana Legal Studies Research Paper No. 104. Bloomington: Indiana University School of Law.

Dench, Geoff. 2010. *What Women Want: Evidence from British Social Attitudes.* London: Hera Trust.

Dey, Ian. 2006. "Wearing out the work ethic: population ageing, fertility and work-life balance." *Journal of Social Policy* 35 (2, April): 86–94.

Diprete, Thomas A., S. Phillip Morgan, Henriette Engelhardt, and Hana Pacalova. 2003. "Do cross-national differences in the costs of children generate cross-national differences in fertility rates?" *Population Research and Policy Review* 22: 439–477.

Ellingsæter, A. L. 2003. "The complexity of family policy reform." *European Societies* 5: 419–443.

———. 2007. "Old and new politics of time to care: three Norwegian reforms." *Journal of European Social Policy* 17: 49–60.

Ellingsæter, A. L., and L. Gulbrandsen. 2007. "Closing the childcare gap: the interaction of childcare provision and mothers' agency in Norway." *Journal of Social Policy* 36: 649–669.

Ermisch, John F. 2003. *An Economic Analysis of the Family.* Princeton, NJ: Princeton University Press.

European Commission. 2009. "Parental allowance (*Elterngeld*) an innovative policy." *European Employment Observatory* (Spring): 27–31.

European Commission and European Foundation. 2003. *Perceptions of Living Conditions in an Enlarged Europe.* EF/03/114/EN. Dublin: European Foundation for the Improvement of Living and Working Conditions.

European Commission, Directorate-General for Employment, Social Affairs and Equal Opportunities. 2005a. *Social Agenda,* No. 11.

———. 2005b. *Confronting Demographic Change: A New Solidarity between the Generations—Green Paper.* Luxembourg: OOPEC.

Field, Frank. 2004. "Eleanor Rathbone and the Politics of Citizenship." Eleanor Rathbone Memorial Lecture. University of Liverpool, December 9.

Gauthier, Anne H. 1996a. "The measured and unmeasured effects of welfare benefits on families: implications for Europe's demographic trends." In *Europe's Population in the 1990s.* ed. D. Coleman, pp. 295–331. Oxford: Oxford University Press.

———. 1996b. *The State and the Family.* Oxford: Clarendon Press.

———. 2007. "The impact of family policies on fertility in industrialised countries: a review of the literature." *Population Research and Policy Review* 26: 323–346.

Gauthier, Anne, and Jan Hatzius. 1997. "Family benefits and fertility: an econometric analysis." *Population Studies* 51: 295–306.

Gauthier, Anne H., Timothy M. Smeeding, and Frank F. Furstenberg. 2004. "Are parents investing less time in children? Trends in selected industrialised countries," *Population and Development Review* 30: 647–671.

Gerson, K. 1985. *Hard Choices: How Women Decide about Work, Career and Motherhood.* Berkeley: University of California Press.

Goldin, C., and L. F. Katz. 2002. "The power of the pill: oral contraceptives and women's career and marriage decisions." *Journal of Political Economy* 110: 730–770.

Gornick, Janet C., and Marcia K. Meyers. 2003. *Families That Work: Policies for Reconciling Parenthood and Employment.* New York: Russell Sage.

Grant, Jonathan, Stijn Hoorens, Suja Sivadasan, Mirjam van het Loo, Julie DeVanzo, Lauren Hale, Shawna Gibson, and William Butz. 2004. *Low Fertility and Population Ageing: Causes, Consequences and Policy Options.* Report to the European Commission. Cambridge: RAND.

Hakim, C. 2000. *Work-Lifestyle Choices in the Twenty-First Century: Preference Theory.* Oxford: Oxford University Press.

———. 2003a. *Models of the Family in Modern Societies: Ideals and Realities.* Aldershot: Ashgate.

———. 2003b. "A new approach to explaining fertility patterns: preference theory." *Population and Development Review* 29: 349–374.

———. 2003c. *Childlessness in Europe.* Report to the Economic and Social Research Council. London: London School of Economics.

———. 2004a. *Key Issues in Women's Work: Female Diversity and the Polarisation of Women's Employment.* London: Glasshouse Press.

———. 2004b. "Lifestyle preferences versus patriarchal values: causal and non-causal attitudes" In *Changing Life Patterns in Western Industrial Societies,* eds. J. Z. Giele and E. Holst, pp. 69–91. Oxford: Elsevier.

———. 2005. "Sex differences in work-life balance goals." In *Work-Life Balance in the Twenty-First Century,* ed. D. Houston, pp. 55–79. London: Palgrave Macmillan.

———. 2006. "Women, careers, and work-life preferences." *British Journal of Guidance and Counselling* 34: 279–294.

———. 2008. "Is gender equality legislation becoming counter-productive?" *Public Policy Research* 15: 133–136.

———. 2010. "(How) can social policy and fiscal policy regognise unpaid family work?" *Renewal* 18: 23–33.

———. 2011. *Feminist Myths and Magic Medicine.* London: Centre for Policy Studies.

Hakim, C., K. Bradley, E. Price, and L. Mitchell. 2008. *Little Britons: Financing Childcare Choice.* London: Policy Exchange. www.policyexchange.org.uk.

Hattery, A. 2001. *Women, Work and Family.* Thousand Oaks, CA: Sage.

Heitlinger, Alena. 1991. "Pronatalism and women's equality policies." *European Journal of Population* 7: 343–375.

Henrekson, M., and M. Stenkula. 2009. "Why are there so few female top executives in egalitarian welfare states?" *The Independent Review* 14 (2): 239–270.

Hoem, J. M. 2005. "Why does Sweden have such high fertility?" *Demographic Research* 13: 559–572. www.demographic-research.org.

Huang, Qinghai, B. M. El-Khouri, G. Johansson, S. Lindroth, and M. Sverke. 2007. "Women's career patterns: A study of Swedish women born in the 1950s." *Journal of Occupational and Organizational Psychology* 80 (3): 387–412.

Ilmakunnas, S. 1997. "Public policy and childcare choice." In *The Economics of the Family and Family Policies,* ed. I. Persson and C. Jonung, pp. 178–193. London: Routledge.

Jones, Rachel K., and April Brayfield. 1997. "Life's greatest joy? European attitudes toward the centrality of children." *Social Forces* 75 (4): 1239–1270.

Jonung, C., and I. Persson. 1993. "Women and market work: the misleading tale of participation rates in international comparisons." *Work, Employment and Society* 7: 259–274.

Lappegard, T. 2010. "Family policies and fertility in Norway." *European Journal of Population* 26: 99–116.

Lewis, Jane, and Susanna Giullari. 2005. "The adult worker model family, gender equality and care: the search for new policy principles and the possibilities and problems of a Capabilities Approach." *Economy and Society* 34: 76–104.

McDonald, Peter. 2005. "Fertility and the state: the efficacy of policy." Paper presented to the 25th IUSSP International Population Conference in Tours, France, July.

McIntosh, C. A. 1983. *Population Policy in Western Europe: Responses to Low Fertility in France, Sweden and West Germany.* New York: M. E. Sharpe.

OECD. 2002–2005. *Babies and Bosses: Reconciling Work and Family Life,* vols. 1–4. Paris: OECD.

Overell, Steven. 2005. "Work-life balance." *Financial Times,* May 9, p. 15.

Penn, Helen. 2009. *Early Childhood Education and Care.* Brussels: EC Directorate-General for Education and Culture.

Pezzini, Silvia. 2005. "The effect of women's rights on women's welfare: evidence from a natural experiment." *Economic Journal* 115: C208–C227.

Philipov, Dimiter. 2005. *Comparative Report on Gender Roles and Relations and Summary Policy Implications Regarding Gender Roles.* DIALOG/IPPAS Report Nos. 16/17. Vienna: Institute for Demography.

Plantenga, J., and C. Remery. 2009. *The Provision of Childcare Services: A Comparison of 30 European Countries.* Brussels: EC Directorate-General for Employment, Social Affairs and Equal Opportunities.

Rabusic, L., and B. C. Manea. 2009. "Hakim's preference theory in the Czech context." *Demography* 42: 46–55. http://www.czso.cz/csu/redakce.nsf/i/demografie.

Randall, Colin. 2005. "Middle class mothers will be paid to start le baby boom." *Daily Telegraph,* September 20.

Ronsen, M. 2001. *Market Work, Childcare and the Division of Labour: Adaptation of Norwegian Mothers before and after the Cash-for-Care Reform.* Report 2001–03. Oslo: Statistics Norway. www.ssb.no.emner/03/04/30/rapp_200103/rapp_200103.pdf.

Schone, P. 2004. "Labour supply effects of a cash-for-care subsidy." *Journal of Population Economics* 17: 703–727.

Sipila, J., K. Repo, and T. Rissanen. 2010. *Cash-for-Childcare: The Consequences for Caring Mothers.* Cheltenham: Edward Elgar.

Sobotka, Tomas. 2004. *Postponement of Childbearing and Low Fertility in Europe.* Amsterdam: Dutch University Press.

Stahli, M. E., J.-M. Le Goff, and E. Widmer. 2009. "Wishes or constraints? Mothers' labour force participation and its motivation in Switzerland." *European Journal of Sociology* 25: 333–348.

Suzuki, Atsuko. 2007. *Gender and Career in Japan.* Melbourne: Trans-Pacific Press.

Thörnqvist, C. 2006. "Family-friendly labour market policies and careers in Sweden—and the lack of them." *British Journal of Guidance and Counselling* 34: 309–326.

Tsui, Amy Ong. 2001. "Population policies, family planning programs and fertility: the record." *Population and Development Review* 27 (Suppl.): 184–204.

Vere, James P. 2007. "'Having it all' no longer: fertility, female labor supply, and the new life choices of generation X." *Demography* 4: 821–828.

Yajima, Yoko. 2007. "Policies on fertility decline and gender equality in Japan." Paper presented to the CGP-SSRC Public Symposium on Fertility Decline and Work-Life Balance, Tokyo, May 26.

Chapter 10

The Future of Fertility

*Future Trends in Family Size
among Low Fertility Populations*

**Wolfgang Lutz, Stuart Basten,
and Erich Striessnig**

A famous quote attributed to both Winston Churchill and Konrad Adenauer goes, "People will always want to have children." In the case of Adenauer, this comment was supposedly made in reaction to experts stressing that Germany's pay-as-you-go pension system was vulnerable to the possibility of declining birth rates. But with the baby boom dispelling any such caution, such an attitude seemed almost self-evident until very recently, and the low fertility rates in some countries were attributed to problems in achieving one's ideal family size rather than lack of want.

Yet new data show that ideal family size also seems to be on the decline in many countries (Goldstein et al. 2009). Is there a chance that Churchill and Adenauer were wrong after all? The "low fertility trap hypothesis" discussed below gives plausible reasons why indeed fewer and fewer people may want to have children in the future. But it is not only desires that change: there may also be new obstacles to actually *having* the number of children that people still want. While discussion has taken place concerning the problems for women to combine work and family, disturbing new findings on declining sperm counts have emerged that suggest that, in places such as Denmark, it is likely that about 20 percent of young men today will not be able to father a child naturally (Jensen et al. 2004; Jensen 2007; Jorgensen et al. 2001). These two recent developments alone suggest that one might profitably look much more closely at the forces that may influence tomorrow's birth rates.

All major population projections currently assume that fertility in the countries with the lowest levels will recover or at least not decline any further. The United Nations Population Division assumes that all countries will eventually fluctuate around a mean period total fertility rate (TFR) of 2.1, while Eurostat makes slightly lower assumptions with TFRs in 2060 assumed to average for the EU27 at 1.68 with individual countries ranging from 1.51 to 1.99 (UNPD 2011, Eurostat 2012).

Yet, should birth rates defy these projections and continue to decline, then the populations concerned would shrink and age much more rapidly than currently assumed. In that case we would have to substantially revise the demographic basis for all assessments of the possible consequences of aging and population shrinking. These would range from the considerations of the European Union's Economics and Finance ministers (EU-EcoFin) to those concerning future family care patterns of the elderly and much more.

Since there is no comprehensive theory that can guide us in thinking about the future level of the birth rate in low fertility countries, it can only be understood through a broad and truly interdisciplinary research program that combines biomedical factors (both on the female and male sides) with evolutionary anthropology as well as sociological, economic, and psychological approaches. Demography is well positioned to serve as the interface between the different disciplines by converting discipline-specific approaches and contributions into one common currency, the future number of births. In the following pages we will discuss a few considerations that could possibly lead to such a new and ambitious research endeavor.

The Lack of a Theory with Predictive Power in Post-Demographic Transition Populations

Explanations and projections of fertility trends in different parts of the world have generally been guided by the paradigm of the demographic transition, which assumes that after an initial decline in death rates, birth rates—after a certain lag—also start to fall. In this general form, the model has received overwhelming empirical support in capturing the remarkable fertility changes of the twentieth century.

The demographic transition began in the late eighteenth and nineteenth centuries in today's more-developed countries (MDCs) and spread to today's less-developed countries (LDCs) in the latter half of the twentieth century (Davis 1991, 1945; Notestein 1945; Coale 1973). The conventional theory of demographic transition predicts that as living standards rise and health conditions improve, mortality rates first decline and then, somewhat later, so too do fertility rates. Demographic transition theory has evolved as a generalization of the typical sequence of events in what are now MDCs, where mortality rates declined comparatively gradually from the late 1700s and then more rapidly in the late 1800s and where, after a gap of up to 100 years, fertility rates also declined. Different societies experienced transition in different ways, and today various regions of the world are following distinctive paths (Tabah 1989). Nonetheless, the broad result was, and is, a gradual transition from a small, slow-growing population with high mortality and high fertility to a large, slow-growing or even slowly shrinking population with low mortality and low fertility rates. During the transition itself, population growth accelerates because the decline in death rates precedes the decline in birth rates.

Unfortunately, the demographic transition paradigm—although useful for explaining global demographic trends during the twentieth century and having strong predictive power in terms of projecting future trends in countries that still have high fertility—essentially has nothing to say about the future of fertility in Europe (Lutz 1996; Lutz et al. 2006). The recently popular notion of a "second demographic transition" is a plausible way of describing a bundle of behavioral and normative changes that took place recently in Europe, but it has little or no predictive power in terms of informing us about likely future fertility trends in Europe (Van de Kaa 1987; Raley 2001; Lesthaeghe and Neels 2002). In fact, the social sciences as a whole have yet to come up with a useful theory to predict the future fertility level of post-demographic transition societies. In the absence of such a theory, all that forecasters can do is try to define a likely range of uncertainty. As the fertility transition is irreversible, we are quite sure that the fertility rate will not return to pre-transitional levels of, say, more than 3.0. There is no equally convincing argument about a lower bound, although many demographers tend to think that fertility is unlikely to fall below 1.0 for long periods. But, as we will see from the discussion below, there are reasons to think that fertility could fall even lower than this, and there is a real possibility that future fertility will exhibit the strong fluctuations, in terms of booms and busts, that we have seen over the past decades.

Six Dimensions Shaping the Future of Fertility

So how can we meaningfully talk about the future of fertility when there is no consistent theory? Much research has been carried out over the past decades trying to identify and study specific determinants of fertility and the individual-level covariates of fertility and specific settings. But little has been achieved so far in terms of drawing a comprehensive picture of what will drive overall birth rates in the future.

1. **The trend in ideal family size and the strength of individual desires for children**: Although answers to ideal or desired family size questions in surveys cannot be treated as direct predictors of fertility at the individual level, shifts in responses over time can provide some indication of the direction in which the desire for children is moving. Empirical data show that personal ideal family size tends to be higher than actual family size at the aggregate level in most European countries (Goldstein et al. 2003). Owing to several obstacles and competing desires, many couples have fewer children than they claim they desire. With all its problems, this indicator still comes closest to the most fundamental question concerning the future of reproduction: to what degree do people still want children, and how strongly do they value children in comparison to other things that life has to offer?

   Unless it is somehow part of human nature that people on average always seek to have at least two children, changing social norms can lead to sub-replacement ideal family sizes and, possibly in the future, even lower levels than we have already witnessed. This is the focus of the low fertility trap hypothesis, which is based on the assumption that norms about ideal family size among the next generation are being influenced and shaped by what they see around them during their period of socialization. Hence, with a certain time lag, low actual fertility may translate into low fertility norms (Lutz et al. 2006). Later on, we will turn our attention to China where the one-child family policy of the past has produced a sort of natural experiment for testing the low fertility trap hypothesis.

2. **Trends in the pattern of education and work, including the proportion of time dedicated to the professional side of life:** It is widely acknowledged that the expansion of education for both men and women in most European countries has been associated with a significant postponement of childbearing. Entry into professional life after education has become more difficult and, if one is lucky enough to get a job, working life has tended to become ever more competitive due to the effects of globalization. In many European countries where young employees in the past enjoyed positions that were more or less permanent, today many have to jump from one short-term contract to the next. Under such conditions it becomes less attractive to establish a family and, subsequently, to avoid dedicating all of one's time and energy to pursuing a professional career. Furthermore, globalization and the flexibility goals pursued under the Lisbon Agenda of the European Union are often at odds with the secure and sheltered conditions required for the first years of family formation. How this balance of time and energy allocation between work and private life will develop in the future is anybody's guess. However, we would expect these pressures to have immediate consequences on the rate of childbearing.

3. **Changing macro-level conditions (government policies, childcare facilities, housing conditions, etc.) that influence the cost of children in a broader sense:** Although other factors tend to dominate the decision to have children, economic considerations likely play a role for couples when deciding how many children to have. For instance, both the economic incentive structures and the costs of children differ greatly among European countries. The French experience shows that a massive redistribution (in the tax system as well as through direct child benefits) from those with no or few children to those with three or more carried out consistently over many decades did indeed prevent fertility from showing the same declines as were experienced by most neighboring countries (Toulemon et al. 2008). While the effectiveness of specific policy measures aimed at increasing fertility is difficult to assess due to the complexity of the entire incentive structure (ranging from the social security system to the

housing market and cultural factors), there is little doubt that significant changes *do* influence fertility—and in the case of a high desired family size this is probably easier to achieve than in cases where desired family size has already declined. We will return to the possible effect of public policy on fertility toward the end of this chapter.

4. **The changing nature and stability of partnership:** Notwithstanding social changes and developments in assisted reproductive technology (ART), the most common family form is still one male and one female who embark upon a long-term commitment. For at least eighteen years, children bring a significant change to the lifestyle of their parents and, in most cases, the responsibility is considered a lesser burden when shared among both parents (Goldsteen and Ross 1989). But couple relationships, whether marriages or non-marital unions, have become less stable over time. In almost all Western societies, rates of divorce and separation have risen. Because births are most intimately linked to partnerships, trends in the nature and stability of partnerships also affect birth rates. This said, there can be effects in opposing directions. Women may decide not to have children if they cannot count on their partners to stay with them and take part in the childrearing—particularly given the strain on relationships that childbearing has been shown to bring (Lillard and Waite 1993). On the other hand, a new partnership after separation may provide an incentive to have an additional child with the new partner. Finally, while the number of women who become single mothers by choice—that is, decide on parenthood completely independently of any relationship with another adult—is comparatively very small, this number has been rising in recent years (Bock 2000). The net effect of all of these forces is culture specific and difficult to predict.

5. **Changes in the population composition and differential trends in population subgroups:** Largely as a result of international migration, many national populations in Europe have become more heterogeneous over the past decades. Specific ethnic or religious subgroups of the population have fertility rates that are twice the national average. Even in the second generation, the fertility rates of those groups often remain somewhat higher (Coleman and Dubuc 2010). Over time, the share of these high fertility groups in the total population has a tendency to increase as a direct consequence of their higher fertility and, in many countries, through continued immigration of new group members. The future national-level fertility rates can be significantly influenced by such changes in population composition. The extent of this upward pressure

on the national birth rate depends on the persistence of ethnic fertility differentials and on the rate of future migration.

6. **Changing biomedical conditions:** Biomedical considerations have been largely absent from the social science discourse about the determinants of fertility because it has typically been assumed that it is the conscious decision to have a child that is decisive. This assumption has already been criticized with respect to the prevalence of unplanned pregnancies (Bouchard et al. 2006; Kuroki et al. 2008). Retrospective surveys show that generally some 10–30 percent of all births are classified as unplanned (by the interviewed women themselves) with great variations across countries and by birth order (Lakha and Glasier 2006; Fleissig 1991). Future progress in contraceptive technology could therefore reduce the birth rate even further if it reduced the still surprisingly high proportion of unplanned pregnancies (Glasier 2009; Fleming 2009). Another highly relevant biomedical factor on the female side is the combination of continued postponement of childbearing to higher and higher ages and the fact that fecundability (the monthly probability of conception) starts to decline around age 30 and is already significantly reduced after age 35. The age pattern of fecundability has proven remarkably stable over time due to the finite number of egg cells a woman has. As a consequence, one observes *both* a dramatic rise in fertility treatment rates *and* an increase in involuntary childlessness (Lechner et al. 2007; Letherby 1999; Shanley and Asch 2009; Todorova and Kotzeva 2003; Van Balen 2008). Future improvements in assisted reproductive technologies or behavioral changes with respect to the age at which women decide to have their children may therefore have important effects on future birth rates. Finally, on the male side the above-mentioned concerns about sperm counts and quality and their uncertain future trends belong in this category.

The future of the birth rate will be a function of the interaction of these six dimensions of change. The future trend in each of these dimensions is uncertain and their interaction is even more so. Yet we are not completely ignorant about the likely forces that will shape these dimensions. Much research has been conducted over the past decades on individual factors of change. What is lacking is the interdisciplinary integration of these different aspects. We need to integrate all the social and economic forces that determine ideal family size and birth timing (for both men and women) into a single model. This must encompass their partnership dynamics, educational and professional careers, and biomedical aspects. An integrated analysis cannot be carried out at the aggregate level using population averages because there is great interpersonal variation along all six dimensions. Thus a more promising avenue of research is to apply methods of agent-based modeling, which have the potential to combine biomedical and behavioral aspects under one rubric.

From "Lowest-Low" to Ultra-Low or Moderately Low?

In the early 2000s, Kohler et al. coined the expression "lowest-low" fertility, referring to societies where TFR fell below 1.3—*far* below the replacement level of 2.1 (Kohler et al. 2002, 2006). Levels this low, "characterized by a rapid shift to delayed childbearing, a low probability of progression after the first child (but not particularly low levels of first-birth childbearing) [and] a 'falling behind' in cohort fertility at relatively late ages (in southern Europe)" were expected to not only persist in certain eastern and southern European countries, but also spread elsewhere (Kohler et al. 2006). Numerous scholars expressed pessimism about the likelihood of a significant upswing of fertility rates (Lesthaeghe and Willems 1999), and low fertility rates were written into national forecasts—most notably in Japan, which forecast TFRs of below 1.3 persisting until 2055 (Kaneko 2008). The low fertility trap hypothesis can be viewed as central to this pessimistic view (Lutz et al. 2006).

Recently, however, a TFR upturn has been reported in a large number of settings (Goldstein et al. 2009; Frejka and Sobotka 2008). Investigating the *reasons* for this shift is clearly crucial. An important study by Myrskylä et al., for example, suggests a link between societal development (as measured by the Human Development Index) and fertility rates, with a reversal of TFR decline taking place after a critical level (Tuljapurkar 2009; Myrskylä et al. 2009). However, perhaps the more influential reason for the recent change in TFR patterns is "tempo distortion" caused by steadily rising average ages of child-bearing (Sobotka 2004; Bongaarts 2002). In other words, as the *postponement* of births reduces the number of births in a given period, TFR appears lower than it really is, viz. the "real" TFR (i.e., a woman's completed fertility at age 45) will be higher than the period TFR. As such, once this tempo distortion is "worked through," TFRs should rise (Goldstein et al. 2009). This assumption permits Goldstein et al. to assert that "it appears that the widespread decline of TFRs to very low levels that began in many parts of Europe and East Asia in the early 1990s is nearly over, at least in Europe." It will be interesting to observe the TFR trends during and after the current economic crisis and see whether this assertion will hold.

Low Fertility in East Asia

The tempo-distortion effect within Europe is undoubtedly significant, and Goldstein et al. remark upon the same pattern of fertility upswing being tentatively reflected in East Asia. Rates across the region fell heavily during the economic and financial crises of the 1990s (Jones et al. 2000). While TFRs are still very low, they *have* risen in a number of East Asian settings. However, these small upswings are hardly indicative of a clear and sustained rise.

Any examination of fertility patterns in China, meanwhile, is even less clear. There is, for example, considerable debate regarding the severity of the official undercounting of births and the effect that this might have in the future (Merli 1998; Merli and Raftery 2000; Zhang 2004; Morgan et al. 2009). Despite this, a number of scholars have either played down the significance of underreporting or have created tests and weights to counterbalance the effect (Cai 2008; Feeney and Jianhua 1994; Retherford et al. 2005; Yi 1996). This debate is usefully restated in a paper by Lutz et al. (2007), who present not one, but *thirty-one* different estimates for the TFR of China in 2000 gleaned from the methodologies of nineteen different authors. These *national* TFRs range from 1.22 (China Statistics Press 2002) up to 2.3 (Liang 2003) with the most recent international studies suggesting a level of 1.4–1.5 for current TFRs (Chen et al. 2009).

However, in a country as large and diverse as China, there are strong regional differentials in TFR, which have been identified by numerous sources. As Chen et al. (2009) note, "In 1975, only two provinces—Beijing and Shanghai—had below-replacement fertility, but by 2000, twenty-nine out of thirty-one provinces had below-replacement fertility. Among these twenty-nine provinces, twenty-two had a total fertility rate (TFR) below 1.7, and twenty provinces had a TFR below 1.5."

Calculating the *number* of people in China living in "lowest-low" fertility regimes (i.e., with TFRs of 1.3 or below) is important to gauge the scale of the issue in East Asia, given the relative population sizes of these provinces compared to the average European country. Goldstein et al. (2009) used provincial data based upon the 2000 census to calculate this figure. They found that twelve provinces experienced a "lowest-low" fertility regime in 2000, accounting for 464.0/473.4 million people, or roughly 36 percent of China's total population (Goldstein 2009, 58–59).

In 2005, however, an inter-censual population survey was performed on a 1 percent national sample by over 200,000 enumerators (Weimim 2005; Nailin 2006). Although continuing problems have been identified with the inter-census survey regarding undercounting (Nailin 2006), on the whole a large number of improvements were made upon the 2000 census with specific measures incorporated to minimize undercounting and quality control methods designed to offset sampling bias (Zhang et al. 2007; Zhu et al. 2009). After adjusting for sample size, the initial impression from these data is of a general increase in both the number and proportion of the Chinese population living under lowest-low circumstances since 2000. Much further work, however, needs to be performed on the 2005 survey before concrete evidence can be presented. And hopefully the 2010 census will provide more useful information on this issue.

The total size of the Chinese areas reported by Goldstein et al. to have had a TFR of under 1.3 numbers 790.8 million, greater than the population of Europe and Russia combined (Goldstein et al. 2009). However, the authors proceed to state that "reliable data are unavailable and lowest-low fertility there may be largely dictated by strict government policies promoting one-child policies." In the remainder of this chapter, we focus on one particular province—Shanghai—in an attempt to get a clearer picture of the state of fertility there and the mechanics underlying the particular demographic state.

Shanghai

Shanghai is the largest city in China, and one of the largest in the world. It has seen phenomenal growth in the past thirty years as a financial, commercial, and industrial center. The "headline" population of Shanghai in 2008 is given as 18,884,600. To put this in context, this is 1.42 percent of the total population of China, greater than the Netherlands and roughly the same size as all of the Balkan States combined. This figure, however, is the *resident* population as calculated by the Shanghai Statistical Bureau. One of the most significant problems in defining the true demographic characteristics of Shanghai involves the number of temporary migrants to the city. They are locally referred to as the "floating population" as they are not registered locally. In 2000, the resident population of Shanghai was calculated at 16,086,300 while the *registered* population was 13,096,300, giving a floating population of 2,990,000 (or 18.58 percent). By 2008, the "floating" proportion had risen to 27.38 percent. Furthermore, if one includes the estimated number of migrants resident in Shanghai for less than six months (1,248,500) the floating proportion increases to 33.95 percent (Shanghai Statistical Bureau 2009). The consequences of such a large body of migrants in the city are addressed later in the chapter. At this point it is sufficient to note that the fluidity of Shanghai's population presents many difficulties in defining demographic characteristics with any certainty.

Calculating TFRs for China is fraught with difficulties and so a wide array of figures have been posited (Lutz et al. 2007). This problem is magnified when attempting to calculate TFRs at provincial or local level. The most systematic attempt has been performed by the Chinese National Bureau for Statistics and the East-West Centre in Honolulu (NBS 2007). By their estimates, Shanghai was, by some margin, the first province in China to experience a sustained TFR below 1.7. The TFR of Shanghai fell as low as 0.64 in 2002–2003, rebounding slightly to 0.89 by 2007. On the one hand, it is possible that the higher levels of surveillance possible in large urban centers such as Shanghai make the TFRs presented more accurate than in a rural province. However, the city's large floating population is a potentially significant problem for accuracy. Yet even if one builds in an undercount of 20 percent these numbers are still incredibly low: among the very lowest in China, if not the world (Retherford et al. 2005).

Beyond the existence of low fertility rates in the *present,* an examination of surveys of fertility desires and intentions can help to provide an impression of what the *future* of fertility might be in Shanghai. In 2003 and 2008, the Shanghai Municipal Population and Family Planning Commission surveyed 12,000 males and 20,649 females between ages 20 and 45 (Shanghai Municipal Population and Family Planning Commission [SMPFPC] 2008). They discovered that the number of Shanghainese who intend to remain childless more than doubled between the two surveys, from 3.37 percent to 7.93 percent. Most significant, however, is the finding that the average ideal family size is just 1.07. Indeed, 81 percent of respondents to the 2003 survey preferred to have one child, with only 14.5 percent stating they wanted a second. Furthermore, the "floating population" or migrants from predominantly rural areas only report a slightly higher ideal family size.

A further striking finding is the effect of siblings on desired family size. It appears that growing up alone has a non-negligible effect on *decreasing* fertility desires.

Why Are Actual and Desired Family Size in Shanghai So Small?

I am earning a good salary and it's fun and exciting to be a part of the company. I learn new things every day. Things are still exciting with my husband too. I don't want to have kids. Maybe I will change my mind when things get boring, but not right now.—twenty-four-year-old Shanghainese woman (Nie and Wyman 2005).

I don't want children. I don't want to lose my figure and become fat. I think it's OK if I have one child, but too many will be bad for my body.—twenty-two-year-old Shanghainese woman (Nie and Wyman 2005).

I don't want a second child. One is enough, and I hope it is a girl. It is very nice to be the only child; you don't need to share or grab things from others. You can have all your parents' attention. My parents have brothers and sisters, but when my grandparents died they quarrelled over the legacy. That was horrible and hurtful. Being the only child, you won't have those problems.—twenty-five-year-old Shanghainese expectant mother (Branigan 2009).

The gradual diminution of the importance of the one-child policy in Shanghai allows us to test the low fertility trap (LFT) hypothesis (Lutz et al. 2006). In the LFT model a key driver is a decline in ideal family size that results from the socialization in a low fertility environment. In Shanghai this low fertility environment was created—at least in part—by government policy. With TFRs having fallen to a very low level for an extended period, the evidence from Shanghai suggests that by now small families have also become the norm. The depiction of small families in the mass media, cartoons, and posters reproduces this social norm. It is further reinforced through government slogans such as "With two children you can afford a 14 inch TV, with one child you can afford a 21 inch TV" (Hesketh and Zhu 1997). Therefore, while the circumstances by which small family sizes emerged differ from those in Europe, the *effect* is consonant with LFT: a self-reinforcing mechanism in which low actual fertility promotes low desired fertility among the following cohorts, which in turn leads to lower actual fertility.

This finding is particularly salient for urban China since the one-child policy is becoming less important. For example, where both partners are only children themselves, they are permitted a second child. The number of couples in such a position—who are thus "free" to have two children—is large. Indeed, in Shanghai this figure is estimated at well over 70 percent of couples (Sun *pers. comm.* 2009). As such, removing the one-child policy completely is unlikely to have much effect on fertility in Shanghai and other similar Chinese urban centres.

While Shanghai's low fertility rates were undoubtedly forced down by China's unique policy, they appear to be staying low for cultural, social, and economic reasons. As such, this natural experiment suggests that, under certain circumstances, the LFT hypothesis *can* be shown to be in effect. Elsewhere, the implications may be even greater. We saw how recent research predicts a likely end to lowest-low fertility over the forthcoming years. The evidence from Shanghai questions this assumption. It avers that low levels of fertility can become normalized and, therefore, deeply entrenched. This problematizes the inevitability of a fertility turnaround. Indeed, we must at least consider a steady-state alternative in which there is a continued majority of one-child families accompanied by moderately high rates of childlessness and only small numbers of families with two or more children. This of course prompts the question of sustainability: are lowest-low fertility rates compatible with broader social goals, or should all countries try and aim for replacement-level fertility?

The Normative Side of the Coin: An "Optimal Fertility Rate"?

So far in this chapter we have considered arguments about the question of what *is* likely to happen to fertility levels in the future. In the seemingly most worrisome of these scenarios, we drew the conclusion that many societies might end up being caught in a low-fertility trap. However, is this quite so bleak as widespread public concern might suggest? In order to answer this question, we rotate the coin—from "is" to "ought"—to focus on its normative flipside. Let's assume fertility is a policy variable and we can choose between various pathways. Many reflexively assume that a replacement-level TFR of around 2.1 is optimal. But we shall show that this is not necessarily the case. Indeed, we need to question our assumptions and ask what the criteria for prioritizing one fertility trend over another are. Once this normative analysis has been conducted, section 4 will revisit—and challenge—the conventional wisdom that low fertility is a major problem. This prompts us to endorse the unorthodox policy position that sub-replacement fertility may well be an optimal goal even in the face of aging and shrinking populations.

The Goal of Replacement-Level Fertility

When asked what a desirable fertility level for populations in Europe might be, most politicians, journalists, and even social scientists would say it is around two children per woman, which constitutes replacement-level fertility. The reasons given for seeking this level of fertility (which in most European countries is higher than that currently reported) usually include maintaining the size of the labor force and stabilizing the old-age dependency ratio. But a closer look at the demographic models that underlie this reasoning reveals that the supposedly precise replacement level of 2.1 (actually more like 2.06 under low mortality conditions) is only derived from a highly stylized theoretical model of stable population. It has little to do with maintaining the size of the labor force in *actual* contemporary European societies. These have an age structure that is highly irregular due to past fluctuations in fertility and net migration. Furthermore, in much of western Europe immigration has added to the labor force to the same effect that higher fertility would have done.

But even in the absence of migration, countries with a high share of young people (i.e., with positive population momentum) should aim for fertility to be well below replacement level if the goal is to maintain the absolute size of the working age population. Conversely, in countries with relatively few younger people (i.e., that have already entered a phase of negative momentum) fertility should be significantly above replacement level if the goal is to maintain the working age population. Lutz et al. (2003) showed that Europe's population entered the phase of negative momentum around the year 2000. Hence, in the context of real European populations, replacement-level fertility makes little sense if the goal is to maintain the size of the labor force.

Others who back replacement-level TFR as a goal cite individual preferences and the supposedly natural desire for a man and a woman to have two children together to replace themselves and hence continue living on through their children. Yet here we need to distinguish between population-level replacement and individual-level replacement (Lutz and Scherbov 2008). At the individual level it is sufficient to have one child (under low child mortality conditions) if the primary goal is to pass on your genes and continue to live on in the next generation. In the absence of cloning it takes a partner of the opposite sex to produce this one offspring. As such, the child is made up of only half each parent's genes. Yet, having two or three children does not make the offspring more similar to you. It would of course spread your genes more widely, but this is a very different aim from replacement. If spreading one's genes is the goal then, naturally, you should have as many children as possible and there is certainly no reason to stop at an "optimal" two. But to achieve individual-level replacement one surviving child is enough.

There may clearly be other individual-level reasons for having a second child such as providing your first child with a sibling, but again this is not related to the question of replacement. We only mention this important distinction between societal and individual-level replacement here in order to make sure that the following discussion of optimal fertility at the societal level is not confounded with that of personal optimal fertility.

When thinking about the optimal level of fertility in the long run for any given population, one must first specify the criteria one is using. In the context of current European populations, most of the concern in the discussion of demographic trends centers on the economic and social security consequences of population aging. In this context the criteria for optimality are to minimize the projected increase in old-age dependency and, more generally, to maximize the economic well-being of the average citizen in the population studied. But in a period of heightened concern over global climate change, the impact of demographic change on greenhouse gas emissions should also be taken into consideration.

With respect to this environmental dimension, there is little doubt that fewer people would be better. Still, the major challenge is how to quantify this effect and how to weigh it against the impact of population aging. Of course, there may be a third, quite powerful, criterion for determining a society's long-term optimal fertility level. We may label this criterion "national identity," reflecting a population's fears of having a smaller population in relation to its rivals. This can operate at both inter-state and intra-state levels (Goldstone et al. 2012). This may explain the prevalence of high birth rates among both Palestinians and Israeli Jews despite the relatively high level of education in both societies (Fargues 2000).

While at some point such cultural criteria must be taken into consideration because they exert a significant influence in real world discussions, in the following we focus solely on economic criteria while explicitly taking education into account. In 2004, Lutz, Sanderson, and O'Neill published the population balance model, which directly addressed the question of optimal fertility. The welfare indicator used to assess optimality was sensitive to age- and education-specific productivity, and the cost of pensions and education. They asked whether the per capita welfare decline caused by rising dependency ratios could be counterbalanced by the improved education of the smaller young cohorts. This might increase their productivity, offsetting the costs of rising dependency ratios, while at the same time smaller young cohorts cost less at a given level of education expenditure per child.

The effects of alternative levels of education on welfare were evaluated in the context of different fertility scenarios. Each steady-state level of fertility produces a distinct age structure that becomes stable in the long run. The results are shown in Figure 10.1. They clearly indicate that in the case of relatively uneducated societies (low education), the optimum TFR peaks around two children. Even at a TFR of 2.5 or 3, the society would be close to its optimum.

Of course, more educated populations achieve higher levels of welfare (indicated by the dark, solid curve in Figure 10.1) than less educated ones (brighter, dashed and dotted curves). This is due to the fact that higher education is associated with higher productivity of adults. But it costs a great deal to educate young people. At TFRs over 4, therefore, the burden of education spending becomes so crushing as to outweigh the benefits.

Most societies seek to increase aggregate education levels to achieve the high welfare levels shown by the solid curve in Figure 10.1. But they must take care to lower fertility so as to reduce the size of the young cohort and bring down the cost of education enough to realize a "profit" from their education spending. At low levels of education (dotted curve), the optimal TFR is around 2. But as

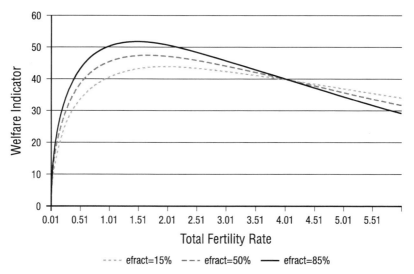

Figure 10.1 Welfare Indicators for Stable Populations

Note: Value of welfare indicator at different levels of fertility and levels of fraction of population educated (efract). Y-axis values refer to the value of the welfare indicator at the respective level of fertility in the respective year.

Source: Lutz, W., W. C. Sanderson, et al. 2004. "Conceptualizing Populaiton in Sustainable Development: From 'Population Stabilization' to 'Population Balance.'" In W. Lutz, W. C. Sanderson and B. C. O'Neill (eds.), *The End of World Population Growth in the 21st Century: New Challenges for Human Capital Formation and Sustainable Development*, 315–334. London: Earthscan. Relevant equation on p. 326.

societies reach for higher education levels (needed to raise per capita welfare), the optimum TFR moves to the left and comes to rest *below the replacement level,* at only around 1.4–1.7 children per woman. This illustrates that under stable conditions, societies can choose to invest heavily in a below-replacement number of children and achieve higher welfare than a society with lower educational investments in an above-replacement number of children per woman.[1]

We will now further expand this analysis, conduct sensitivity studies, and, most importantly, apply the model to the actual age and education structures of selected European countries. Here we highlight our findings to date.

Using the IIASA/VID data and projections on educational attainment the population is first divided into four education categories (none, primary, secondary, and tertiary).[2] We then apply different weights to these categories, both with regard to the dependency burden of education cost and to the differential degree of support that people in the various working-age groups can offer to the economically inactive. This is a somewhat more sophisticated and realistic extension of the conventional support ratio model, where every person of working age is assumed to make the same contribution to the support of the dependent population.

Since there is overwhelming evidence that in virtually every society the more educated are more productive in economic terms, the better educated are given higher productivity when calculating the contributors (numerator) in the support ratio.[3] In the web figures the specific assumptions made are listed in the box on the upper left where "ed1_weight" refers to the weight given to working age people with only primary education (this is usually set to 1.0), "ed2" refers to those with at least junior secondary, and "ed3" to those who have at least a completed first-level tertiary education. In all other respects this analysis makes the same simplifying assumption as the usual support ratios (that everybody of working age who no longer attends school is in the labor force, there is no unemployment, etc).

As far as the dependents (denominator of the education-weighted support ratio) are concerned, retirees get the same weight (here assumed to be 0.8), but the ages of labor market entry and exit are education-specific. In other words, primary and secondary educated people are assumed to move from being dependents (the denominator of the support ratio) to contributors (numerator) after age fifteen, while the tertiary educated follow ten years later at the age of twenty-five. We also assume that those getting secondary and tertiary education require a higher education input after the age of ten. Here the assumed values on the web figures are listed under "edcost" where the cost is 1.0 for everybody up to age ten. It is then increased to "ed2_cost" for those with secondary education up to age fifteen and to "ed3_cost" for those going on to study to age twenty-five.

But education has benefits as well as costs. When retiring from the labor market and thus returning to the denominator, the primary educated are assumed to make the transition at age fifty-seven, the secondary educated at sixty-one, and the tertiary educated at sixty-five. This resembles the current pattern in a sample of European countries, though current trends across the continent strongly suggest these ages will rise over the coming decades. For simplicity, the retirement ages are assumed to be the same for men and women, but this could easily change. So too could our other assumptions regarding the productivity-enhancing benefits of education and the age of transition from contribution to dependency.

In the context of real populations with non-stable age distributions, the time dimension becomes extremely important in this exercise. If the time horizon for optimization is only ten or twenty years, the optimum for increasing the support ratio is very different from that of a longer time horizon. In all of the figures on the web site, it is assumed that fertility shifts from its current level to the target level (listed on the x axis) by 2015 and then remains constant.[4]

Extremely low fertility is optimal[5] for all time horizons in which these fewer children do not yet affect the size of the labor force but only bring down young age dependency. In these cases, no children is best. Such a policy increases the support ratio, but is of course very short-sighted because it will begin to starve the economy of workers after fifteen years. But in the full, long-run model—as can be seen after 2075 in these figures—the optimal TFR generally stabilizes below the replacement level.[6]

Also, we examine the sensitivity of the education-weighted support ratio to alternative educational structures. The standard assumption for all education trends is the global education trend (GET) scenario—defined as the baseline in the IIASA-VID education projections. It assumes further gains in education level as countries converge upon a tertiary level of education of 60 percent, the most advanced level. A less optimistic scenario assumes constant education levels based on current (2010) age-specific school enrollment rates. Comparing these two scenarios, we find that more education not only brings a higher support ratio (and hence a higher level of per capita material well-being) but also that the optimal TFR is lower in an educated population than in one with lower average education.[7]

Again, this effect is due to the balance of total education costs (which are lower for fewer children at any given level of per capita expenditure), increased productivity due to education, and the proportion of pensioners at any given point in time. The time frame is important for understanding this. Thus, despite the fact that bigger cohorts of schoolchildren imply larger cohorts of productive adults in the future, they also beget future large cohorts whose education costs will outweigh the prospective benefits. At any point in time, the ratio of schoolchildren to productive adults remains less favorable under conditions of high fertility.

While it is beyond the scope of this chapter to show all the sensitivity analyses and alternative model calculations that we have performed (see Striessnig and Lutz 2011), we still want to highlight a few important findings. General changes in the education weights for the numerators (ed_weight) and denominators (ed_cost) mostly influence the level of the support ratio and have only minor influences on the shape of the curve, that is, the resulting optimal TFR. But, as might be expected, the shape of the curve is sensitive to changes in the pension age as well as the ratio of pension costs to working age contributions. The higher the level of pension payments relative to the education-specific support capacity of active people, the greater the dependency ratio (implying lower welfare) and the higher the optimal level of fertility.

In other words, under this scenario of massive wealth transfer to pensioners, more children are required in order to expand the workforce to pay for pensioners. For the case of Germany, a pension level of 0.8 results in an optimal fertility of 1.78. If we increase the pension level to 1.2, it would be optimal to have 2.27 children.[8] But one can also read this in a different way to find the pension level that would be optimal for a given level of fertility. Then the result is that the support ratio improves as pension cost declines. An alternative means of improving the support ratio is to raise the retirement age. An increase of the average pension age by two years not only raises the general welfare level as measured by our support ratio but also lowers optimal fertility. Compared with our results in Web Figure 10.1, optimal fertility in 2100 is reduced to 1.63 (from 1.78). At lower TFRs, people have to stay in the labor force longer as the emerging young cohorts are relatively small.

In conclusion, this brief exercise in education-specific population dynamics shows that it is far from evident that replacement-level fertility is optimal. If education is factored in, below-replacement TFR is typically optimal. Only very high pension incomes relative to workers' earnings result in higher optimal fertility. But this comes at the cost of vastly reduced levels of general well-being. There is a caveat: our numerical exercise only covers the quantifiable economic burden associated with population aging. If global environmental change is factored in, the optimal TFR will fall to still lower levels. What, then, does this mean for public policy?

What Should Be the Goal of Population Policies in Low Fertility Countries?[9]

In international enquiries, many governments in Europe report dissatisfaction with the current demographic trends in their countries. The further one moves east in the continent, the stronger the concern. The prime minister of Bulgaria calls his country's "demographic crisis" the number one policy priority; the president of Belarus speaks of a national "demographic security crisis," implying that this requires drastic action on par with a military crisis. Less dramatic in tone but equally urgent in its message, the president of the European Commission repeatedly refers to Europe's demographic trend as one of its three major challenges.

What do these policy-makers have in mind when they refer to demographic crises? In the eastern part of Europe, where most countries—with the notable exception of Russia—have experienced significant population declines since 1990, concerns revolve around the fear that the nation will lose its population base. Bulgaria, for example, had close to 9 million inhabitants in the late 1980s; in 2008 just 7.6 million remained and that number is projected by Eurostat (2008) to shrink to 6.5 million in 2035 and 5.5 million in 2060. In western Europe and Russia (which received many Russians from other former Soviet republics), the story has been less dramatic because thanks to migration gains, only very few countries are already on a declining trajectory, and the public policy concern is mostly with respect to the implications of population aging.

This loss of more than one-third of its entire population alongside very rapid population aging is indeed significant for countries such as Bulgaria. But this is only so in the context of traditional thinking, where more population meant more soldiers and more power. Moreover, throughout human history, population shrinking has always been associated with misery and national decline (Goldstone et al. 2012). Thus, while the sense of crisis is understandable, it may not reflect future realities.

In the global-level policy debate, the notion of population stabilization has been the guiding principle and the explicit goal of virtually all population-related policies for decades. This is so within the United Nations (UN) system and outside. This goal corresponds nicely to the UN projections, which used to assume that in the longer run, all countries of the world would converge in their fertility rates to replacement level. This would result (together with an assumed leveling-off of life expectancy) in long-term stabilization, that is, constant world and national populations.

Population stabilization is likely to please government officials who do not want to see their populations disappear or explode in the long run. The only problem with this politically attractive concept is that the real world does not conform to it. A majority of the world's population already has below-replacement fertility and there is little reason to assume that all countries will eventually converge to replacement level (Lutz et al. 2006). Actually, the most recent projections by IIASA indicate a probability of more than 85 percent that world population will peak during this century and then begin to decline—a very different story from the UN's stabilization picture (Lutz et al. 2008).

The notion becomes even more problematic at the level of individual countries. What does the goal of population stabilization imply for Bulgaria? Does it call on the government to bring the population back up to the 9 million mark of the late 1980s, keep it constant at the current 7.6 million, or stop it from declining below 7 million? None of these seems realistic. In that case, what would be an appropriate target for a country like Bulgaria? This is not obvious. We counsel that per capita welfare is key, therefore a more useful and comprehensive policy paradigm must include educational structures alongside the current focus on total population and age structure.

Human Capital

> People are the wealth of nations. But it is not only the number of people that counts, it is also the skills, abilities and health status of the people that matter. All these aspects viewed together can be called the human resources base, or human capital in more economic language. This broadened view of population also implies that political goals should not be defined in terms of population size but rather in terms of human resources available for producing the best possible quality of life for all citizens. —Wolfgang Lutz, population adviser to the Bulgarian government.

This shift in paradigm, from a focus on mere population size to one that aims at a fuller picture that encompasses their skills, is not an easy one for many to digest. For centuries, population size has been the primary target of national and world population policies. Throughout European history, it was assumed that the bigger a kingdom/republic in terms of population, the more powerful it would be and so the better off its citizens (Coleman 2006). The rationale behind this view is military: the bigger the population, the more potential soldiers and the greater the possibilities to defend, or expand, the national territory. But there has been economic reasoning behind this view as well: more people imply greater markets with more trade, and higher population density furthers the division of labor and technological progress—all things that are considered to be conducive for economic growth (Haas, in Goldstone et al. 2012). Yet in our interdependent world, self-sufficiency is less important. In the specific case of Bulgaria, the accession to the European Union brought a huge increase in the market even under conditions of population decline.

The opposite view—that population growth is detrimental to human well-being—also has a long pedigree. It dates from the late-eighteenth-century views of Thomas Malthus. Here the reasoning has been that the resource base is limited for any national population and that population growth eventually surpasses the carrying capacity of a given territory. This leads to lower quality of life and even starvation and death. Based on such reasoning, the Netherlands and England were considered overpopulated in the nineteenth century.

In reality, however, through colonization and international trade, the resource base of these countries expanded to accommodate the increase. Technological progress resulted in a much higher quality of life despite increased population density. A modern version of this Malthusian view is reflected in the Limits to Growth study by the Club of Rome (Coleman 2006) and, more recently, in the notion of the "ecological footprint." This claims that a rising number of people in a country increases consumption, which has ecological consequences far beyond its territory. There have been many discussions of what the optimal population size of a given country should be. While this discussion has been inconclusive, the majority of researchers in the field have understood that it makes little sense to maintain a one-dimensional focus on absolute population size. What really matters is the change over time and, most importantly, the composition of the population. For this reason this chapter considered the question of optimal fertility from a vantage point that includes education alongside traditional concerns about age structure and population size.

Demographers tend to study the composition of the population mostly with respect to age and sex. Changes in the age structure of a population matter because producers must support consumers. Significant changes in the support ratio can be associated with decreases in the well-being of the population. In terms of pension systems, the expectation is that as the population ages, with the proportion over sixty years of age increasing rapidly, there will be growing pressure to act. But the process of population aging has only begun. Significant future aging is already pre-programmed into the existing population age structure as a consequence of a history of low fertility.

There is little doubt that population aging will pose a challenge to European societies. The more rapidly the proportion of the elderly increases in a population, the greater the challenge will be. In this sense—at least at the national level—population aging is clearly more relevant than declines in absolute population size when it comes to potentially diminishing the welfare of individuals. Therefore, should a population policy seek to minimize the speed of population aging? This is clearly a more meaningful goal than trying to target a particular population size because it is more directly related to the well-being of the population.

Yet—as we showed—this is not the full story. Whether a smaller young cohort actually translates into a decline in total welfare depends not only on the crude number of workers but on their productivity. If productivity per worker increases at the same rate as the number of workers declines, the effect is neutral (although a distributional issue still remains). There are many factors that contribute to the growth of productivity, but the most important seems to be human capital, a consequence primarily of education as well as health and motivation. In other words, the rate of human capital improvement is a crucial intervening factor that will govern the extent to which population aging and decline have negative consequences for the well-being of the population. This focus on human capital is not new in the history of demographic thinking. In 1958, Alfred Sauvy, in the context of the German economic miracle, after its total destruction in 1945 and the fact that it had to absorb five million refugees, wrote,

> Why this success, contrary to the forecasts of all doctrines ... ? Because these men without capital came with their knowledge, their qualifications. They worked and they recreated the capital that was lacking, because they included a sufficient number of engineers, mechanics, chemists, doctors, sociologists, etc. If five million manual workers had entered Western Germany instead there would be five million unemployed today. (Sauvy 1963)

Despite the prominence of Sauvy, mainstream demography has not really incorporated this important line of thinking. Instead such qualitative dimensions were considered too difficult to measure and largely left to economists. The more advanced demographic tools of multi-state population dynamics, pioneered by IIASA in the 1970s, permit us to fully integrate the educational attainment dimension into formal demography. As the title of an article by Lutz, Goujon, and Doblhammer, "Adding Education to Age and Sex," suggests, it is high time we more systematically applied the human capital approach to population analysis and policy (Lutz et al. 1999).

The concept of human capital development combines concerns about population size with those of age structure and human capital. It goes beyond population stabilization, which is not a viable policy goal for Bulgaria or most other countries in Europe over the coming decades due to the momentum of population decline. The human capital paradigm, on the other hand, brings education and health on board alongside age and sex. This does not imply that the three determinants of population size and age structure—fertility, mortality, and migration—do not matter. They continue to be the key drivers of change but must be viewed in interaction with education. In the case of migration, for instance, under the human capital perspective, it would not only be the numbers of migrants that count but their skills and qualifications. This is the view that has long been taken by successful immigrant countries such as Canada. There are also important interactions between education and fertility (with better-educated women giving birth later but also having better educated children) and mortality (more educated people are generally more healthy) that need to be considered in the formulation of policies.

Conclusion

Further scientific research (including alternative projections and considerations of the criteria of optimal fertility as described earlier) as well as dialogue among scientists, stakeholder groups, civil society, and government are needed to find the way forward. But in order to be useful in this process, demographers need to venture beyond their traditional comfort zone and include both quantitative information on education as well as relevant qualitative dimensions in their models. This demands that broader societal concerns such as development and poverty reduction, climate change, and even such difficult issues as national identity need to be integrated into existing analyses. The explicit modeling of human capital is a first step into this direction. To further advance it is a demanding task, but vitally important for our collective future.

Notes

1. Note that age-specific mortality rates were held constant in all of these fertility scenarios.
2. For European countries the first category is irrelevant. In order to assess the welfare impact of different long-term patterns of fertility we use a simple population model that enables

us to calculate education-weighted support ratios, based on observed initial (2010) population structures and survival probabilities as reported by the UN in its 2008 revision of the World Population Prospects.

3. The specific weights at this stage are rather arbitrarily chosen. In the future we aim at having these weights based on empirical analysis. However, as sensitivity analysis conducted in IIASA-IR (forthcoming) reveals, the optimum does not respond greatly to the choice of these weights. Rather they affect the level of the support ratio.

4. For the results of the baseline scenarios for Germany and Spain for different points in time see Web Figure 10.1 and Web Figure 10.2 on the book web site.

5. See Web Figures 10.1 and 10.2 on the book web site.

6. It is also interesting to note that the curve declines more steeply to the left for cases of extremely low fertility and somewhat slower to the right for cases of high fertility. The TFR that shows the highest level of our welfare indicator is also indicated for different points in time in the box in the lower right corner.

7. See Web Figure 10.3 on the book web site for the case of Germany with all other weights as in the baseline case.

8. See Web Figure 10.1 on the book web site.

9. Part of this section has previously been published by Wolfgang Lutz as a commentary in VYPR 2008.

References

Baochang, G., W. Feng, et al. 2007. "China's Local and National Fertility Policies at the End of the Twentieth Century." *Population and Development Review* 33(1): 129–148.

Billari, F. C. and H. P. Kohler. 2004. "Patterns of Low and Lowest-Low Fertility in Europe." *Population Studies* 58(2): 161–176.

Bock, J. D. 2000. "Doing the Right Thing? Single Mothers by Choice and the Struggle for Legitimacy." *Gender and Society* 14(1): 62–86.

Bongaarts, J. 2002. "The End of Fertility Transition in the Developed World." *Population and Development Review* 28(3): 419–443.

Bongaarts, J. and G. Feeney. 2006. "The Quantum and Tempo of Life-Cycle Events." *Vienna Yearbook of Population Research*: 115–151.

Bouchard, G., J. Boudreau, et al. 2006. "Transition to Parenthood and Conjugal Life: Comparisons Between Planned and Unplanned Pregnancies." *Journal of Family Issues* 27(11): 1512–1531.

Branigan, T. 2009. "Shanghai Encourages Second Child for Eligible Couples: Move Marks Dramatic Shift Away from 30-Year Priority of Keeping Population Down." *The Guardian* (UK) (Online). London: GMG.

Cai, Y. 2008. "An Assessment of China's Fertility Level Using the Variable-R Method." *Demography* 45(2): 271–281.

Chen, J., R. D. Retherford, et al. 2009. "Province-Level Variation in the Achievement of Below-Replacement Fertility in China." *Asian Population Studies* 5(3): 309–328.

Coale, A. J. 1973. "The Demographic Transition." In *Proceedings of the International Population Conference.* (International Union for the Scientific Study of Population, Liege, Belgium, 1973), vol 1.

Coleman, D. 2006. "Europe's Demographic Future: Determinants, Dimensions, and Challenges." In P. Demeny and G. McNicoll (eds.), *Population and Development Review* 32: 52–95.

Coleman, D. A. and S. Dubuc. 2010. "The Fertility of Ethnic Minorities in the UK, 1960s–2006." *Population Studies: A Journal of Demography* 64(1): 19–41.

Davis, K. 1945. "The World Demographic Transition." *Annals of the American Academy of Political and Social Science* 237: 1–11.

Davis, K. 1991. "Population and Resources: Fact and Interpretation." In K. Davis and M. S. Bernstam (eds.), *Resources, Environment and Population: Present Knowledge,* 1–21. Oxford: Oxford University Press.

Eurostat. 2012. *Population Statistics Database,* Eurostat, Brussels. http://epp.eurostat.ec .europa.eu/portal/page/portal/population/data/database. Accessed July 20, 2012.

Fargues, P. 2000. "Protracted National Conflict and Fertility Change among Palestinians and Israelis." *Population and Development Review* 26(3): 441–482.

Feeney, G. and Y. Jianhua. 1994. "Below Replacement Fertility in China? A Close Look at Recent Evidence." *Population Studies* 48(3): 381–394.

Fleissig, A. 1991. "Unintended Pregnancies and the Use of Contraception: Changes from 1984 to 1989." *British Medical Journal* 302(6769): 147.

Fleming, C. F. 2009. "Long-Acting Reversible Contraceptives." *The Obstetrician and Gynaecologist* 11(2): 83–88.

Frejka, T. and T. Sobotka. 2008. "Overview Chapter 1: Fertility in Europe: Diverse, Delayed and Below Replacement." *Demographic Research* 19: 15–46.

Glasier, A. 2009. "Should Healthcare Professionals Be Advocating Long-Acting Reversible Contraception?" *Women's Health* 5(1): 1–4.

Goldsteen, K. and C. E. Ross. 1989. "The Perceived Burden of Children." *Journal of Family Issues* 10(4): 504–526.

Goldstein, J. R., W. Lutz, et al. 2003. "The Emergence of Sub-Replacement Family Size Ideals in Europe." *Population Research and Policy Review* 22(5): 479–496.

Goldstein, J. R., T. Sobotka, et al. 2009. "The End of 'Lowest-Low' Fertility?" *Population and Development Review* 35(4): 663–699.

Goldstone, J., E. Kaufmann, and M.Duffy Toft. 2012. *Political Demography: Identity, Conflict and Institutions.* New York: Oxford University Press.

Hesketh, T. and W. X. Zhu. 1997. "Health in China: The One Child Family Policy: The Good, the Bad, and the Ugly." *BMJ: British Medical Journal* 314(7095): 1685–1687.

Jensen, T. K., A. M. Andersson, et al. 2004. "Body Mass Index in Relation to Semen Quality and Reproductive Hormones among 1,558 Danish Men." *Fertility and Sterility* 82(4): 863–870.

Jensen, T. K., N. Jorgensen, et al. 2007. "Self-Rated Health and Semen Quality among 3,457 Young Danish Men." *Fertility and Sterility* 88(5): 1366–1373.

Jones, G., T. Hull, et al. 2000. "The Social and Demographic Impact of the Southeast Asian Crisis of 1997–99." *Journal of Population Research* 17(1): 39–62.

Jorgensen, N., A. G. Andersen, et al. 2001. "Regional Differences in Semen Quality in Europe." *Human Reproduction* 16(5): 1012–1019.

Kaneko, R. 2008. "Population Projections for Japan: 2006–2055. Outline of Results, Methods, and Assumptions." *Japanese Journal of Population* 6(1): 76–114.

Kohler, H. P., F. C. Billari, et al. 2002. "The Emergence of Lowest-Low Fertility in Europe During the 1990s." *Population and Development Review* 28(4): 641–680.

Kohler, H. P., F. C. Billari, et al. 2006. "Low Fertility in Europe: Causes, Implications and Policy Options." *The Baby Bust: Who Will Do the Work? Who Will Pay the Taxes?*: 48–109.

Kuroki, L. M., J. E. Allsworth, et al. 2008. "Is a Previous Unplanned Pregnancy a Risk Factor for a Subsequent Unplanned Pregnancy?" *American Journal of Obstetrics and Gynecology* 199(5): 511–517.

Lakha, F. and A. Glasier. 2006. "Unintended Pregnancy and Use of Emergency Contraception among a Large Cohort of Women Attending for Antenatal Care or Abortion in Scotland." *The Lancet* 368(9549): 1782–1787.

Lechner, L., C. Bolman, et al. 2007. "Definite Involuntary Childlessness: Associations between Coping, Social Support and Psychological Distress." *Human Reproduction* 22(1): 288–294.

Lesthaeghe, R. and K. Neels. 2002. "From the First to the Second Demographic Transition: An Interpretation of the Spatial Continuity of Demographic Innovation in France, Belgium and Switzerland." *European Journal of Population* 18(4): 225–260.

Lesthaeghe, R. and P. Willems. 1999. "Is Low Fertility a Temporary Phenomenon in the European Union?" *Population and Development Review* 25(2): 211–228.

Letherby, G. 1999. "Other than Mother and Mothers as Others: The Experience of Motherhood and Non-Motherhood in Relation to 'Infertility' and 'Involuntary Childlessness.'" *Women's Studies International Forum* 22(3): 359–372.

Liang, Z. (2003). "An Alternate Estimation of China's Total Population and Women's Fertility in 2000." *Chinese Journal of Population Science* 6: 9–16.

Lillard, L. A. and L. J. Waite. 1993. "A Joint Model of Marital Childbearing and Marital Disruption." *Demography* 30(4): 653–681.

Lutz, W. 1996. *The Future Population of the World : What Can We Assume Today?* London: Earthscan.

Lutz, W., A. Goujon, et al. 1999. "Demographic Dimensions in Forecasting: Adding Education to Age and Sex." *Frontiers of Population Forecasting* 24: 42–58.

Lutz, W., B. C. O'Neill, et al. 2003. "Europe's Population at a Turning Point." *Science* 299(5615): 1991–1992.

Lutz, W., W. Sanderson, et al. 2008. "The Coming Acceleration of Global Population Ageing." *Nature* 451(7179): 716–719.

Lutz, W., W. C. Sanderson, et al. 2004. "Conceptualizing Populaiton in Sustainable Development: From 'Population Stabilization' to 'Population Balance.'" In W. Lutz,

W. C. Sanderson and B. C. O'Neill (eds.), *The End of World Population Growth in the 21st Century: New Challenges for Human Capital Formation and Sustainable Development,* 315–334. London: Earthscan.

Lutz, W. and S. Scherbov. 2008. "Exploratory Extension of IIASA's World Population Projections: Scenarios to 2300." In *IIASA Interim Report IR-08-022.* (IIASA, Laxenburg, Austria, 2008).

Lutz, W., S. Scherbov, et al. 2007. "China's Uncertain Demographic Present and Future." *Vienna Yearbook of Population Research*: 37–59.

Lutz, W., V. Skirbekk, et al. 2006. "The Low-Fertility Trap Hypothesis: Forces that May Lead to Further Postponement and Fewer Births in Europe." *Vienna Yearbook of Population Research*: 167–192.

Meadows, D. H. and Club of Rome. 1972. *The Limits to Growth; A Report for the Club of Rome's Project on the Predicament of Mankind.* New York: Universe Books.

Merli, M. G. 1998. "Underreporting of Births and Infant Deaths in Rural China: Evidence from Field Research in One County of Northern China." *China Quarterly* (155): 637–655.

Merli, M. G. and A. E. Raftery. 2000. "Are Births Underreported in Rural China? Manipulation of Statistical Records in Response to China's Population Policies." *Demography* 37(1): 109–126.

Morgan, S. P., G. Zhigang, et al. 2009. "China's Below-Replacement Fertility: Recent Trends and Future Prospects." *Population and Development Review* 35(3): 605–629.

Myrskylä, M., H. P. Kohler, et al. 2009. "Advances in Development Reverse Fertility Declines." *Nature* 460(7256): 741–743.

Nailin, F. 2006. "Lessons Learnt From the 2005 One-Percent Population Survey of China and Initial Plans for 2010 Round of Census." In *The 11th Meeting of the Heads of National Statistical Offices of East Asia Countries.* (Tokyo, 2006).

NBS. 2007. "Fertility Estimates for Provinces of China, 1975–2000." *National Bureau of Statistics of China.* Honolulu: Beijing and East-West Center.

Nie, Y. and R. J. Wyman. 2005. "The One-Child Policy in Shanghai: Acceptance and Internalization." *Population and Development Review* 31(2): 313–336.

Notestein, F. W. 1945. "Population—The Long View." In T. W. Schultz (ed.), *Food for the World,* 36–57. Chicago: University of Chicago Press.

Raley, R. K. 2001. "Increasing Fertility in Cohabiting Unions: Evidence for the Second Demographic Transition in the United States?" *Demography* 38(1): 59–66.

Retherford, R. D., M. K. Choe, et al. 2005. "How Far Has Fertility in China Really Declined?" *Population and Development Review* 31(1): 57–84.

Sauvy, A. 1963. *Fertility and Survival; Population Problems from Malthus to Mao Tsetung.* New York: Collier Books.

Shanghai Statistical Bureau. 2009. *Shanghai Statistical Yearbook.* Shanghai: Shanghai Statistical Bureau.

Shanley, M. L. and A. Asch. 2009. "Involuntary Childlessness, Reproductive Technology, and Social Justice: The Medical Mask on Social Illness." *Signs* 34(4): 851–874.

SMPFPC. 2008. *Briefing on SMPFPC Fertility Survey 2008* (2008 年11月11日下午，上海市人口计生委召开2008年度上海人口和计划生育情况驻沪领馆通报会。) Shanghai: Shanghai Municipal Population and Family Planning Commission.

Sobotka, T. 2004. "Is Lowest-Low Fertility in Europe Explained by the Postponement of Childbearing?" *Population and Development Review* 30(2): 195–220.

Sun, C. 2009. pers. comm. S. Basten. Shanghai.

Tabah, L. 1989. "From One Demographic Transition to Another." *Population Bulletin of the United Nations* (28): 1–24.

Todorova, I. L. G. and T. Kotzeva. 2003. "Social Discourses, Women's Resistive Voices: Facing Involuntary Childlessness in Bulgaria." *Women's Studies International Forum* 26(2): 139–151.

Toulemon, L., A. Pailhé, et al. 2008. "France: High and Stable Fertility." *Demographic Research* 19: 503–556.

Tuljapurkar, S. 2009. "Demography: Babies Make a Comeback." *Nature* 460(7256): 693–694.

UNPD. 2011. *World Population Prospects: The 2010 Revision.* New York: United Nations.

Van Balen, F. 2008. "Involuntary Childlessness: A Neglected Problem in Poor-Resource Areas." *Human Reproduction* 2008 (1): 25–28.

Van de Kaa, D. J. 1987. "Europe's Second Demographic Transition." *Population Bulletin* 42(1).

Weimim, Z. 2005. *China's Inter-census Survey in 2005.* Beijing: National Bureau of Statistics of China.

Wu, J., S. Meldrum, et al. 2008. "Contraceptive Nonuse among US Women at Risk for Unplanned Pregnancy." *Contraception* 78(4): 284–289.

Yi, Z. 1996. "Is Fertility in China in 1991–92 Far Below Replacement Level?" *Population Studies* 50(1): 27–34.

Zhang, G. 2004. "Very Low Fertility in China in the 1990s: An Illusion of Birth Underreporting?" *Annual Meeting of the Population Association of America (PAA).* (Boston, 2004).

Zhang, W., X. Li, and H. Cui. 2007. *China's Intercensus Survey in 2005.* Beijing: China Population Publishing House.

Zhu, W. X., L. Lu, et al. 2009. "China's Excess Males, Sex Selective Abortion, and One Child Policy: Analysis of Data from 2005 National Intercensus Survey." *BMJ (Clinical research ed.)* 338.

Index

Abortion, 140; China's one-child policy, 98

Achieved fertility, 3; circumstances affecting, 12, 21; desired fertility and, 208–209; expected change in happiness owing to childbearing, 56–60; future well-being and fertility, 57–60; parenthood and subjective well-being, 68; Shanghai, 215–216

Adaptive women: divisions of domestic labor and, 118, 167, 171; preference theory, 179–188

Adema, Willem, 165

Adenaur, Konrad, 205

Adopted children, 54–55, 84–85, 92

Age: division of domestic labor, and marital satisfaction, 124; individual fertility of women in 45 countries, 139(table); optimal fertility, 219–221; optimal fertility levels, 218; parenthood and type of civic engagement, 39–40; perception of future well-being deriving from children, 58–60; postponing childbearing, 2–3, 80–81; preference theory, 184–185; religion, fertility and, 12

Aging population, 206, 207–208; biomedical factors in future fertility, 211; challenging society, 226–227; China's one-child policy and, 107; Europe's increasing ethnic gaps, 145–146; impact of children on well-being controlling for partnership, 64–65

Algerian Muslims, 147–148

Allocation Parentale d'Education (APE; France), 190

"The Angel Plan," 163

Anglo-Saxon countries: family-career tradeoff for women, 20. *See also specific countries*

Antinomian countercultural values, 137

Artificial reproduction, 79–89; anonymity of donor insemination, 82, 90, 92(n3), 92(n4); marketing, 89–90; policy recommendations, 90–92

Artificial reproductive technologies (ARTs), 79–89

Ashino, Yuriko, 159–160

Australia: artificial reproductive technologies, 81, 83; female unemployment rates, 13; parenthood and civic involvement, 34; personality traits and fertility, 55; work-family reconciliation policies, 166

Less-developed countries (LDCs): demographic transition, 207
Liberal nationalism, 150–151
Life-cycle well-being, 49–56
Lifestyle preference, 178–188, 179
Limits to Growth study, 226
Lisbon Agenda, 209
Living standards, 207
Low fertility countries: future birth rate levels, 206–207
Low fertility trap hypothesis, 206, 208–209, 216–217
Lowest-low fertility, 157, 212; feminists' view of, 159–160; implementing work-family reconciliation policies, 168–173
Lutheranism, 7(table), 141, 143, 145
Luxembourg: female unemployment rates, 13

Macro-level conditions and theories, 141, 196, 209–210
Mahon, Rianne, 165
Malthus, Thomas, 226
Marital equity, 119–129
Marital satisfaction: among childless women, 126(fig.); among women with children at home, 127(fig.); division of labor, 115–117, 119–129; traditional versus egalitarian marriages, 127–129
Marital status: childbearing and marital satisfaction, 55; civic involvement, 35; fertility rates, religious practice and family size, 9–10; individual fertility of women in 45 countries, 1999–2000, 139(table); interfaith and interethnic marriages, 148; lifestyle preferences, 182(table), 187; parenthood and well-being, 51, 53–54; utility gains of parenthood, 50
Marital trends, 210
Marriage: attributes of married couples, 123(table); division of labor and marital satisfaction, 113–115; flexible views of marriage correlating with high fertility rates, 167–168; Japan's fertility decline following marriage rate decline, 159–160; motherhood and perceived marital unfairness, 117–119; religious affiliation and family size, 9

Mass media, 136–137
Material factors in declining fertility, 21
Maternal attachment, 53
Maternity leave. *See* Parental leave
Men's fertility, 81
Mental health: China's one-child policy and, 107–108; civic engagement fostering, 32; only children versus sibling children families, 100
Migrant population: Shanghai, 214–215
Military view: importance of human capital, 225–226
Minnesota Twin Register, 50–51
Moderately low fertility, 212
Modernization. *See* Secularization
Moldova: total fertility rate and civic engagement, 31(table)
More-developed countries (MDCs): demographic transition, 207
Mormons, 140, 141
Mortality rates, 32, 207
Motivations for having children, 51
Mukuno, Michiko, 163
Multidimensional Personality Questionnaire (MPQ), 50–51
Multiple births, 81
Mundy, Liza, 81
Muslim population: correlating religiosity and fertility, 140–141; correlating religiosity and future fertility, 145–148; Europe's future demographic, 149; family-career tradeoff for women, 20; impact of religious practice on fertility, 10; increasing OECD populations, 4; lifestyle preferences, 186–187; religious practice and family size, 11; sanctity of children, 78; WVS-EVS data, 7(fig.)

National identity, optimal fertility level and, 219
National Longitudinal Study of Adolescent Health, 51, 120
Neotraditional model of domestic labor division, 118–120, 123, 125–128, 127(fig.)
Netherlands: artificial reproductive technologies, 90; correlating religiosity and fertility, 141, 142; ethnonationalism

About the Editors and Contributors

Alícia Adserà is Research Scholar and Lecturer in Economics at the Woodrow Wilson School of Public and International Affairs, Princeton University. Her research interests are in economic demography and development. She is co-director of Princeton University's Global Network on Child Migration. Her recent work focuses on the determinants and consequences of low fertility and migration. Her work has been published in the *American Economic Review P&P, Journal of Population Economics, Population Studies, Journal of Law Economics and Organization,* and *International Organization,* among others.

Stuart Basten is Research Fellow in the Department of Social Policy and Intervention at the University of Oxford. He is also Research Fellow in the Sociology Group at Nuffield College, Oxford, and in the Department of Social Work and Social Policy, National Taiwan University. His research concerns past and future trends in partnership and family formation in East Asia as well as the global relationship between gender issues and fertility. His most recent publications include "Baby Longing and Men's Reproductive Motivation" (with Anna Rotkirch, Heini Väisänen, and Markus Jokela), *Vienna Yearbook of Population Research* 9 (2011), and "Gender Equality and Fertility Intentions Revisited:

Evidence from Finland" (with Anna Rotkirch and Anneli Mietinnen), *Demographic Research* 24, no. 20 (March 2011).

Jeffrey Dew is a faculty fellow at the National Marriage Project and an assistant professor of Family, Consumer, and Human Development at Utah State University. His recent publications include "Beyond Employment and Income: The Association Between Young Adults' Finances and Marriage" with J. Price (*Journal of Family and Economic Issues* 2011), "Financial Disagreements and Marital Conflict Tactics" with J. Dakin (*Journal of Financial Therapy* 2011), "Financial Issues and Relationship Outcomes among Cohabiting Individuals" (*Family Relations* 2011), "If Momma Ain't Happy: Explaining Declines in Marital Satisfaction among New Mothers" with W. B. Wilcox (*Journal of Marriage and Family* 2011), and "Motherhood and Marriage: A Comment" with W. B. Wilcox (*Journal of Marriage and Family* 2011).

David J. Eggebeen is Associate Professor of Human Development in the Department of Human Development and Family Studies at Pennsylvania State University. He is currently involved in three projects: exploring the patterns of intergenerational exchanges of support in American families; the role of values—especially religious values—in the family formation processes of young adults; and the implications of fatherhood for men. His work on family formation behavior among young adults has focused on the role of religious beliefs and behavior in adolescence on the subsequent likelihood and timing of marriage and cohabitation. Finally, the work on consequences of fatherhood on men has most recently focused on the cumulative effects of fatherhood for men's social connections at middle age.

Catherine Hakim is a social scientist and Senior Research Fellow in the Centre for Policy Studies, London. She is an internationally recognized expert on women's employment, social policy, and labor market trends and is a frequent contributor to media debates on women's position in society and gender equality issues. Her publications include over 100 papers published in social science journals and edited collections, as well as textbooks on research design and research methods. Recent books include *Work-Lifestyle Choices in the 21st Century: Preference Theory* (Oxford University Press, 2000), *Social Change and Innovation in the Labour Market* (Oxford University Press, 1998), *Models of the Family in Modern Societies: Ideals and Realities* (Ashgate, 2003), and *Key Issues in Women's Work* (Glasshouse Press, 2004).

Eric Kaufmann is Professor of Politics at Birkbeck College, University of London. He is the author of *Shall the Religious Inherit the Earth? Demography and Politics in the Twenty-First Century* (Profile, 2011), co-editor of *Political Demography: Identity, Institutions and Conflict* (Oxford, 2012), author of *The Rise and Fall of Anglo-America* (Harvard, 2004) and *The Orange Order* (Oxford, 2007), co-author of *Unionism and Orangeism in Northern Ireland since 1945* (Manchester, 2007), and editor of *Rethinking Ethnicity: Majority Groups and Dominant Minorities* (Routledge, 2004). He is also an editor of the journal *Nations and Nationalism*. He has written on religion and demography in academic journals as well as for *Newsweek International, Foreign Policy,* and *Prospect* magazines.

Hans-Peter Kohler is Frederick J. Warren Professor of Demography in the Department of Sociology, and Research Associate at Population Studies Center at the University of Pennsylvania. Prof. Kohler's primary research focuses on fertility and health in developing and developed countries. A key characteristic of this research is the attempt to integrate demographic, economic, sociological, and biological approaches in empirical and theoretical models of demographic behavior. Prof. Kohler has widely published on topics related to fertility, health, social and sexual networks, HIV/AIDS, biodemography, and well-being in leading scientific journals, and his work has had substantial influence on policy and media discussions related to demographic change. He is currently the principal investigator of the *Malawi Longitudinal Study of Families and Health* and the Chair of the Graduate Group in Demography at the University of Pennsylvania.

Ying Liu, a research analyst at the Population Studies and Training Center (PSTC) of Brown University, obtained her PhD in nutrition epidemiology and has been trained in sociology and biostatistics at Carolina Population Center, the University of North Carolina at Chapel Hill. She serves as the statistical consultant to faculty and graduate students in PSTC. She is an expert in analyzing the multiple-facet and complicated national surveys such as Add Health, DHS, NCES, SIPP, and CHNS. She also has research interest in social networks and health behaviors of children. Publications include "Trends in Eating Behaviors among Chinese Children (1991–1997)" (*Asia Pac J Clin Nutr* 2006).

Wolfgang Lutz is Founding Director of the Wittgenstein Centre for Demography and Global Human Capital (a collaboration among the International Institute for Applied Systems Analysis [IIASA], the Vienna Institute of Demography [Austrian Academy of Sciences], and the Vienna University of Economics and

Business [WU]). He is also Professorial Research Fellow at the Oxford Martin School for 21st Century Studies. He holds a PhD in demography from the University of Pennsylvania (1983) and a second doctorate (Habilitation) in statistics from the University of Vienna. He has worked on family demography, fertility analysis, population projection, and the interaction between population and environment. Lutz is author and editor of twenty-eight books and more than two hundred refereed articles, including seven in *Science* and *Nature*. In 2008 he received an ERC Advanced Grant, in 2009 the Mattei Dogan Award of the IUSSP, and in 2010 the Wittgenstein Prize, the highest Austrian science award.

Elizabeth Marquardt is editor of FamilyScholars.org and directs the Center for Marriage and Families at the Institute for American Values in New York City. She is author of *Between Two Worlds: The Inner Lives of Children of Divorce* (Crown, 2005) and co-investigator of the influential studies "My Daddy's Name Is Donor: A New Study of Young Adults Conceived via Sperm Donation" and "Hooking Up, Hanging Out, and Hoping for Mr. Right: College Women on Dating and Mating Today." Her writings have been published in the *New York Times, Washington Post, Los Angeles Times, Huffington Post, Slate, Atlantic* online, and elsewhere.

Leonard Schoppa is Professor of Politics at the University of Virginia where he is Associate Dean of Social Sciences. His research focuses on the politics and foreign relations of Japan and comprises several distinct projects. He recently completed work on a project examining the transformation of Japan's system of social protection as it has been buffeted by the pressures of globalization and changing gender role aspirations of women. In *Race for the Exits: The Unraveling of Japan's System of Social Protection* (Cornell University Press, 2006), he explained the failure of the Japanese to modify their system in the face of these pressures by building on Albert Hirschman's exit-voice framework. He has also written extensively about Japan's economic negotiations with the United States in a book titled *Bargaining with Japan: What American Pressure Can and Cannot Do* (Columbia, 1997) and about Japan's policy immobilism in *Education Reform in Japan* (Routledge, 1991).

Susan E. Short is Professor of Sociology at Brown University. She specializes in demography with an emphasis on social and policy contexts and their intersection with family processes, gender dynamics, and health inequalities. Recent research includes population-level analyses of changes in the composition of households of mothers of young children; the relationship between policies, prenatal care, and fertility; and family organization and child well-being. Short has served as Associate Director of the Population Studies and Training Center at Brown University and as a member of the Board of Directors of the Population Association of America.

Erich Striessnig is a Research Assistant with the World Population Program at International Institute for Applied Systems Analysis, Austria, and FWF-project staff member at the Vienna University of Economics and Business.

W. Bradford Wilcox is Director of the National Marriage Project at the University of Virginia, Associate Professor of Sociology at the University of Virginia, and a member of the James Madison Society at Princeton University. His research focuses on marriage and cohabitation and on the ways that gender, religion, and children influence the quality and stability of American family life. He has published articles on marriage, cohabitation, parenting, and fatherhood in *The American Sociological Review, Social Forces, The Journal of Marriage and Family,* and *The Journal for the Scientific Study of Religion.*

Hongwei Xu is a Faculty Research Fellow at the Survey Research Center, Institute for Social Research, University of Michigan. His research interests include health inequalities, epidemiologic and nutrition transitions, child well-being, and the residential segregation of ethnic groups. He is currently working as a research team member on the Chinese Family Panel Studies, one of the largest longitudinal data collection projects in contemporary China. Recent publications include "Health Insurance Coverage Rates in 9 Provinces in China Doubled from 1997 to 2006, with a Dramatic Rural Upswing" (*Health Affairs,* 2011), "Concurrent Sexual Partnerships among Youth in Urban Kenya: Prevalence and Partnership Effects" (*Population Studies,* 2010), and "How Chinese Children Spend Their Time" in *Applied Demography in the 21st Century,* edited by Steve H. Murdock and David A. Swanson.